A YANKEE AND THE SWAMIS

TIBET

COUNTY LIBRARY

H I M A L A Y

Bhutan

Nepal

Ganges

Sarnath

East
Pakistan

Gaya

Benares

Budh-Gaya

Khatra
Bankura

Jayrambati

Kamarpukur

Bishnupur

Calcutta

BURMA

West Bengal

Cuttak

Bhubaneswar

Konarak

BAY OF BENGAL

Puri

Sri Sarada Math

Rahara

Dakshineswar

Willingdon Bridge

Waltair

Baranagore Monastery

Cossipore Garden House

Belur Math

Baranagore Burning Ghat

0   1 MILE

Madras
Tirukalikundram
Mahabalipuram

Grand Trunk Road

Cossipore Road

Hooghly (Ganges) River

25°

20°

15°

10°

Baghbazar Section

Balaram Bose's House
Udbodhan

Howrah Bridge

Howrah Station

rameswaram

Ceylon

85°

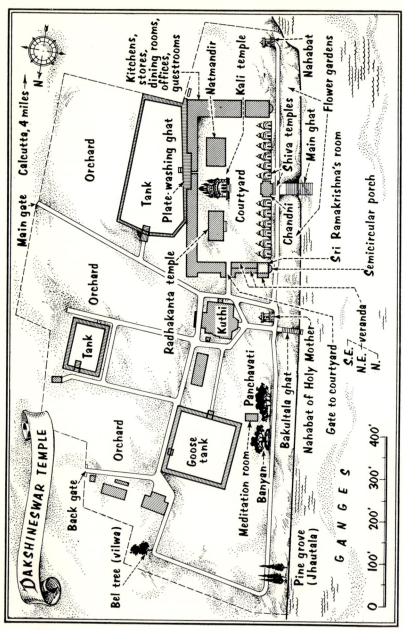

1. Map of Dakshineswar

A Yankee

AND

the Swamis

JOHN YALE

Ruskin House

GEORGE ALLEN & UNWIN LTD

MUSEUM STREET LONDON

PRINTED IN GREAT BRITAIN
in 10pt. Plantin type
BY C. TINLING AND CO., LTD
LIVERPOOL, LONDON AND PRESCOT

CONTENTS

CONTENTS

ILLUSTRATIONS

For full annotation of the illustrations
see pages 222-224

CHAPTER I

BELUR MATH ON THE GANGES

IT will soon be eight years since the events took place which are described here. As I think back to the time and happenings which prompted this book I see that nothing is the same. Or rather, the people and places it touches may not have changed so much. I hope they have not. They were quite wonderful as they were. But I have changed. I needed to. I could never again make a journey like the one described in this book or write about it as I have done; for the aggressive inquirer is gone. The younger man who did the research, who observed and made notes, who judged and came to conclusions, is no more.

'I'! These two hundred pages are filled with 'I's. I am sorry for this. Pride does not dictate this usage. It is only that there is no way to tell this story with the immediacy it should have except through the first person singular. My purpose throughout has been to describe for the alert Westerner interested in religion the things he might like to know about the 'home base' of an important and growing new spiritual movement. He will want to see it inside and out—its heroes, its objectives, its problems and hopes and accomplishments. It has seemed that this could best be done by placing before him an informant through whose eyes he could see and through whose emotional system he could feel. That informant is this 'I'.

Who is this individual so necessary to the story and yet later so changed? He is a man who has been essaying to be a monk at the Hollywood branch of the Ramakrishna Order of India for the past ten years. He has another name beside the one used on the title page. That was his name in the world and it is used because it is Occidental and is easily spelled and pronounced. The name of this man in religion is Brahmachari Prema Chaitanya. What a brahmachari is will soon be described; and the meaning of both 'prema' and 'chaitanya' will also appear in the narrative. Both his religious name and his monastic status this man bears proudly and seeks to live up to.

Before this 'I' came to the Vedanta Society of Southern California he had lived in as satisfying a manner as possible in the 'world'. He had grown up in the Midwest of the USA. He was from a middle-class family whose religion was fundamentalist Protestant. His mother was of English stock and his father had been born in Vermont. After college this 'I' went into the publishing business in Chicago, where he made a fair professional and financial success, allowing him to taste many of the so-called good things of life.

But as he left the twenties and entered his thirties, the writer began to feel inside himself some crippling lack. Possessions and pleasures were not enough. A sadness came over him. 'Is this all?' he asked. At the far end of the tunnel old age and death already could be seen waiting; the conveyance to which he was fastened moved toward them slowly; but it did move, and this made him afraid. So this man began to search. He tried to be kinder and more service-minded in his work. He looked into the remedies of psychotherapy, and solutions offered by the social sciences. What he really longed for was to be religious; but he didn't know where to find a faith with which he could feel compatible. The religion of his early years seemed childish now. Perhaps the Episcopalian Church or the Roman Catholic would have something more to offer. He attended these and studied their creeds. Again, a rank provincialism assailed him, so out of step with the realities of history and of modern knowledge.

Then in the Christmas season of 1947-48 this man was in New York on a business trip. The interior crisis had far advanced. He recalled a review in *Time* magazine which had attracted his attention a year or two before, concerning a new translation of the Bhagavad-Gita, made by a Swami Prabhavananda, assisted by Christopher Isherwood and Aldous Huxley. This man walked out in the snow on a Saturday afternoon to a bookstore and bought a copy of that Gita. He went back to the hotel and began to read. He thought: 'I am generally repelled by Oriental things—yogis and snake charmers and naked fakirs and foolish ladies chattering about trances and emanations. But let me sample this reputed spiritual classic, at least.' He finished the book without putting it down. That was the most hopeful Saturday night he had spent in a long time! He felt he had found a clue to the answer which his heart had always told him must surely be waiting somewhere and which could cope with the state of emergency his life had reached. And in a curious way he felt as though the message of the book were capable of reawakening the happy condition of pure faith he had formerly enjoyed as a child; hence healing the psychic breach which the emergence of discrimination had caused.

With much uncertainty this man sold his share of the business in which he worked and moved to California. He went to the Vedanta Society in Hollywood and sought out its leader, who was the Gita's translator. He told Swami Prabhavananda his troubles and his hope for a new pattern of behaviour that would satisfy his head and his heart. He associated himself with the Society. In course of time the Swami was kind enough to let him enter the organization as a monastic probationer. That was in the spring of 1950. He has been there ever since and hopes that he will spend the rest of his days within the Order. The bogeymen at the end of the corridor seem now not so fearsome; while progression through life, even though still in their direction, has become pleasant and peaceful.

This 'I' was very self-confident in 1950. He also believed himself to be scientific-minded. Since life in the Hollywood ashrama was an extension of the practices and policies of the Ramakrishna Order of India, he reasoned that it might be useful to go to India and see the organization on its home grounds. He would be able to understand the programme in Hollywood better, and an acquaintance with the institutions and leading spirits of the movement would be valuable. He wanted, also, through visiting places associated with the life of Sri Ramakrishna, to draw near the Order's nineteenth-century founder. There were also mundane considerations. Before throwing in his lot forever, before taking vows and surrendering the little nest egg he had accumulated, it might be wise to see fully what he was getting into. This man went to India in 1952-53 with the idea of taking a critical look at renascent Hinduism.

This man visited all the Vedanta Societies in the United States, England, and France on the way to India. He travelled five thousand miles in India itself and stopped at thirty-eight of the Order's centres. He went to places associated with the life of Sri Ramakrishna and the first apostles of the Ramakrishna movement. He sought out the major holy places of the country, entering the most famous and most closely guarded shrines of Hinduism as a worshipper. He attempted to live as an Indian monastic, while maintaining the coolness of judgment of a Western observer.

When this 'I' came home he began to set down impressions of his journey for publication in a magazine called *Vedanta and the West*, put out by the Vedanta Society of Southern California. These were travel stories filled with interpretations of what he had experienced. To the Indians who read these essays, many parts probably seemed superficial or presumptuous. The Indian's attitude, perhaps, would be something like this: 'As a Westerner you noticed externals too much. The externals in India are not very satisfactory. But then they are also to us not very important. You should have tried more to feel the inner spirit of the country. When a person goes to a shrine or meets a holy man he should put aside appraisal and try to catch their essential spirit. Feel the glory of God; don't try to evaluate it. The Real cannot be caught in the net of anybody's description. Even revelation itself is defiled a little as it passes through the mouth of man.' There is merit in this viewpoint and the writer somewhat subscribes to it now. On the other hand, everyone must start from where he is, and this applies also to the Westerner who would be a Ramakrishna devotee. The reporter's-eye-view of Ramakrishna's India furnished by this 'I' told exactly the things that Western students of the new movement wanted to know. These impressions were appreciated for their candour and for the inside information they imparted; so much so that it was decided they should be brought together in the more permanent form of a book.

I wish to make two things clear. First, as I have already said, I do not want this to be a book about me. And second, I maintain a hope that this may prove to be something beyond a mere travel story.

The 'I' is a necessary device. But what I most desire is that the men of luminous character whom I met should shine forth. What I hope the reader can gain is a sense of the consuming longing for God that is noticeable in India, and the freedom that is permitted to people to go about seeking him in their individual ways. The idea is that man and his present concerns are nothing. God is everything. I must find him. Vast numbers of people live out their days, direct all their activities, toward this end. And they do find him. This picture of others—of seekers and finders—I wish to impart.

Several years ago *Life* magazine ran a series of articles on the great religions of the world. In the article on Hinduism the following very interesting and indeed surprising passage appeared: 'Hindus themselves think their religion is not only the most ancient in the world but also the most modern and the best suited to resolve the problem of the world's many conflicting faiths. To Christians who have a first-hand acquaintance with Hinduism this claim is not as far-fetched as it may sound to Western ears. In a recent issue of *The Christian Century*, the leading Protestant publication in the United States, Philip Ashby wrote: "A respected and eminent Indian Christian, high in the councils of world Christianity, recently said to me that he is convinced the Hindu . . . argument that all religions are equally valid may well sweep the world in the next twenty-five years. He found this thesis congenial to the contemporary European and American mind. . . . The Hindu considers himself to be the representative of twentieth-century understanding, and the Christian, along with the Moslem, to be the epitome of religious exclusiveness and bigotry which must disappear in the modern world." '

This concept is what brought me to Vedanta and moves me to wish to give the rest of my life to its service. I can be religious without being provincial. The Ramakrishna movement is in the forefront of this new teaching of universality. Ramakrishna's special emphasis was that all roads lead to God if reaching God is one's objective. This revelation he established by his experience.

In following Ramakrishna I could also be progressive in my religious outlook. Growth and decay is a law of life. Like everything else, religions rise, flower, and then decline into periods of lessened vitality. Christ brought a quickening in the religion of the Jews, as did Buddha within Brahmanism. Hinduism has been revitalized again and again, by Rama, by Krishna, by Shankara, by Sri Chaitanya. Ramakrishna Vedanta is one more renewal within Hinduism, which in addition has implications for the refreshment and broadening of all the religions of the world.

This leads to my second point. I have not wanted this to be simply a travel book. I dare hope more than that, to have made a souvenir which will add something to the contemporary knowledge of an important work and trend. Suppose someone present in the area of the Mediterranean Sea in A.D. 100 had noted down impressions concerning the direct disciples of Christ—what they were like, their memories of the old times, the concerns that moved them. Such information would be of inestimable value. My position is that these are comparable times, and that I have met and written of equally significant men. Do I grant them too much, and in doing so, do I aim too high ? In all realism, I think not. Anything we may know about these early days of the Ramakrishna Order and movement is presently of interest and potentially of extreme importance. Thus my hope is that I have gathered and saved a few evidences which will add to the record of these early drawings of the more unified age to come.

Finally, a word about the title of this book: *A Yankee and the Swamis*. It has a double meaning.

Yes, here are incidents about a conservative American going to India and living with Hindu swamis. He had an impact on them, as they had on him. That the 'I' is a real Yankee will be seen in Chapter VI, in which the reader will learn that he is a relative of Elihu Yale. The effect of representatives of two very different cultures operating on each other is interesting to observe. But the roles of Yankees and Indians since the 1700s are shifting. A reversal is developing which adds to the interest of the present situation. Old Eli, born in New England, went to India to make his fortune. As governor of Madras he did just that, so that he was able to be generous enough to have a college named after him. He thought of Indians only as subjects to be made use of. No white man could have much to learn from them; whereas these Asians had everything to gain by emulating him. Now the situation is somewhat the opposite. In the art of living at peace with oneself it is growing evident that now as in the past it is the West which must be the learner, with the Oriental the teacher. 'A Sahib and the Sadhus' would be an equally apt title for this book. 'Sahibs' are, of course, white masters; and the word 'sadhu' is a general Indian term for monastic.

But I have intended the title to have a larger significance. According to the classic Hindu view of life, each of us moves deliberately, through many existences, from being a separate, suffering individual to becoming free and in unitive contact with all life. Swamihood—or sannyas—is the fourth and final stage of life in the Indian scheme. The meaning of formal sannyas is detailed in Chapter X. The status of sannyas is the noblest man can know. A swami is free because desire has been killed in him. He is Christ's lily of the field, Christ's bird of the air. His provider is

God; his relatives are everyone; his home is this world and all other worlds.

We all start out as Yankees of one sort or another. We commence as persons of respectability, perhaps, or failures; as humanitarians, fanatics, hypocrites, liars; as neurotics; as alcoholics; as Boston or Indian Brahmins; as western or Indian sudras. From where we start we must journey toward the final stage of life, in which we are not limited and defensive, but part of the unity. We must journey towards freedom. To enjoy this state is what we long for and this is what God's destiny for each of us eventually is.

God has come periodically to show man how to make this progression. A basic premise of this book is that he has returned in recent times to emphasize the old message again. He is telling us as before, to start from whatever condition of Yankeeism one may find oneself in, and progress toward the unlimited.

It is mid-evening, and I am standing at the little bar of the Philippines Airlines plane, talking to an Englishman also getting off at Calcutta. Behind us in the dark interior are dozing people—all sorts of international travellers, including several Philippinos going on around to their homeland. The date is November 5, 1952. We left Rome last night, and Karachi just two hours ago, where we learned that Eisenhower had won the election.

It is only a Coca-Cola, but I drink it hungrily, and salute with it. One for the road, an unknown road. I guess I have never been so nervous in my life. Here I am, a one-hundred-per-cent Occidental, setting myself down untutored and alone in an order of Hindu monks. In response to my request for indoctrination, Swami Prabhavananda, my teacher, told me: 'Just be natural and you'll be all right.'

'But Swami, what about etiquette, customs?'

'Take the dust of the feet of every swami when you first meet him; and take the dust of the feet of the President every time you meet him.'

That is precisely the extent of my orientation.

The Englishman isn't helping things any. Western brahmacharis don't wear any distinctive dress, and I haven't told him the nature of my visit to India. I have simply said I am spending the winter there.

'Good heavens, you must be crazy,' is his rejoinder. 'I have to live here for business reasons, and I just hate it. With all the other places there are in the world, why would anyone choose to come to India, or take a holiday here?'

'Well, you see, it isn't exactly a holiday,' I say. 'It's more in the nature of a research trip.'

'And what do you expect to find?'

'I'm a student of Indian philosophy.'

He is really disgusted. 'Oh, one of those—another would-be Larry in

2 Belur Math on the Ganges

Dakshineswar

3 Josephine MacLeod (Tantine) in her later years

Swami Sankarananda

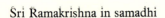

Śri Ramakrishna in samadhi

Śri Sarada Devi with Margaret Noble (Sister Nivedita)

another impossible *Razor's Edge*. Well, you're in for some disappointments.'

Now I have to tell him. 'I'm an American member of the Ramakrishna Order,' I say, 'and I've come to India to see things for myself. I expect tonight to be sleeping at headquarters, at Belur Math.'

My companion is mollified a little. 'Oh, the Ramakrishna Mission,' he says. 'They do some good things—perhaps the best native organization there is.' But now he returns to his previous tone: 'But of course you know that Belur is in Howrah, which is one of the most malarious districts in the whole world.'

A plump little shaven-headed swami, dressed in the characteristic pinkish-tan of the gerrua dress of the Indian sannyasin was waiting for me. I made my way toward him loaded with topcoat, briefcase, and portable type-writer, and, I fear, carrying gloves. A nervous moment when I had to deposit all this paraphernalia on the ground and make my first pranam—to touch each of his feet and then my forehead. This is 'taking the dust of the feet.' Making this gesture is a simple way in India of showing respect for elders and men of character, comparable to the Catholic's practice of kneeling before the Pope. Basic etiquette for a junior of the Order, the pranam would not, however, be expected from lay visitors, Western or Indian.

It is said that when India gained her freedom she retaliated for the in-dignities previously inflicted on her nationals by drafting customs prac-tices which include everything Western countries follow, and more besides. Even with the aid of the swami, it took me an hour to fill up all the forms. By the time I was through I realized how incongruously I was dressed. My wool jacket and flannel trousers had turned into steamy Turkish towels, and the very sight of the topcoat was unpleasant.

We started off in what I now know to have been a real luxury and at an expense rarely incurred by Indian sadhus: a taxi to Belur Math some miles distant. It was a pre-war, right-hand-drive Chevrolet, re-upholstered in figured calico. No street lights anywhere, and the night very dark and close. Once we were stopped by soldiers and the car thoroughly inspected. Nobody seemed to know the reason for the search. Perhaps smuggling of goods between India and East Pakistan was the reason. Then we crossed the Ganges and entered the Belur grounds. I was taken to my room—a corner of the second-floor veranda of the old guesthouse. In the wavering electric glare of a little bulb high up in the ceiling I saw my bed: a cotton pad on a wooden bench, with an overhanging mosquito net. A mosquito net! An old, old movie scene of Tallulah Bankhead in a house-boat on some humid, swamp-choked Far Eastern river rose to my mind. I was in the Orient, very much so.

It was 2.30 a.m., and I went to sleep instantly the minute I crawled into that unyielding bed. But India is geared to a schedule which permits two-thirds of your sleep at night and one-third at siesta time. Here Ganges-side factory whistles start blowing at 4.45 a.m.; dogs—and the numerous jackals which roam the Calcutta suburbs—bay at this time; and all the commotion of sunrise services from the infinitude of nearby temples pours out to assault you.

Before six o'clock the young man who was to help orient me had entered, to urge me to do what all other occupants of the Math do at the beginning of the day—make the rounds of the various temples on the grounds, to receive the blessing of the holy personalities they commemorate. His name was Manik Maharaj, a brahmachari of about thirty who had been a fiery independence worker before entering the Order. His head was shaved like those of the swamis, but with a difference. A small tuft was retained at the crown. Brahmacharis keep this lock until after ten years or so of novitiate they take the vows of sannyas. The tuft is the insignia of the brahmachari and is cut and burned when a man takes this final step of renunciation.

All morning Manik took me about, introducing me to other brahma-charis and to swamis of all grades of seniority. I was an object of intense interest, and the people who saw me stared with that frankness which only the unaffected dare to show. With as good a technique as I could manage I namaskared my equals with folded palms, and touched the feet of the swamis. The Math manager, Swami Nirvanananda, whose informal name is Sujji Maharaj, asked me about my requirements—whether I wanted a servant to prepare separate meals for me, if I needed someone to wash my clothes, and so on. I told him I hoped to enter the life of the Math as much as I could and didn't want any special attentions at all. I wanted to try to be a 'real' Indian brahmachari. It was the right answer, although I didn't know then just all that was involved!

Think of the Ganges, muddy at this point and more than half a mile wide, flanked by tropical vegetation, old houses and temples, and new factories. A few miles to the south is the heart of Calcutta, where the Howrah bridge goes across. Ocean-going ships come up this far, from the Bay of Bengal, some hundred miles away. To the north is another bridge, named after Lord Willingdon, once Viceroy of India. Just beyond this, on the opposite bank, is the temple of Dakshineswar, the locale of Sri Ramakrishna's adult life-drama. You can see its nine-towered main shrine from Belur. There is a mad variety of traffic on the river: little skiffs handled by one boatman; big freight vessels whose decks bend under the weight of bales of goods and a dozen oarsmen who stand and drive the craft forward to rhythmical chants; a few dilapidated launches and steamers; and a gun-boat or two.

The atmosphere of Belur Math is like a benediction. You rise in the cool dawn, perhaps in time to see the monks 'getting up the Lord' with chanting, ringing of a bell, and waving of little candles. Now the men, women, and children of the neighbourhood come through the gate, to use the Belur bathing ghat for their morning baths. There is a solemnity to the performance; indeed, it has the elegance, the stylization of a holy rite. Math inmates and visitors are now bowing before the temples, and many are sitting in meditation or calling out the sonorous words of some Sanskrit scripture. Breakfast is eaten at 7.00 a.m. At 8.30 the Math offices open, to close again about 11.00. During the morning, daily worship is performed in each of the temples. Then lunch. Now the sun has gone high and it is sleepy-time. Everything stops. Really, this is the only genuinely quiet time of day or night. Then it is four o'clock and the offices open again until vespers, which is at sunset. As it grows dark hundreds or thousands of devotees pour in from Calcutta and farther. Vespers is an impressive ceremony, with tremendous openhearted singing to the sound of cymbals, gongs, and drums. The monastic members sit on the floor nearest the shrine, with the laymen behind them, and the women and children farthest back. There is a ceaseless commotion of humanity coming up to bow before the deity—a most mobile, various, and colourful crowd.

Then the grounds empty, the gate is closed, and it is time for meditation. You sit on your bed under your net—for the mosquitoes are just fantastic in their numbers and voraciousness here—and seek to place your mind in the Lord. Supper is served at nine o'clock. Finally bedtime at ten-thirty. And as the immediate noises cease, it comes to you how busy life is outside, and how much of it there is. The squeaking, scurrying, fluttering is a rumble, and above this come the noises from the river: instrumental music and plaintive songs in an unfamiliar key.

Belur Math is a big place. The property must extend a thousand feet along the Ganges, and wider at some points and narrower at others, run back half a mile to the Grand Trunk Road. The district is suburban in feeling, although some industries are at work along the river front. The site where Belur Math began was once occupied by a boat-works. As the organization grew, adjacent parcels of land were acquired, so that the compound now is made up of properties containing buildings, tanks, walls, gardens, and even an ancient ruin or two, and is most irregular in shape.

From the river six major buildings stand out. These are the old headquarters building, the Swami Brahmananda temple, the Sri Sarada Devi temple, the Swami Vivekananda temple, the old guesthouse, and the main temple, dedicated to Sri Ramakrishna, rising long and high behind. But the grounds contain far more than this, for there are dormitories, kitchens, dining halls, a college, an industrial school, a post office, a free clinic, an experimental farm with a good dairy, a library, a salesroom for Mission books and industrial school products, and of course many offices. There is a picture of Belur Math opposite page 14.

I was interested in the guesthouse, because I was staying there, and because I had known Josephine MacLeod, who occupied the second floor on her frequent visits to Belur from 1916 onward. Later I found that this functional two-story structure is characteristic of much of the recent construction to be found in India today. The walls are of brick, plastered outside and in. Floors and ceilings are of concrete, supported on cast-iron girders, which I was surprised to find are cheaper than good wooden rafters. The roof is flat, to serve also as an open deck. The feeling of the interior is more that of a covered porch than of rooms, for there are no windows in the Western sense. There are many openings, but these have only louvered shutters, and vertical iron bars to deter unwanted visitors. Doors, window frames, and shutters are painted in a green oil paint, and the outside walls washed with lime of pale yellow. The guesthouse, like most other such buildings in India, even if newly painted, may give the look of long neglect because of the insistent suns and driving rains. The interior is almost empty, drapes, rugs, lamps, and other heat-catchers being absent. There are just the essentials: chairs, tables, beds, and wardrobes of wood, and clay drinking-water cooler jugs.

As I watched the Ganges traffic from my window I thought about Josephine MacLeod, or Tantine—'Auntie'—as she was usually called. Of all the individualists produced in America in that unhampered last half of the nineteenth century, Tantine would be a stand-out anywhere. When I knew her she was dying, a long skeleton of ninety-odd, but still tremendously strong-minded. Few have ever heard of Tantine now. But in years to come, when the growth of the Ramakrishna movement will make its telling the concern of professional historians, I believe Tantine will be a familiar and favourite figure. There is a picture of her opposite page 15.

Tantine's contribution is twofold. She was a friend and social sponsor of Swami Vivekananda when he brought the message of Vedanta to America and Europe in the late 1890s. She was an instrument of his being introduced into the most widely cultured circles of the day. Leaders of international society, as well as influential thinkers like William James, Max Müller, and Paul Deussen, became his ardent friends. In such a role, Tantine was a pioneer in helping to make Indian thought respectable in the West. And in India Tantine used her money and the influence she had among the British ruling classes—her niece was the Countess of Sandwich —to help a 'native' organization get a healthy start. The swamis still like to tell about the shrewd moves of this formidable Occidental female, of how she helped the Order hold and expand—in the face of British governmental and business pressures—the property of Belur Math.

How many articles have been written, and resolutions taken, endorsing East-West syntheses! But Tantine was a living example of it—one of the first thoroughly international Western persons of this new age.

And as I was first in India, I thought of Tantine in another connection. In her memoirs she tells of her first trip there in 1897 to visit Swami Vivekananda, after his return home as a national hero. She had written asking whether she should come. 'Yes, come,' the answer had been, 'if you want filth and degradation and poverty and many loin cloths talking religion. Don't come if you want anything else. We cannot bear one more criticism.' So she had gone. She had been perturbed, as any visitor is at first, at many things. One that she mentions is the 'primitive' look many Indians have, including many one associates with directly, because of the markings often worn on forehead and arms. The devotee who had come to meet her boat had borne the red stripes of the Vaishnavite. Later on she had happened to mention this to Swami Vivekananda.

'Hands off! What have you ever done?' he said to her sternly.

'I did not know what I had done then,' Tantine tells us. 'Of course I never answered. Tears came to my eyes and I waited. I learned later that Mr. Alasinga Perumal was a young brahmin teaching philosophy in a college in Madras, earning a hundred rupees a month, supporting his father, mother, wife, and four children, who had gone from door to door to beg the money and send Vivekananda to the West. Perhaps without him we never would have met Vivekananda.'

I had made up my mind not to criticize anything, or to show bad reactions, no matter what new or unexplainable experiences might greet me. This resolution was tested almost daily. At first India upset me considerably and I had times when I didn't know whether I could remain.

The second morning after my arrival I left the Belur grounds for the first time, to make my police registration. Swami Prematmananda, or Mahavir Maharaj, who shared the responsibility with Manik Maharaj of my orientation, accompanied me. We had to pass through what must be one of the worst slum sections of the world—yes, even a notch or two more dreadful than those of Harlem, of Chicago's west and south sides, or of Naples. What must have been difficult conditions previously had now been worsened by the arrival of the East Pakistan refugees. Hundreds of thousands of these had just set themselves down in this already overcrowded city.

Two impressions bear upon you in such places—the chaotic jumble of the physical features and the supersaturation of human and other life. Grandiose gates through walls never completed. New buildings reduced in no time to the general level of disorder by ill-conceived additions, little deletions, continual defacements. A feeling for the total effect seems to be missing. A shopkeeper will sweep energetically the little space in front of his establishment, leaving all the refuse at its borders. A hawker will take goods and build them up with infinite patience and neatness into a fine arrangement—right over an open sewer. Or someone will make new rooms on the veranda of an architecturally elegant nineteenth-century house by erecting mud walls on the marble floor between columns of classic Greek perfection.

And the quantities of men, women, children, cows, goats, dogs, cats, chickens, birds, flies, mosquitoes! Such an amount of life following so many destinies. You feel invaded, infringed upon. And there is always that fear, familiar to visitors to the tropics, of invisible sicknesses every-where, seeping out at you from walls, foliage, insects, passers-by. In those first days I felt the environment was rushing at me like a prairie fire, over-taking me, destroying me. The New York subway rider at rush hour travels in isolation compared to the passengers on the Howrah bus. So on that first ride to the police station I appreciated Mahavir Maharaj's con-sideration in manipulating for me the security of a seat, while he, my superior, rode standing.

The other big problem at first was the feeding. The main dining hall at Belur Math was a long alley-like structure, with a corrugated tin roof. At the sound of the gong you leave off your shoes, to enter barefoot and squat in two facing rows. Diners arrange themselves roughly according to seniority, with the older monks at the kitchen end, then brahmacharis, probationers, and men and boy lay visitors. You sit on a mat and eat from a leaf or plate of brass placed directly on the cement floor. Servants and monks walk up and down between the diners, ladling food on to the plates from pails. There is no silverware. Indians eat with their fingers, mixing the components on the plate with a deft wrist motion, carrying the wet morsels to the mouth with a gravity-defying fling. Like a pet extending a wounded paw, as a diner finishes he sits holding out his 'foody' hand. Then on a signal from a senior a closing grace is chanted and everybody rushes outside to the spiggots to wash.

I had trouble getting used to the Indian mode of eating. My main objec-tion was that it was needlessly unaesthetic. During the first few meals—with well over a hundred friendly but very curious people watching me—I managed to proceed just barely short of catastrophe.

But in a foreign land, if a visitor does not like some feature, that is *his* problem; it is not the local people who are wrong. For any guest, it is only good manners to assimilate the manners of the people he is visiting. This pleases them and helps them to accept you; and it helps you to become an insider in the shortest possible time. There is also something else, more subtle. If you merely observe a custom you may think it peculiar or pur-poseless. But if you participate, its inner meaning may reveal itself to you. I wanted to come to know my Indian associates, not as a guest, not as an outside observer looking in; I wanted to become one of them. How could I really grasp anything of India or Indians otherwise? So I kept quiet about the strangenesses and made the plunge. I took my chances with the rest of the standees on the bus. I immersed my fingers in the curry. Pretty soon the dislocations vanished. I was seeing things from *their* standpoint, and with knowledge, understanding and love came.

Before leaving home I had invested in clothing that I presumed would be suitable for the Indian sojourn. I had bought half a dozen pairs of cotton trousers and an equal number of porous sport shirts. But soon I learned that what might be attractive on an American golf course was not necessarily pleasing at Belur Math. The pants implied the 'smell' of sahib, while it appeared that, in Indian eyes, the knitted shirts had an objectionably underwearish look. For a visiting American businessman, professor, or tourist such clothing might be all right, but not for a brahmachari.

I had been watching to find out what the characteristic Indian dress might be. I am still wondering! The absence of some national apparel is typical of that famed variety you encounter in India. In many aspects, life there is rigid. But in certain fields it seemed to me that individuality is given a freer hand than at home. Surely this is true in the matter of clothing. Mass production and mass promotion have brought Americans considerable uniformity in appearance, but not so in India. I asked the Assistant Secretary, Swami Saswatananda, if he thought a typical dress might emerge in India and he said he thought not—and indeed who would want one?; the variety lent something very attractive to the scene.

In much of India the sari is fairly standard for women, although in some parts one will see gypsy-like skirts and satin or cotton trousers. Men wear everything imaginable—pants, jodhpurs, shorts, dhotis wrapped between the legs, dhotis wrapped around like a long skirt. Above are worn sleeveless undershirts, T-shirts, dress shirts, coats, chadars, and nothing at all. And some men wear only a loincloth.

There is, however, a characteristic dress for monks of the Ramakrishna Order. It is the same for brahmacharis as for swamis, except in colour. The colour for the former is white and that for the latter is gerrua. In fact, when one takes his final vows, he can convert his clothing very easily by just dipping his brahmachari apparel in a dye made of powdered gerrua stone and water. I saw this conversion at the time of Ramakrishna's birthday celebration, when fourteen brahmacharis took sannyas.

There are five components of this dress, plus a sixth variant. There is the kaupinam—a loincloth made of two strips of cloth. One strip encircles the waist; the other is run between the legs, over the strip in back, and back under again, to be tied over the waistband in front.

The second is the dhoti. This is the basic element of male clothing throughout India. It is merely a piece of cloth about forty-five inches wide and five yards long. It may be of thin machine-made cotton, costing less than an American dollar. It may be of hand-spun and hand-woven cotton khadi. It may even be of expensive silk. Babus (misters) drape the dhoti up between the legs, producing balloony pants and a kind of tail-like appendage in the rear—one of the most ugly styles, it seemed to me, to be found anywhere in the world. Monks generally, and some householders in the south, simply wrap the dhoti around so that it hangs straight and forms a skirt to the ankles.

The third component is the chadar. This is really nothing but a little portable blanket, serving the same multitudinous purposes as the Mexican poncho. It forms a topcoat, a shawl, a sun shield, a mosquito protection, a coverlet. It can be wadded up into a pillow. When the weather is too hot for it to be worn open, the chadar can be neatly folded lengthwise and placed over the left shoulder. Worn thus it gives one a dressy look, such as a European would gain while carrying gloves. In the south chadars are creased very narrow and knotted around the neck as scarves. Chadars can be of cheap machine-made cotton, khadi, silk, or wool, and are in size from that of a bathtowel to something more than a yard in width and three yards long. Borders are of all kinds, even of gold threads, and much of the style and desirability lies in the excellence of the border.

For Ramakrishna monks there is a little hat, designed by Vivekananda. This fourth component consists of a kind of overseas cap, with added ear flaps reaching past the chin. Normally the flaps are tucked into the upper part, but they may be lowered in cold weather.

The fifth element is the shirt. The old custom is for priests to wear no shirt when performing religious rites. I gathered that the shirt is a debatable item of wearing apparel, to be worn or not worn according to weather, occasion, and individual preference. Ramakrishna monks may leave them off when in their own quarters, but don their shirts when there are visitors or when they go out. Shirts are of many designs, the most common being like little jackets or like American white business shirts, except for having invisible pockets in the sides and being worn with the long tails hanging outside.

Finally, footwear. So many places in India must be approached barefoot that the shoe is a rather ambiguous article. Shoes are left outside shrines, temple compounds, living quarters, and even Indian-style shops. They are not worn even in secular places considered worthy of respect—for example inside a tomb like the Taj Mahal or at the cremation site of Gandhi. Hence in a sense footwear is a nuisance since there are so many places where one cannot take shoes—and there is at the same places the constant likelihood that good shoes will be stolen. A big secondhand footwear commerce exists, supplied from such sources. Protection of devotees' shoes is a concern at Ramakrishna establishments. At many of these a free checking service is provided on public occasions. In places where no formal arrangements exist for the keeping of visitors' shoes, people make their living watching over footwear for the public. Most Indians have developed thick soles on their feet; some thus eliminate the problem by dispensing with shoes entirely. Monks of the Ramakrishna Order may go barefoot in the monastery, or may wear common wooden clogs which can be left about without danger of loss. But when they go out they usually wear neat leather sandals called chapals, or even slippers of suede looking rather like old-fashioned dancing pumps.

So Manik Maharaj brought me a couple of dhotis and chadars and insisted that we go to a nearby tailor to have some shirts made. Put the pants and sport shirts away, he ordered. And he was quite right in forcing me into what at first seemed like a masquerade costume. I am too conservative to have taken the leap without pressure. Wearing the monstica garb proved to have been strategically a very good move, and after the first few times of feeling extremely strange, I began to realize that it was a very fine dress for India.

The dhoti is put on like this. You double it, so that you have a piece about two and a half yards in length, and reaching from the waist to the ankles. You start at the left hip and come around once and then across to the right hip. You tuck it in tightly there, then make an accordion pleat with the left-over material in the middle of the front. For security reasons I wore a belt at first, but soon I found that by rolling the cloth a little around the top you can make the garment snug enough to stay up for hours without adjustment. To put on a chadar properly you first drape it over the shoulders like a shawl with the ends hanging down on either side, the right one a little longer than the left. Then you throw the right end over the left shoulder. Next you run your left arm down under the left end like feeling into a sleeve, and bring the material around and back so that it falls down the left front with the border perpendicular.

I don't mean to give the impression that there is a regulation habit which must be worn in a particular way by members of the Ramakrishna Order. Quite the contrary. The freedom I observed in dress would be indicative of the liberality permitted in Indian monastic practices generally. In India the idea is that renunciation gives one the right of progressive freedom. There a worldly man must obey countless outward observances. But should he become a full-time religious aspirant, society ceases to expect particular responsibilities from him. It is felt that he has now earned the privilege of pursuing any individual behaviour which may be of spiritual aid. This would apply equally to women as to men. In India women of the home live almost as in confined orders. But if a woman chooses a religious life, she may move about the world freely, boldly. No one will think her immodest; no one will harm her. I saw several of these wandering sannyasinis.

So when I give this description of the monastic dress of the Ramakrishna Order I mean only that it is approximately as stated. Innumerable variations are to be seen. One great opportunity for personal expression is in the manner of wearing the cap. Ear flaps in, ear flaps out, ear flaps half in and half out, ear flaps tilted in a certain way—so that from great distances individuals can be recognized from the outline of the head. In the West swamis of the Ramakrishna Order wear the dress of the country in which they are residing. And, by the way, there are no distinguishing insignias for the higher echelons. Senior swamis, trustees, and officers wear precisely the same kind of clothes as everyone else. In addition to the freedom, I was pleased to note this very good expression of democracy.

Anybody brought up to the reassurance of trousers at first feels exposed, undressed in a dhoti. The material is light in weight, and the garment is open to updrafts and likely to fly apart past the knee with each step. But I found a great joy in wearing 'the cloth'. I admire its simplicity and cleanliness. One washes his clothes every day, just as he bathes every day. Being merely a long piece of yardage, the dhoti can be easily dried in the sun. It dries without a wrinkle, as though ironed. If you want it to look especially nice you may fold it precisely and place it beneath your mattress for further pressing. Putting on your dhoti each day is like wrapping yourself up in fresh air and sunlight. Frankly, I felt lucky to be wearing enlisted man's white rather than officers' gerrua. One feels so stately in white—so immaculate, so classic!

Putting on the cloth took me out of the category of foreign guest and helped me to be taken seriously as a sadhu. It was astonishing to see how magically this worked. When you wear their dress you are compared to Indians; the monastic community begins unconsciously to think of you as Indian. I would hear them speaking of me as resembling this or that acquaintance. In India beauty is more in lightness of colour than regularity of features. So it seems I not only was regarded as an Indian but even as a kind of ideal Indian! I was constantly spoken of as being able to pass for a Kashmiri brahmin.

I didn't shave my head; pure vanity restrained me. Fortunately everybody agreed to my not doing so, although on a different basis; they were afraid I would catch cold. Nor did I adopt the kaupinam. I continued to wear my boxer shorts—which worked out fine, except when I was caught between an observer and strong, low sunlight. Then the silhouette of the unorthodoxy beneath the orthodoxy caused amusement, which I also shared.

When I was in Rome on the way to India, the Vatican reminded me of a fortified Renaissance city. There are walls and palaces; there are soldiers and grand personages—a glittering court.

In contrast, Belur Math is like a timeless rural village. It has its main street, its market place, its fields and recreation areas. Cows graze on the lawns. It has a full and complex human society. But there is little observation of any protocol, and great informality prevails. I have no doubt that personal squabbles occur as in any community, together with a certain amount of 'political manoeuvring'. But nobody seems to press his own personal motives very seriously. Mostly it is amiability, tranquillity, ingenuousness—and what a Yankee might consider to be a touch of indolence—that one encounters.

It is peculiar what an effect these qualities can produce in the brash Westerner. Just as a charming child or pet can make the most coldhearted person turn soft in his presence, so the people I met at Belur Math brought out in me traits I had forgotten I possessed. 'What a loving person you must be to come so far to pay us a visit,' they would say, looking at me affectionately. All this imputation of their own goodness on to me had the effect of making me good—or at least better—too. I found myself all softened up, manifesting a simplicity of feeling and reaction that had not been a part of my character for years.

The organization inspired by Sri Ramakrishna, founded by Swami Vivekananda in 1897, and headed during the formative two decades by Swami Brahmananda, has one purpose: to help people realize God. Monastic members are encouraged to do this through those usual spiritual practices which are a part of Hindu monastic tradition, and through something new in Indian monasticism—selfless service to mankind irrespective of caste and creed. This service consists of teaching the Vedanta philosophy in India and abroad as revitalized and extended by Sri Ramakrishna, and of sponsoring social service activities in India: schools, hospitals, relief stations, Red-Cross-type disaster works, agricultural experimental activities, and many more. The monastic training programme is carried on by the Ramakrishna Math, and the public service programme by the Ramakrishna Mission. Two organizational set-ups are preserved for the sake of appropriate collection and allocation of funds, but in effect there is one organization, since both have common officers, trustees, and to a large extent personnel, and both have headquarters at Belur Math.

The president is Swami Sankarananda. There is a picture of him opposite page 15. And he is in a group photo taken when he visited Madras in January (turn to page 113). This latter is like an old-fashioned school class graduation portrait. We are lined up in two rows: the brahmacharis standing in the back, and the swamis seated in front, with President Maharaj resting in a big armchair in the precise centre, a flower garland around his neck.

In the pictures President Maharaj looks, as he does in person, kind and grandfatherly. You soon grow to realize he is far more than that. The President of the Ramakrishna Order is chosen by the trustees on the basis of seniority and spiritual competence. He is the spiritual head of the organization. As chief guru he is considered the primary channel for the transmission of spiritual power. It is he who initiates aspirants into spiritual life. It is he who solemnizes monastic vows.

In India holiness is regarded as more valuable than rubies. Anyone believed to possess it is enormously revered. It is felt that one may ingest virtue himself by being in the presence of virtue—by seeing, by touching a possessor of it. This process is referred to as obtaining darshan. Thus it is the custom at Belur Math, or wherever President Maharaj is in residence, for the monastic members to come in after morning meditation to greet him, bowing before him as he sits in his big chair, touching his feet. At this time bits of news are exchanged and inquiries made into the health and welfare of each member. In the evening after vespers and on holy days Swami Sankarananda takes his place in a reception room, where the public is permitted to come to him. It is at these times that persons whom he has initiated visit him, or persons who are seeking initiation make their requests known.

Two brahmachari attendants and a sannyasin secretary look after the President's physical needs, help him with his wide correspondence, and regulate his visitors to some extent. But little formality is followed. On public days, if the crowd of people wishing to receive darshan of President Maharaj pushes too precipitously at him, some attempt to form them into an orderly line may be made. If a caller remains for an unseemly long time, one of the attendants may make some move to hurry the interview to a close. But it is all kept casual, informal. The President has no office. His bedroom is his workroom and his audience chamber. There is no paraphernalia of status at all.

Mahavir Maharaj took me to call on President Maharaj a day or two after my arrival. I was nervous because I respected him so much—he had known many of the original disciples of Sri Ramakrishna and as a young man had been Swami Brahmananda's attendant and private secretary for many years. Also I didn't want to disgrace my guru through failure to follow correct etiquette. Mahavir Maharaj made a full-length prostration and then introduced me. I saluted the President with folded palms and stooped to take the dust of his feet. He seemed full of joy to see me and pointed to a chair on his right, asking me to sit down. We talked enthusiastically for a long time, discussing the work in Hollywood and all that I had seen at the other Vedanta Societies I had visited in America and Europe on the way to India. It was not until I was ready to leave that I realized that Mahavir Maharaj had remained seated on the floor. Embarrassment exploded inside of me. I recalled some Hindu injunction that juniors are supposed to sit on a level below that of seniors—and who could be more senior than the President or more junior than I? I knew that I had committed a serious breach of good form in taking the chair. I felt bad about it ever afterwards; the memory of my mistake still fills me with shame.

Since that painful episode I have tried to comprehend why President Maharaj invited me to take the chair. As time has passed I have perhaps begun to understand. His action was the result, I now see, of the attributes of holiness, where so-called logical gestures or normal motives do not apply.

This is the explanation I have reached. A deep and unqualified respect for others—even for the 'undeserving'—is one of the qualities of the holy man. As a Westerner I was a chair-sitter, not a floor-squatter. This President Maharaj knew, so that his natural act was to invite me to take a chair. The comfort of his child from the West (not any question of respect or disrespect toward himself) was the topmost concern in his mind.

In addition, my mistake, I am sure, had no effect upon him. If he noticed what I did at all he probably never thought of it again. He was not affected. (And if I am to be honest, hurt ego was the sole reason actually that making the mistake bothered me.) This is the second observation I would make as to the quality of sanctity. Like God, saints look at our shortcomings and are not disturbed by them. Indeed, if we love them, I think they are almost blind to our transgressions.

But see what effect the attitudes of saintliness have upon *us*. Although we are ignorant of how ignorant we are, we are not abandoned. By being treated with respect and acceptance—which is the saint's pure love—we begin to love in return. And as we begin to love the holy man, we commence to emulate him, so that quite naturally and painlessly, we correct ourselves.

An equally vivid event occurred when I was presented to the General Secretary. My anticipation in meeting Swami Madhavananda was great. The holder of this office is the top executive of the Math and Mission. And Swami Madhavananda was and is known as a razor-sharp administrator, and has a distinguished reputation as an author and Sanskrit scholar as well. He rarely leaves his room; he sleeps but little. His responses are brief and honest when he is asked for opinions or directions. His time is so efficiently scheduled that—despite the fact he has few of the usual accessories of power—he does a mountain of work and carries on his spiritual practices without seeming busy at all.

When I went to meet Swami Madhavananda he was sitting in a lounge chair with his feet stretched out; I believe he was reading proof. Like a soldier preparing to salute a general, I thought when I stooped to make my pranam, 'I must do this with as good form as I can muster.' I reached forward to touch his feet.

'No, no,' shouted Swami Madhavananda.

I pulled back and rose, extremely disconcerted. We had a short talk, with me standing.

Later I found out that the General Secretary had been troubled with a skin irritation so that he found it painful to have people touch him.

But this awkward start opened the way to what I felt to be a warm relationship. I never attempted to bow to this very senior sadhu again and I was relieved not to feel a need to. Having worked in the West for several years in the late 1920s, Swami Madhavananda knew, I think, that such salutations do not come too easily to Westerners. I always felt he regarded external evidences of respect as botherations also. At least such was my interpretation.

I saw Swami Madhavananda often, pleasantly, informally. Toward the end of my stay I presented myself before him with a prepared list of searching questions on the state and conduct of the Order. It would have been easy to consider me bumptious. But Swami Madhavananda gave me a straight answer to everything I asked about.

I wish I could describe all the other inmates of Belur Math. They parade now before my inner eye—young and old, smart and simple, fatty and underweight—a wonderful aggregate of individuality and good-heartedness. There was the elder swami with the Santa Claus beard and mane who died while I was there and was cremated in the Math ground beside the Ganges. There was the sadhu who, even on hot days, went about heavily enwrapped in a wool blanket, with only his eyes peering out. I assume some tropical disease must have harmed his circulation. One old monk habitually wore Victorian gaiters. One wore earrings, necklaces of holy beads the size of acorns, and conch-shell bracelets. It is said that in his relationship to God he took the attitude of being a hand maiden of the Divine Mother. Some sadhus carried staffs. Foreheads were unadorned or marked with white or red, according to personal viewpoint.

Perhaps the tendency is for young swamis and brahmacharis to maintain more outward austerity than do seniors, who have at last graduated to the freedom of being fully themselves. It is said that the mind becomes the guru in time. Most of the brahmacharis impressed me as enthusiastic, hard-working, business-like—not so different from idealistic college-age men in the United States. There were a few very young pre-probationers of perhaps seventeen or eighteen.

The head musician at Belur Math is Prahlad Maharaj. The first time we met I went to him to obtain recommendations as to the names of good phonograph records of Indian music to take back to Hollywood. Because several other visitors from America had come to him to learn the Math songs, he thought that was my purpose too. But if there is anything I cannot do and have no interest in, it is singing. Prahlad Maharaj's English is sketchy, and Bengali is totally foreign to me. A state of confusion existed for a long time, while he demanded with growing excitement that I just try a few notes, and I tried more and more irritably to get him to give me the titles of some recordings. Finally an English-Bengali speaking swami from the next room, weary at last of the pandemonium, came and straightened things out.

I was not able, in India, to grasp much of the ins and outs of the caste system. Its workings are too subtle for my powers of observation. But I suppose the hired helpers at Belur Math—of whom there must have been at least twenty-five—were of lower castes, and castes appropriate to the work they did: yard and room cleaning, cow herding, gate keeping, and policing at the time of large crowds. But I did see this, that these servants were attractive persons, seemingly well adjusted vocationally, and treated with consideration by the monastic personnel. I still fondly remember Govinda, who trudged in tousle-headed at dawn to wash my floor and fetch the day's drinking water. There was the clear-eyed, laughing youngster always moving about with wheelbarrow and long broom of twigs, whose job it was to keep the grounds tidy. And I can still see the fine-looking temple guard in neatly pressed uniform of khaki blouse and shorts, but barefoot, who always saluted me smartly with his baton.

India has had many invaders. She has been conquered in succession by the Persians, the Greeks under Alexander, by Bactrians, Scythians, Afghans, Moguls, and finally the British. Still, if India cannot claim many victories, at least in the long run she has never lost a war. With the exception of the British, each wave of invaders came as foreign conquerors and remained to be Indian subjects. They lost their allegiance to their homelands, intermarried, and settled in India permanently. Gradually they adopted many of the customs of the country, enriching the country also by sharing features of their own civilization with the inhabitants. They came to speak local languages and even—with the exception of the Mohammedans—began to practise the Hindu religion.

But the British wouldn't let themselves be absorbed. Evidences of their hermetically sealed separateness remain: English countryside churches looking so peculiar with palms and plantain trees around them, and now going rather out of repair; cantonment areas in the European style, snobbishly established outside the city limits; clubs in the best quarters with porticos grand and ominous. The British wouldn't let themselves be absorbed, and in India they did not colonize. So they had at last to retreat.

Hence the sight of an 'Englishman' seriously studying Indian knowledge, purposely trying to get himself absorbed, was a big attraction whenever visitors came to Belur Math. I would see little children pulling at their mothers and whispering to them to look around and see the curiosity. Students and other young men constantly cornered me, sometimes twenty or thirty at a time, to ask me to please tell them what I saw in their religion. They have been told endlessly that their culture must be inferior because —otherwise why would their country be so poor? Reading American magazines, seeing American movies, and contrasting the material state of the two civilizations, one can make this mistake easily. The Indian doesn't know about the problems of mental disease in the United States, of alcoholism, of material satiety and boredom. For someone to come from America—and especially from Hollywood—as a pilgrim and co-devotee made them regard what was their own with new eyes. It also produced an outpouring of affection which was often embarrassing. I received several letters pledging everlasting friendship. I was induced to exchange addresses with some, and promise to write. Some went to the trouble of bringing cameras, or in one case, taking me to a photographer's salon, to have their pictures taken with me. Everybody wanted to take me home to meet his father. One young man, when I demurred, argued: 'But I am a brahmin.'

This adoration was so fresh, so artless, as to make me ashamed of my inability to return it. Shraddha and Bob Louis are Americans who lived in India for many years. He was in the importing business there. Shraddha told me that Indians are capable of devotion such as we in the West cannot even dream of. She was a student at the Chicago centre, of Swami Gnaneswarananda, who died in 1939. She told me how she went to his home town in East Bengal to tell his family of his last days and to honour her teacher's memory. Not only was she invited into—and actually visited—every house in the entire village; but when she had finished, a bent old lady appeared. This woman had been trailing her for hours and miles from house to house in the heat, always just missing her, with the purpose of honouring her— worshipping her feet, as they call it—with flowers. Painfully she knelt down and placed a blossom between each of Shraddha's toes.

In many externals India is an upsetting country. I fear that the new policy of trying to attract tourists there may do as much harm as good. This land provides few of the distractions Western travellers seek, and the sights of starvation and poverty that cannot be avoided may end in disgusting or confusing them. In terms of the English Lake Country, Paris, the Riviera, the Alps, or Florence, India is simply not a tourist destination. But already I could see that behind the dilapidation a small and secret structure rose in ever-newness and beauty. Could I make my way into that shrine? Had I the qualities of authenticity, would the grace be afforded, that I might reach it?

CHAPTER II

THE GODS AND GODDESSES
OF DAKSHINESWAR

THERE are in Europe and America many places of pilgrimage. Some that we hear about often are Lourdes in France, Assisi in Italy, Sainte-Anne-de Beaupré in Canada, Guadalupe in Mexico, and of course Rome and Jerusalem. Why do people travel to these places? I expect many go just for the fun of it—as one would make an excursion to Coney Island, Brookfield Zoo, or Catalina. There are sights to see, things to do. Perhaps a few travel to spots associated with holy personalities as acts of devotion. Many apparently go in order to win particular favours. For example, I remember a sign at the infirmary cell at Assisi where St. Francis died. It stated that the visitor obtains an indulgence of a certain number of days or of years as a result of having worshipped there. An indulgence is a reprieve of such-and-such an amount of time one may have to remain in purgatory in expiation of earthly sins, even though these have been forgiven through confession and absolution. There is a pale resemblance in this to the Hindu notions of karma and, indeed, of reincarnation. Inadequacies must be compensated for through further effort; and one is 'born into' a place where this can be worked out. However, the Hindu would question the validity of earthly time operating in a non-earthly realm such as purgatory. Finally, as the *Catholic Dictionary* states, Christians go on pilgrimages as penances.

People go on pilgrimages in India, too. In fact, doing so seems to be a national preoccupation. Just as in America one is practically nobody if he has not been to Europe at least once, so in India one's social pre-eminence is improved in accordance with the number, length, and difficulty of one's religious perambulations. And, according to Vedic tradition, some visitation of holy places is important in one's retirement years to round out, to make harmonious, the pattern of his life. There is a gigantic hierarchy of sanctified spots, running upward from the neighbourhood shrine to the so-called four sacred destinations in the four corners of India.

I do not believe Indians go on pilgrimages with the idea of doing penance. The notions of sin and atonement do not seem to be motives in Hinduism. But they certainly go on religious journeys for the other reasons common to Westerners; for the fun of it; to gain a boon; and as an act of devotion. Still, I think, the main reason is different from any of these, and a reason that one cannot grasp unless he has a conception of the Hindu science of 'vibrations'.

As I understand this study, everything in the phenomenal world is conceived of as composed of vibrations or wave lengths or undulating molecules. A chair, a flower, a body—these are nothing but atomic arrangements. Their composition can be known through the five senses, assisted by instruments. So far this Hindu view coincides with the findings of modern physics. But the Indian believes that the mind, too, is material. That bundle of experience and potentiality, that reservoir of knowledge, memory, tendencies, and attitudes which we call a person's mind is also composed of matter, of a very subtle kind. The matter of a chair or flower or body has definite characteristics—weight, colour, smell—which can be perceived by the sense organs. According to the Indian science of vibrations, every mind also has characteristics. These are projected much as weight, colour, or smell are projected, and can be perceived by some subtle apparatus in other minds. Every mind is thus revealing its own particular characteristics; we go about as veritable sending towers, each encompassed in a cloud of his individual signals. The West is straining toward an understanding of this through its interest in field theory. Everyday proof is common. Someone comes into your room in a depressed state. He doesn't need to say a word; you don't even need to see his face. But you can sense his state, and in turn you may become depressed. Likewise, if you go into the presence of a depressed person in a good frame of mind, you may affect him positively. Different minds have different powers of projection and reception, depending on their relative quality of concentration. Mental atmosphere is thus believed to be transferable from mind to mind. The condition of another will affect me when I am in his presence, and my state will affect him. These subtle vibrations are also thought to permeate and remain in gross material objects. You leave a trace of yourself in everything you have had contact with: a piece of work you have done; some article of clothing you have worn; the remainder of food on your plate—and for that matter, even the plate—when you have eaten. These will be steeped in your whole temperamental atmosphere.

One needs to grasp this Hindu science of subtle vibrations if he would hope to understand much of Indian social practice. For example, the unfamiliar notions of darshan and prasad become logical on the basis of this idea. In the first chapter of his *Lead Kindly Light*, Vincent Sheean attempts to explain darshan. After a long analysis he gives this definition: 'Darshan in practice is a form of happiness induced among Hindus by being in the presence of some great manifestation of their collective consciousness. It may be a person, place or thing, and represent past, present or future, so long as it sets up the definite recognizable glow of suprapersonal happiness.' This is needlessly complex. All we need to say is that darshan is getting good vibrations by being in the presence of them. Of course this makes one happy. The effect is believed to be enhanced if one can see, as well as merely be in the field of, the worthy source. But darshan has nothing to do with being or not being a Hindu. This concept is simply a rational explanation of why we are affected by people we associate with or places we go to and why selectivity in the company we keep or the places we frequent is important. If the science of subtle vibrations is true, having darshan is a universal human experience, except that some of the world does not call it that or consciously cultivate it.

As I understand it, taking prasad is the same thing carried a step further. It is the process of getting good vibrations by touching. Prasad is an actual relic of someone, which one accommodates to himself, with the object thus of absorbing its vibrations. To possess a piece of clothing worn by a great soul is the same as having an amulet. Food is considered especially conductive of vibrations. Enjoying food left by an impure person or prepared by a cook whose mind is unclean can affect one adversely, while eating the remainder of food touched by a holy man is believed to be very helpful.

Thus, when an Indian goes on a pilgrimage, what he is really trying to do usually is to gather up holy vibrations. To accumulate such subtle matter in one's mind is to improve the quality of, and in time to purify, that mind. The object of veneration in a temple is believed to be charged with good vibrations. Holy men who have worshipped it have left a residue of holiness. The spiritual attributes of worshippers at the spot remain. A sacred place accumulates good vibrations like a savings bank into which money is deposited; it also has available good vibrations, as a savings bank has money, accessible to any who may wish to make a withdrawal.

The object of veneration at holy places in India is usually an image of one of the many aspects of God. But it need not be. It may be an abstract representation, like a Shiva lingam; it may be a particular part of a river or a confluence of rivers; it may be a special formation of rock. One will even see people in attitudes of worship before what look like very average, ordinary trees. The Indian is sophisticated in matters of religion and mysticism. Of course he doesn't think the infinite Lord is the idol, lingam, water, rock, or tree. What he is straining toward is recollectedness—as constant a running out of the mind toward God as possible. Thus he establishes reminders everywhere. He keeps holy pictures and a shrine in his home. He builds big temples which are also to a certain extent clubs, fair-grounds, recreational headquarters—places to go and focuses for social life. And if he discovers a natural spot which is unusually inspirational, he doesn't build a cocktail lounge or motel there as the American might do, but constitutes it as a place of worship.

C

In the Bhagavad-Gita there is the promise: 'Howsoever you conceive of Me, if you really desire Me, I will come to you in accordance with your conception.' Once designated as holy, an object of veneration will thus have the tendency actually to increase in holiness and to become holy. I set up some representation of divinity. I channel my longing, my devotion for God into and through it. Others come and do the same. Holy men also worship there. Vibrations build up and a genuine place of sanctity is established. In time the accumulation of earnest entreaty may even induce the Reality which is being celebrated there to infuse itself fully into the representation. Then the phenomenon appears of what is known as an awakened deity. (Yes, the word deity is used even for a lingam, a natural formation, a holy tree.) The Lord is considered to be fully present in an awakened deity. Most places of national pilgrimage are places where the deity is considered to be awakened. How compassionate God is: He can be induced by man, can actually be forced, to infuse his power into any representation which it is pleasant and natural for us to establish and worship!

The pilgrim thus seeks to establish connection with God, seeks to absorb good vibrations, through the two procedures of darshan and prasad. To see a deity is important and valuable. I can still hear the shouts of joy from the pilgrims as they entered the temple of Jagannath to catch their first sight of the surrealistic figures of Jagannath, Balaram, and Subhadra. Non-Hindus and unsympathetic foreigners were and to some extent still are not permitted close proximity to a deity. But even these are granted the privilege of darshan. At even the most orthodox temples they are allowed to enter up to a certain point, or look in through a peephole, thus enjoying the deity's darshan. In other words, sudras may receive good vibrations through darshan, without impairing the level of vibrations of the temple through introducing their own. This seems unforgivably snobbish until you realize that the Indian believes that one's caste in the present life may be for some a reflection of the spiritual level gained through struggle in previous lives.

Prasad, being more intimate, is considered more efficacious. It is not surprising that a major part of Indian worship consists in presenting food to the deity, then taking a portion of that food back to be consumed. One considers God a friend, a guest, a son or daughter, a respected elder, a lover. What is more natural than to want the privilege of feeding him? In turn, as a friend, guest, child, elder, or lover he does accept your hospitality —he does consume the food's subtle essence—and gives his leavings to you, which you can enjoy as God's prasad. Clothing is given to him, to be taken back and worn with his blessing; the vermilion or ash placed on the forehead may be offered first—so that when you are wearing the sign of your denomination you are also bearing his mark. The Hindu has the practice of using holy water, too, as Catholics do. But this is not blessed by a priest and sprinkled over one. It is the 'bathwater' of the Lord, taken inwardly in a tiny sip.

I admit these ideas and practices appear fantastic at first. But even if there is nothing demonstrable in the concepts of darshan and prasad, one must notice at least how recollectedness is built up. Hammer, hammer, hammer on the mind, driving in associations between everyday things and God.

I realize that these methods appear hopelessly dualistic—play activities for simple souls. Well, they are, to a large extent, for really what percentage of mankind can think of goodness or beauty or bliss or truth abstractly, divorced from actual exemplifications thereof? But Sri Ramakrishna showed that dualism is a stage on the way to non-dualism; in the highest illumination we become perforce non-dualistic, as we also become non-denominational. The Vedantist would say that you can evaluate an aspirant's level of realization on the basis of how non-dualistic or non-denominational he is. If a person designated a saint continues to emphasize organizational allegiance, the Vedantist would say that that individual's spiritual eye has opened less fully than that of one who has grown less aware of such distinctions.

Hindu religious psychology prepares the way in dualism for non-dualism. The Vedantist knows about and subscribes to the actuality of the Atman—that spirit which is co-equal with God, which actually is God—present in completeness in each human person. He agrees that the purpose of man's life is to uncover this Atman and know one's identity with it. Then one also realizes his brotherhood—indeed, his selfsameness—with everyone else in the world and sees that men and women, Hindus, Christians, and Buddhists, good characters and bad, are not fundamentally different at all, but Spirit which has solidified in so many various forms. The deity outside he sees thus to be only a tangible representation of what is truly inside, but less easy to visualize there. The installation ceremony of an image consists in invoking into the wood or stone the spirit which is known to be within the installer; meditation is to some extent the reverse process, visualizing what is seen outside, inside.

I had no clear idea, when I arrived at Belur Math, of exactly which places of pilgrimage I wanted to visit. I only knew that I had a wish to see the workings of the Ramakrishna Mission in as many installations as possible and to go at least to the Dakshineswar temple and to Sri Ramakrishna's birthplace at Kamarpukur. But gradually a kind of classification scheme developed, which I recommend to anyone making a religious journey to India. I wish I could have carried it out more fully myself.

You may classify the holy destinations under these headings: First, natural spots with religious significance. Leading examples of these would be Rishikesh and Hardwar, where the Ganges issues into the plains from the Himalayas; the meeting of the Ganges and Jamuna rivers at Allahabad; Cape Comorin at the southernmost tip of the subcontinent where the Bay of Bengal and the Indian Ocean flow together; and the Amarnath rock cave with ice lingam, difficult of approach in a formidable section of the Himalayas, said to be the abode of Shiva. Second, old and power-charged temples. Jagannath at Puri is an outstanding example of such; others are the so-called Golden Lotus temple at Madura in the south, Kalighat in Calcutta, the Gadadhar temple at Gaya, the Vishwanath temple at Benares, and the Badrinath temple twelve thousand feet high in the Himalayas above Hardwar. Third, religious communities. These are not necessarily located near auspicious formations of nature nor are they always the sites of great temples. They are simply towns or cities which, either through tradition or because of the spiritual current God-men have generated there, have come to be regarded as having a spiritual atmosphere; Brindaban, Benares, Bhubaneswar, Conjeevaram, and Rameswaram would be examples. Fourth, places associated with the birth, illumination, preaching, or death of incarnations of God. The location of the Bodhi tree at Gaya where Buddha reached nirvana, and the deer park at Sarnath where he gave his first sermon, are such places. Mathura near Agra is revered as the scene of Krishna's birth. The ecstatic love for God Sri Chaitanya thrilled to still vibrates in Puri. And already these have become places of pilgrimage because of their association with Sri Rama-krishna: the remote Bengal hamlet where he was born and grew up; the grove of trees near the Dakshineswar temple where he prayed and medi-tated intensely to realize God; his room at Dakshineswar where he uttered his gospel and trained his disciples; the villa in the Calcutta suburb of Cossipore where he died.

I have listed only a few and the most familiar examples under each of the four headings. They could be added to greatly. Of course, functioning holy places are not the only sites worth seeing in India. There are many archaeological treasures—constructions originally religious, of course—whose connection with religion today is not so close. These would include the Ajanta mural-filled caves, the peculiar monolithic stone city of Mahabalipuram, and the sensational ruined temple of Konarak. I have not mentioned a single Moslem place or structure, not even the Taj Mahal. I have done so purposely. None that I saw appealed to me as having, compared to Hindu places, strong religious atmosphere, nor much of artistic worth beyond a static picturesqueness.

It is 1855. In the United States Franklin Pierce is President. Trouble between the North and South is growing. Abraham Lincoln has just emerged from provincial obscurity into Illinois politics. The British Empire is reaching out, strong and secure, with Victoria already having completed a score of years as queen. Napoleon III, nephew of Bonaparte, is Emperor of a prosperous France. Italy is moving toward unification.

In the realm of ideas fracturing is far advanced. Christianity's hold over man's mind and person has long since broken down, with humanism and naturalism rushing into the vacuum, but hardly doing more than adding to the confusion. Nobody knows what to believe. The God of the Middle Ages has vanished and no replacement has been found. Leading thinkers are now looking to science to provide a new foundation for idealism and faith. It is a time of uncertainty and doubt, which are to increase, rather than lessen, in the hundred years to follow.

In India the British have been in control of the Madras and Bengal areas for fifty years. The land is yet prosperous, with the famines and malaria epidemics which are to devastate the country still some years in the future. But confusion exists in India, too. Centuries of Mohammedan military and religious invasions have disrupted old ways of life in the central and northern parts. In the large cities Christianity and Western rationalism have been introduced. Although they are still talked about a great deal, sound Vedic religious and social practices have deteriorated. Caste regulations have multiplied to a ridiculous extent, and sects and denominations have developed bewilderingly.

Four miles above Calcutta, on the eastern bank of the Ganges, a wealthy woman is bringing to an end the construction of a big temple. Her name is Rani Rasmani. She has made a huge fortune in real estate dealing and property management. She is highly respected and devout. Building a temple is an act thought to be productive of good karma. But there is more here than mere personal self-interest. The Rani is a genuine devotee. Her good heart seeks to build a dwelling place where the Lord may be beautifully housed and fed and well decorated with costly ornaments. She wants to sponsor a headquarters of spirituality where—according to the custom of the country—other devotees such as penniless sadhus and pilgrims in transit can find free sleeping and feeding accommodations, where devotional music may be played, and where the scriptures may be read and pundits may come to discuss religious matters before audiences of the best people.

There is one hitch. The Rani is of the fourth caste. Sudras may not feed deities, nor will brahmins, kshatriyas, or vaisyas accept a sudra's hospitality. The best advice is sought as to how to overcome this hindrance. From a certain scholar-priest comes a formula which is found to be workable. Upon completing it the Rani must give the temple away, placing it in the name of some high-caste person. She may stay on as executive officer and financial provider, but if technically the temple belongs to a brahmin, traditions will not be abused and worship and hospitality may be engaged in acceptable to all. The Rani deeds the temple to her guru and installs the author of the saving prescription as head priest. The temple is consecrated. The total cost of the land, structures, and dedication festivities is estimated to have been at least a third of a million dollars. In addition, there is the daily maintenance cost of the big and busy community, which is enormous.

The new priest is a man of about fifty, having come from the rural Bengal town of Kamarpukur. His name is Ramkumar Chatterjee. Needing assistance, he appoints his nineteen-year-old brother, Gadadhar, as helper. Ramkumar dies a year later, leaving Gadadhar in charge. Except for two or three trips to his home town and a pilgrim journey to Benares and Brindaban, Gadadhar remains at the temple for the next thirty years. He becomes known as Sri Ramakrishna and is acclaimed by a few in his time as an incarnation of God in the modern age.

At the present time the Dakshineswar temple is deteriorating. The great tiled courtyard is uneven; the gardens and woods are unkempt; the south music tower is rotting away, succumbing to jungle vegetation. Maintenance is not a strong point in India. I was saddened to see that this spot of the highest historical value—and which also from a purely religious point of view is already a popular pilgrim destination—should be let to deteriorate so badly. Coloured paper is hung over gaps, and home-made props are inserted to sustain places which should be repaired with solid brick and stone.

In the interest of future generations it should be carefully guarded and lovingly preserved. Some will agree. Some will not regard the matter so seriously. 'Why worry?' might be their attitude. 'Let us get what we can from the atmosphere of this place while it is still standing. Yes, Dakshineswar will decay, but what matter? It is not well to cling too anxiously to mere material relics. Discount the apparent; seek the Real. Anyway, the Lord will come again and again, and there will be many new Dakshineswars.' This attitude, of course, helps to explain why India has little recorded history.

But a hundred years ago Dakshineswar is a splendid place. The reader should consult the map which appears as this book's frontispiece, photograph 2b, and the notes on Dakshineswar on page 222. The establishment has two main parts—the temple compound, and the surrounding grounds. The grounds contain tanks, orchards, and flower gardens, and a grove of trees where Sri Ramakrishna often meditated, the Panchavati. The woods and gardens are well suited to the living habits of wandering mendicants.

The temple group is magnificently conceived. It is laid out in a rectangle surrounding a courtyard. At the corners on the river side are nahabats, amusing circular structures which serve as elevated bandstands. Facing into the courtyard with their backs to the Ganges are twelve shrines dedicated to Shiva. These are on raised platforms, six on each side. In the centre is a splendid portico, which forms an entrance gate leading up from the landing ghat. The Shiva temples are about ten or twelve feet square, identical in appearance, with the upper parts in the design of the thatched roofs of rural cottages, simulated in masonry. Each is bare inside except for a stone lingam.

On the opposite side of the courtyard are three buildings. To the north is a shrine of Krishna and Radha. To the south is a pillared meeting hall. In the centre is the nine-spired main temple dedicated to the Rani's chosen deity, Kali. Its shrine does not open on to the courtyard as one might expect, but faces south, so that audiences gathered in the public hall may have the darshan of the goddess. The north and south ends of the compound are closed in by a string of rooms set behind colonnades. These are guest and staff rooms. The chamber on the north side, directly facing the Ganges, is the quarters of the temple priest. Within its perfectly average confines are to take place the most important happenings of our times. Just outside the compound is a house, called the kuthi, or mansion. This has been built to house the Rani and her family on their visits to the temple.

What an exciting place! From the nahabats orchestral music pours out at dawn, sunset, and noon. The grounds are crowded with holy men, cooking their meals over bonfires, meditating in the open air. There are guests and pilgrim visitors aplenty. Scores sit down at every meal to partake of the prasad food cooked for the deities by an army of servants in the busy kitchens. Beggars and poor people are given help. In the meeting hall groups of listeners gather around scholars who are discussing the fine points of Sanskrit literature, and other groups are enjoying religious songs. Some are bathing in the Ganges. Boats arrive and depart at the ghat. Worshippers move in and out, bowing before the deities. Rituals are being performed simultaneously in all the shrines, with the joyful ringing of bells and pounding of gongs. It is a magnificent place of worship, a salon, a picnic ground, a Himalayan retreat, a charitable institution, a vacation resort, a community centre packed with colour—and all designed to direct the mind toward God.

An incarnation of God, when he comes, is said to do two things. He inspires a return to proved moral standards—that is, he re-establishes a social climate helpful for spiritual aspiration. Hindus call this dharma. And he originates a new approach to God appropriate to his time and sphere of influence. Thus the God-man has a perennial function and a contemporary one.

Krishna gave approval to the classic pattern of life duties of the Hindu, and showed how these must be used to lead him to God-vision. Jesus confirmed the ethics of the Old Testament, while also bringing a new commandment which was to help a Western world grow away from savagery toward the ideals of humanity. Buddha re-established Vedic dharma and demonstrated to a ritual-ridden society that a man can achieve knowledge of the Godhead without priestly intervention, through self-struggle and identification with the Fullness within. Less complete manifestations of divinity do similar things, but with not quite so broad a result. Mohammed taught a creed of fraternity and respect for a common God among self-interested tribesmen. Shankara, coming a thousand years after Buddha, through a sheer tour de force of spiritual rationality, set up once more the principles of pure Hinduism, which had again deteriorated. St. Francis re-emphasized the simplicity, the human-heartedness of Christ at a time when his gospel was becoming depersonalized. In the sixteenth century

Sri Chaitanya showed an age which had degraded religion by mixing sex enjoyment with worship, how to use the drive of the emotion of love as an aid in realizing God.

What was Sri Ramakrishna's function? Of course, no one can catch him in a net of his own personal evaluation. He is all one describes him to be, and always something else and much more. Even his own disciples, who possessed extraordinary insight themselves, were unable to gauge the full significance of their master. But some things seem clear.

Like all other incarnations, Sri Ramakrishna confirmed classic morality. Through his own actions he spurned the valueless additions to dharma but supported what was sound in it. For example, for some time after he came to Dakshineswar the Master cooked his own food rather than accept that provided from the Rani's kitchens. Yet he looked upon the Rani and the members of her family, in their role of spiritual aspirants, as neither inferior to nor different from himself or any other being. The purity code of his caste must be followed by a brahmin; yet that devotion to the Lord erases all caste distinctions is another principle established in very ancient times. The sacrament of marriage is one of the established duties of life for all Hindus except those who choose to be monks. Sri Ramakrishna was a man of the completest renunciation; yet he did marry, to confirm the virtue of the householder state. And, in accordance with pure tradition, he was a teacher, indeed an actual guru, to his wife, while at the same time worshipping her as a symbol of God the Mother. He showed how marriage, if not used for selfish purposes, can contribute to the spiritual advancement of each partner. As was proper, the Master honoured his parents, looking after his widowed mother to the end of her days. He performed all rites and practices expected of a brahmin in completest orthodoxy and then went on to enjoy the liberation from such responsibilities enjoined of a sadhu.

Sri Ramakrishna's contemporary message was: any religious faith, if sincerely followed, is a genuine avenue to God. The Hindu community had been arguing for centuries as to which is the correct view of God and man: dualism, qualified non-dualism, or non-dualism. The dualist preached that God is different from creatures and the universe, an all-powerful being outside them who must be worshipped, propitiated, prevailed upon to grant salvation. Christianity, Judaism, and Islam have remained largely dualistic to this day. In qualified non-dualism the devotee feels that all things and people in the world are God's parts. According to the non-dualist viewpoint, however, there is nothing in the universe except God; appearance makes for apparent separations and differences; but this stems from ignorance, which can be removed in the highest vision of Divinity. A few Christian mystics—Eckhart seems to be one—are believed to have attained non-dualist experience.

Sri Ramakrishna showed that dualism, qualified non-dualism, and non-dualism are not contradictory standpoints, but rather positions on an ascending scale. Dualism is an authentic viewpoint, for God may be realized according to the desire of one who holds it. But this is a lesser vision; after attaining it, if one continues to persist, he will proceed through qualified non-dualism to gain the non-dual knowledge, through which he will see that God is not different from his creation; instead the world and its creatures are known as God sporting in so many disguises.

The Hindu community—like the rest of the world—had also been sorely denominational. The three main sects were those of Shiva, Vishnu, and Shakti. Besides these, there was the circle of the advaita Vedantists and a Hindu reform movement—comparable to Christian Protestantism —called the Brahmo Samaj. Sri Ramakrishna's contemporary message also furnished a basis for sectarian harmony. He did not invent a new eclecticism; he did not synthesize, or preach union or fusion of faiths. He asked an individual to be a serious devotee of his own path or Chosen Ideal, whatever that might be, following fully the practices ordained for the worship of that Ideal. Each Ideal is a particular congealing of Divinity in a form easy for devotees to appreciate. Hence all Ideals are true and eternal, and God is present fully in each. Just as dualism, followed sincerely, conducts a devotee to non-dualism, so sectarian observances, persisted in, bring one to a convergence in the central Godhead. How can anyone thus, if he has such an understanding, deprecate another's religion? What a doctrine of harmony for a world which was becoming one in every branch—except ideology!

Sri Ramakrishna was able to pronounce his new findings on the basis of experimental evidence. Providence had not inspired the Rani for nothing to the unusual performance of installing in one temple deities of all three of the contending sects of Hinduism. The Master scientifically established the law of harmony of approaches at this local level first, before moving out into the international area. Through practice of them one after another, he realized God by way of the established procedures of Shaivism, Vaishnavism, Shakti, advaita, and even gave his blessing to the Brahmo Samaj. Then he pushed on, to see God through Jesus, Mohammed, and others. Although Sri Ramakrishna attained knowledge through worship of established incarnations, what happened was that those to whom his new law of non-contradiction appealed saw him as the incarnation of the new day and became devotees of Sri Ramakrishna himself.

The Master, of course, saw what was happening and used to joke about it. One day he said, 'A man had a tub of dye. Such was its wonderful property that people could dye their clothes any colour they wanted by merely dipping them in it.' But this is not all. 'A clever man,' he went on, 'came and said to the owner of the tub: "Dye my cloth the colour of your dyestuff".'

Bearing all this in mind, then, it was with intense anticipation that I made the trip to Dakshineswar about a week after landing in India. A good-looking young swami named Upen Maharaj went with me; he was in transit to the Mission's big Rangoon, Burma, hospital and had a few days of leisure at Belur Math while waiting for his visa to arrive. We took a bus north on the Grand Trunk Road from the Math drive to the end of the Willingdon Bridge, then a bicycle rickshaw over the bridge and around to the entrance of the temple compound. I was proceeding with such reverence that the scattering of souvenir shops lining the main approach jolted me. It shouldn't have, for commercial enterprises hug pilgrim spots the world over. Everything from handsome carved stone dishes to over-coloured pictures of Sri Ramakrishna were pushed at us by enterprising hawkers. Then a little boy of about four or five ran up, chattering excitedly, and threw his arms around my legs in a miniature football tackle. Upen Maharaj explained that this was a shoe-check concessionaire, taking no chances on failing to obtain our patronage. We left our footwear with him and went into the courtyard.

On our right, the twelve identical Shiva temples, inside each a lingam about three feet tall, of black stone, with an appliquéd silver emblem near the top. Around the bottom a circular basin to catch the liquid offerings poured on the head of the lingam—water, milk, buttermilk, honey, yogurt—and carry them off through a spout to the right. This non-representational figure is the deity of the Shiva worshipper throughout India. I saw it again and again; the stone pillar, sometimes thin and as tall as one and a half to three feet; often hardly bigger than, and rounded like, a softball. And always the saucer-like trough below, with the spout on the right. No one seemed able to explain it to me and I am still unclear about it. Upen Maharaj gave me an inward smile when I asked him for enlightenment and said he understood but couldn't find the right words.

There is, of course, the idea that the lingam is a fertility symbol, an abstract male phallus, with the basin below representative of the female generative structure. This is an easy assumption to make; but according to Swami Vivekananda the interpretation is without grounds. He stated that the lingam is a vestige of the sacred post at which sacrifices were performed in the Vedic period. No doubt in times and places of decadence the sexual possibilities of the symbol have been exploited and will be again. That is the characteristic of an abstraction: you can read into it whatever is in your own mind. I doubt that any sex idea about the Shiva lingam ever enters the heads of most of the thousands of people I saw paying reverence to it. I can still hear the groans of resentment from many of my Indian friends over the article in *Life* magazine in October of 1951 written by the American diplomat and fact-finder, William C. Bullitt. In discussing India's over-population problem, Bullitt attributed it to the influence of Shiva worship. He implied that Indians go to their temples to worship a sexual symbol—sometimes, he complained, eight and a half feet high—thus becoming motivated to rush home and breed more children.

Who or what is Shiva? In one guise he is the dancing Nataraja whom one finds so often, especially in South India, exquisitely commemorated in bronze. Here is jubilant spirituality. Beneath Nataraja's feet is the prostrate body of the demon, ignorance, conquered through attainment of true knowledge. A ring of fire encircles the god, symbolic of the joy, the radiance which flames out from one who has gained wisdom.

Nataraja has four arms. What is the purpose of representing Hindu deities, which look like human figures in every other feature except this, with more than the normal number of arms, and in some cases, heads? This mixture of the symbolic with the realistic used to bother me. Now I see it as simply a resourceful solution to the problem of portraying in one figure the manifold attributes of a supranormal being. Nataraja's upper right hand carries a drum for beating the rhythm. It is said that this stands for sound, the conveyer of revelation, of the Word, from which the world evolves. In the upper left hand is a dart of flame, for lighting the funeral pyre, symbolic of death, destruction. See the grand symbolism: the counterpoise of creation and destruction, evolution and involution, in the play of cosmic dance? The second right hand forms a gesture of benediction, betokening God's protection and peace, while the remaining left hand points downward to the feet, to re-emphasize the reason for the dance, the conquest of maya. Meditate upon this figure. Pry open the tremendous idea in it and learn to overcome the world. Then you can dance through life and death, too!

Shiva appears in other forms. In one he is the lord of ghosts and goblins, with his favourite haunt the cremation ground. Here he is seen, with his wife, Devi, drunken and surrounded by inebriated imps. Here he is the refuge of the mad, the strange, the lost. He would come down this far to save us.

Again, we see Shiva as a great ascetic. I have a strongly coloured print of him in this guise before me now, showing an ash-smeared sadhu, sitting in meditation on a tiger skin. The eyes are indrawn. It is one of those bright-as-day full-moon nights, and the forest is alive with beings. Snakes twine about Shiva's perfectly still body; squirrels, birds, and other children of nature play beside him, unafraid. Nearby is his mount, a white brahmini bull, Nandi. Shiva's hair hangs down long and untended; some of it is done up in a little knot on the top of the head. From this flows the Ganges.

Then there is Shiva of the Shiva-Shakti conception. In this figure, Shiva is the male half of an icon half male, half female. We cannot know the Absolute, but when we try to personalize it, the first and primal unfolding of the non-sexed Brahman is into the opposites of male and female principles. Shiva is the male principle: Purusha, soul, Self. Shakti is the counterpart: Prakriti, energy, maya. Life and death, soul and nature, cause and effect, stillness and movement—we see the two everywhere. Each is completed by the other, with the truth found in a combination and transcendence of both.

Who or what is Shiva ? This symbol stands for so much, the possibilities in it are so fabulous, as to overwhelm you. From one standpoint Shiva is archetypal dancer and reveller. He is total activity: life's energy, aimless, playful. 'Tonight I shall storm heaven and bring down the sacred fire! I shall claw apart the veil, make naked the mystery, and possess it!' You must run through all experience that in time you may be able to renounce it.

For Shiva is also archetypal ascetic. His primary significance is in the control and utilization of the primal urge. If you can contain this jetting need it will force something open inside you. So Shiva is total tranquillity, total renunciation absorbed in the Self. He is God the Father. Shiva knows everything, and all the evil of the world he accepts. His throat is blue in many of his pictures, forever scorched by the poison he drank in mythological times to save our forebears from death. When shown in company with Kali, he lies beneath the wildly beating feet of Maya in perfect inward recollectedness.

Although such a generalization is not fully accurate, for the sake of convenience we may think of Shaivism as the path of renunciation, austerity. Shaivism teaches the control and sublimation of our human-nesses. It is an approach to God through emphasis on the impersonal. Sri Ramakrishna once gave this explanation: 'Do you know the significance of the Shiva emblem?' he asked. 'It is the worship of the symbols of fatherhood and motherhood. The devotee worshipping the image prays, "Oh Lord, please grant that I may not be born into this world again; that I may not have to pass again through a mother's womb".' How fitting, then, that Shiva should be represented by an abstraction. No, I do not understand the meaning of the lingam rationally. But as I grew familiar with this symbol, first at Dakshineswar and then afterwards many times all over India, I grew dimly to perceive an utter appropriateness, some wonderful latency, in it.

In Vishnu we have the opposite side of the coin. Vaishnavism stresses the personal, the intimate, and uses these to take us to God. The incarnations of Vishnu are superlatively human, humanity carried to divine lengths.

For example, there was Rama. He was the idol of the heroic age, and is still worshipped as the embodiment of truth and of morality—the ideal son, the ideal husband, the ideal father, and the ideal king. Then followed Krishna. He is known to us in three guises, as Gopal, the most delightful of all babies; as a cowherd youth, Govinda; and as the mature sage who spoke the Bhagavad-Gita.

The Vishnu shrine at Dakshineswar celebrates the Govinda phase. In their own temple facing into the courtyard stand the images of Govinda and Radha, about thirty inches tall. He is a darling cowherd lad with a peacock feather in his hair, playing a flute. Radha, chief of the milkmaids, leans toward him adoringly. This Radha-Govinda symbol is one of the most popular forms in which God is worshipped throughout all India. It objectifies the pursuit and attainment of him through ecstatic love. He plays forever in that Brindaban idyl, the most delicious of all beings. We lose ourselves, like the country girls did, in blind adoration of him. Yes, God may be impersonal; he may be a remote power and the pervasive Atman inside us all. But let me just idolize this delightful lad; let me lose myself forever as his adoring playmate.

Once Sri Ramakrishna said: 'A man born with an element of Shiva becomes a jnani; his mind is always inclined to the feeling that the world is unreal and Brahman alone is real. But when a man is born with an element of Vishnu he develops ecstatic love of God. That love can never be destroyed. It may wane a little now and then, when he indulges in philosophical reasoning, but it ultimately returns to him increased a thousand-fold.'

So far so good. The Shiva idea and the Vishnu idea are not completely remote from the previous experience of one who has been brought up a Christian. But the concept of Shakti is, and at first seems totally bizarre. There are Radha, Sita, Parvati, Durga, and others. But of all the female aspects, Kali especially on first acquaintance appears just too incomprehensible. Indeed, not only incomprehensible, but heathenish. Perhaps, the idea flashes through your mind, the gossip about her circulated by our missionaries is not without some foundation after all!

But how can we ever have the idea of the noumenal without the idea of the phenomenal, or of the phenomenal without that of the noumenal? No doubt ultimate Truth is beyond them both, but in the meantime it is through comparison and contrast of pairs of opposites that we progress to understanding. The mind proceeds, as it were, by feeling along both walls. You cannot claim that God is being without admitting he is also becoming.

In Hinduism, God as becoming is thought of as female. Rama was an incarnation of God and his figure is eternal; but he is completed by his wife Sita. As Rama was ideal man, Sita was ideal woman, and her glories as such are sung by countless Indians to this day. Sita's has become an eternal figure also. The fullest value of the form of Christ is present when that of the Virgin Mary is present likewise. Christianity has ever been richest when God as mother is given recognition. Mary is as true and as timeless as Jesus. About the Radha-Govinda representation, Sri Ramakrishna once explained as follows: Sri Krishna is the eternal conscious Principle; Radha is his Shakti, the primal power. The two are Purusha and Prakriti. What is the meaning of this figure, the conjoined images of Radha and Krishna? It is that Purusha cannot exist without Prakriti, and Prakriti cannot exist without Purusha. If you mention one, the other is understood. It is like fire and its power to burn: one cannot think of fire without its power to burn; again, one cannot think of fire's power to burn without fire. Therefore in the conjoined images of Radha and Krishna, Krishna's eyes are fixed on Radha and Radha's on Krishna. Radha's complexion is golden, like lightning; so Krishna wears yellow apparel, Krishna's complexion is blue, like a dark cloud; so Radha wears a blue dress; she has also decked herself with blue sapphires. Radha has tinkling anklets; so Krishna has them, too. In other words, there is inner and outer harmony between Purusha and Prakriti.

The Kali image at Dakshineswar is smaller than I had expected it to be. Somehow I had always visualized her as massive and overwhelming, but she must be only about four feet tall. She stands on a base shaped like a full-blown lotus, made of silver, within a silver pavilion. Although the Kali temple is of a generous size, Kali herself occupies only a very small shrine. What use the remainder of the building is put to I do not know. Really, the shrine is hardly more than a niche in the south wall, with room for one priest in front of the image and space for not more than half a dozen worshippers crowded together at the top of the marble steps outside. Being used to Christian churches where the object of veneration is placed, like an actor in centre stage, in clear view of hundreds or thousands, I found this Hindu plan of practically secreting the deity in a closet very hard to understand. Later I came to know some of the reasons for it. I went to Dakshineswar four times altogether but I never felt I had a full view of Kali. This was partially due to her position and partially to the fact that it is the custom to bedeck deities with flowers, and Kali was always so loaded with garlands that I could never get much of an idea of what she really looks like.

But I know this, that Kali is one of the most potent concepts ever entrusted to man. She meant nothing to me at first except a grotesquery in questionable taste. But now I can say this, that having placed my mind in this figure for some time, I find in it the most exciting spiritual possibilities.

She is a woman of dark colour, standing upon a prone Shiva. A mass of black hair streams down her back, and she is clothed only in a girdle of amputated arms and a necklace of skulls. Kali has four arms. The lower left hand holds a severed human head, while the upper grips a blood-stained sabre. One right hand offers boons and the other forms a gesture of protection. The goddess's tongue protrudes; some say in an exaggerated gesture of coyness, once common to country women in Bengal; some say because she is licking blood.

Can you stand it? Is this merely a statement of the dreadful fact that, yes, death does conquer all? Surely it is that—maya triumphant over man's dream of release. But if you can look squarely at Kali's hideous side and sustain it, in time a transformation will be felt. She begins to grow tender and to turn her benign side toward you. She picks you up and mothers you, lifts you over her carnage to the realm beyond good and evil, life and death. To push into this figure is to see how dynamic it is. Starting at where we are, enveloped in maya, in misery and joy, we are carried around and finally behind to where mere understanding must leave off and revelation take over. Yes, Shiva is lying prostrate, Reality inert beneath triumphant Appearance. But we also find him smiling up at his conqueror, for she is likewise true; and besides, his undisturbed adoration of her makes her his captive in turn. Who has conquered whom? On first appearance Kali seems to be self-assured, all-powerful, terrible. But as you look again you see a certain coquettish fragility there; she is trembling to be mastered. At first sight she is awesome, ugly; but after a time you perceive that this woman is beautiful. She is daughter, wife, mistress, mother. Round and round you may go, extracting wider symbolism, further meaning. Then Kali's own duality falls back into the larger twofold idea of Shakti-Shiva, and this in turn fades into the formless Brahman whence it comes. Kali is true, yet she is only a projection, relative truth in tangible form. She is maya, real when she is seen to be real, unreal when what is behind her is known. This is God as Shakti, as Divine Mother of the Universe. No incarnation has come unaccompanied by her; no aspirant can make progress until he has made his peace with her.

Ramprasad was a back-country minstrel who lived and died in Bengal some two centuries ago. He started life as a clerk, but had to give up regular employment when the meaning of Mother took possession of him. For the rest of his life Ramprasad remained in his provincial home singing new songs to Kali, elaborations of the theme of her indifference which turns to compassion when she is sincerely implored. These verses help us to force open the inner meaning of this figure. The following is typical, containing some ideas which will at first seem strange to any Westerner but upon acquaintance will be found to express deep truth. 'Lotus feet' appears in line four. The feet, it should be remembered, are considered special conductors of spirituality and our own humility is expressed in bowing down to them. The lotus, which appears often in Hindu literature and art, stands for the ultimate in beauty and purity. To seek to realize God's lotus feet is to seek, with a strong sense of one's unworthiness and his excellence, to realize God.

> Mother, do you believe me
>   your weak and unfavoured child?
> Well, your red eyes cannot terrify me!
> My fortune is your lotus feet,
>   which Shiva holds upon his breast.
> Yet when I ask for this inheritance
>   I meet with excuses and delays.
> A deed of gift I hold in my heart,
>   attested by your husband Shiva.

And if I must, I shall sue
for this heritage and shall win it.
Oppose me and learn what kind
of a mother's son am I!
This bitterly contested suit
between Mother and son
is a grand game, says Ramprasad.
But I shall never stop tormenting you
until you yield the fight
and take me in your arms at last.

I shall never forget my first sight of Mother because—just like a woman
—she took advantage of my solemnity to play a trick on me. I walked up
those marble steps faint at the thought of all that had transpired there.
Here Sri Ramakrishna had functioned as priest for so many years. Here
he had sung to the goddess and danced before her. Here he had suffered
in an agony of separation, begging her to become real. And here she had
emerged from the basalt and shown herself as his blissful Mother, so that
he had lived for the rest of his life in full confidence as her child. You could
even say that this was a headquarters from which for a time the entire
universe was operated. The eternal conscious Principle and its manifestation played together in this little shrine—which play *is* the universe.

When I went to Mother that first time I was not weaned entirely from
silverware. Knowing I was going to have lunch later at the office of the
Bengali magazine of the Ramakrishna Order, I had brought along a
teaspoon as a safety measure, in case the menu there should contain
something too liquid for me to manage with my fingers. The spoon was
in my shirt pocket. In great sobriety I mounted those steps and prostrated
before Mother. Then out came the spoon, crashing down upon the marble
sill and producing startled responses from the worshippers seated there
and profound embarrassment in me.

But playing this trick on me was Mother's grace. For that mishap gave
a blow to my puritanism. 'Do you see what I think of your sanctimonious-
ness?' Mother seemed to say. 'You and your dourness. You and your
dark nights of the soul. Christ wasn't that way; where did the church get
this idea of dolour as a necessary part of religion, anyway? Religion is fun,
and if you hope to progress in your study of it you will have to become
acquainted with me; you will have to learn to sustain a capricious element
which—once you get over being scandalized about it—will simply delight
you. This world is not so very earnest, for, remember, it is not so very real.
And what can you do about it anyhow? It is I who am running everything.'

Thus Mother let me in on one of her secrets. I have been thankful for
this disclosure, for whenever things grow a little grim, it is usually possible
to remember this truth and to relax.

Upen Maharaj and I now went to the park and to the nahabat where Sri Ramakrishna's wife lived. The park is chiefly noted as the locale of the Master's classic struggle to realize God in his many aspects. Under the big banyan tree he meditated. Beyond this, near the north property line, is a bel tree beneath which he practised the disciplines of the Shakti approach. And in between these is a little hut replacing one where the Master remained in non-dual samadhi for three days, culminating his advaita practice.

Sri Ramakrishna's wife was called Sarada, a favourite name in India, meaning 'giver of the quintessence of life'. But she was usually known as the Holy Mother. When you see the ground-floor room of the north nahabat where she lived on and off for some fourteen years at Dakshineswar you can hardly believe that this could be the habitation of a human being, let alone of a personage regarded by many as the incarnation of God as Mother of this age. This bandstand cannot be more than fourteen to sixteen feet in diameter, and of that, most is circular porch. The second-floor centre room may be a little more commodious, and here Sri Rama-krishna's ancient mother resided until she died. But the ground-floor room is not high enough for anyone to stand up in. It reminded me of a good-sized fireplace. In Holy Mother's time the porch around it was hung with screens, to give the privacy old-fashioned Indian women considered proper and to add some additional usable space.

Consider this wonderful woman who habitually got up at three o'clock in the morning so that she could take her Ganges bath without anyone seeing her and meditate before dawn, then spend the day preparing endless betel rolls and cooking for Sri Ramakrishna and the unpredictable numbers of devotees who came to see him. As I peeped into that tiny apartment I could just see her, a plain woman squatting before a little blaze in that smoky pocket, day in and day out, in what we would call a condition of drudgery. Holy Mother worked and served so inconspicuously that many never knew of her existence. When she went to bed at night she simply stretched out in this chamber, with all her cooking pots around her and provisions for future meals hanging from the ceiling. Beside her labours as cook and housekeeper, Holy Mother nursed her mother-in-law for years and was hostess to the many women devotees who came to Ramakrishna. As if this were not enough, she also had the job of looking after a husband who had a most sensitive constitution, who hardly ever slept, who ranged daily through innumerable states of God-intoxication, and who frequently felt himself to be a helpless child of the Divine Mother, whom he considered her to be! Besides, as time went by and people more and more began to recognize her for what she was, the Holy Mother was called upon to act as spiritual adviser herself. The Holy Mother was the ultimate in Indian woman—servant of all and so queen of all. Is it any wonder that in Hinduism Mother is regarded as Power?

D

And so around at last to Sri Ramakrishna's room, to me the most interesting spot at Dakshineswar, and for that matter perhaps in all the world. On the later occasions when I visited the temple I paid scant attention to its other features but went directly to the Master's room, where I simply sat on the floor as near to his bed as possible and tried to open my mind to its holy darshan.

The room is sizable—perhaps twenty feet square. A veranda leads into it from the courtyard, and on the other side is another veranda facing Holy Mother's nahabat. To the west, overlooking the Ganges, is a semi-circular porch. On his first visit to Dakshineswar it was by this doorway that Narendranath Dutta, later Swami Vivekananda, entered the Master's room. The chamber is sparsely furnished, like most rooms in India. A large water jar stands in one corner. A few built-in shelves remain, on which clothes, food, and other personal items were kept. Pictures of various deities adorn the walls. The floor, of concrete in the Master's day, has now been covered with tile. In the southwest corner are two beds or rather a bed and a couch. These are perfectly everyday wooden cots— a bit termite-eaten now—but they are priceless relics to the devotee. On the larger bed in the corner Sri Ramakrishna slept. And on the couch in front is where he sat as he talked to his disciples and visitors.

One feels it would be appropriate if the Ramakrishna Order could obtain possession at least of the Master's room. But Dakshineswar continues to be in the control of Rani Rasmani's descendants. As an increasingly important pilgrim destination it must be a profitable holding. For it is the custom when visiting shrines for every pilgrim to leave some offering. Priests, quick to encourage a contribution and distribute a bit of prasad food in return, are much in evidence. Worship is performed in Sri Ramakrishna's room now. Pictures of him stand on the large and small bedsteads. They are garlanded daily and lights waved and incense burned before them. It is not unusual, within the course of an hour, for more than a score to several hundred people to pass through this room, prostrating before the beds, dropping coins in the offering box, perhaps pausing for a while to meditate.

As I sat there that first day, thrilled with having actually reached this place whose every inch I already knew from the Master's Gospel, I thought of how it must have been in the crescendo years of Ramakrishna's life in the early 1880s. Still of boyish beauty although nearly fifty, he lounged there on the couch, joking, telling funny stories, giving out his message, going in and out of samadhi. The floor would have been covered with mats, where the visitors could sit. The Master formed an inner circle of a few young monastic disciples; these came to him at any time of day or night and often stayed overnight, just stretching out to sleep on the floor or outside on one of the verandas—a practice not so very different from the way most Indians go to bed to this day. Householder devotees came when they could, usually on week ends and holy days. Sometimes the boys would bring instruments and sing, or professional musicians would come and there would be scenes of high fervour in which Ramakrishna and his visitors would dance. The Master is reported to have been a superlative mimic. For hours at a stretch he would convulse his visitors with imitations of recognizable human types, particularly female. He spoke the old-fashioned up-country Bengali—what we would call patois. His speech was plain and often earthy, with illustrations taken from the full range of experience of everyday men and women.

All kinds of people came to Sri Ramakrishna: members of super-orthodox brahmin subcastes—the most exclusive aristocracies on earth; progressives who had taken on Western ideas and perhaps even affected a preference for speaking English; businessmen, pundits, sadhus, poor old widows, pure youngsters barely in their teens; Christians, Moslems, Buddhists, Jains, Sikhs; money-lenders, prostitutes, drunkards. All found something different in the Master, and each discovered there some attractive personification of the Divine that elevated his mind. To Mathur Babu, the Rani's son-in-law and business partner, Ramakrishna was God the Father. A devout matron saw him as Lord Krishna in the baby Gopal phase and remained in continuous ecstasy visualizing herself looking after God as infant. Girish Ghosh, the genius tycoon of the Bengal theatre and a confirmed man-about-town, became fully transformed through his perception of Ramakrishna as master and himself as servant. To Rakhal, later Swami Brahmananda, Ramakrishna was father and mother.

Who were you, Ramakrishna? How could you appear to one individual after another like this, forever different and forever his own preferred Ideal? Were you young or old, a sage or a child, male or female? The Master—who himself enjoyed God around a full spectrum of different standpoints—often joked that he hardly knew himself. Well, that is a characteristic of God as understood in Hinduism. Out of compassion for limited mortals he permits our yearning to fashion him into that form which we find most attractive and helpful.

Something happened to me in Sri Ramakrishna's room that day. At last God was no longer the stern patriarch with a white beard, wild accusing eyes, and a jabbing finger pointing toward hell—surely a figure difficult for anyone with taste to accept. I saw that he could be as charming, as marvellously appealing as the many fascinating people I have known and loved in this world—and much more so. He became dynamic, too—not only the tragic figure of the cross—but also the Christmas babe, the vigorous young male who had followed stern disciplines and had won his realization, the happy guest at a wedding feast. The New Testament account took on new meaning, and in the context of great yogi and avatar, Jesus at last became understandable. And I knew now that God is also Mary, the world Mother, and Sita and Radha. The same God is Krishna and Rama. God is Buddha; God is the Chinese sages; God is Moses and Mohammed and Sri Chaitanya. God is that ideal of polar tension called

Shiva. God is also, in a sense, delicious maya. Yes, God is good enough to be even Kali who will play roughly with us, and befoul us, if that is what we want; who is ready, too, to clean the soiled child when he has had enough.

I had sought him with longing down the serpentine corridors of the Great Maya. Now he had come again in my time: a contemporary Lord—still equally the embodiment and fulfilment of those others. And I was his great grandson. My guru's guru was his spiritual heir. And here I was, where he had lived and communed with God—where God had lived and communed with man—only two generations before!

Something broke open in my mind, then. I ran from that wonderful room to the semicircular porch where Swamiji had first come in, and wept. For I saw that I had reached home at last. I could finally enter into peace with myself and with my world. That neurosis, that painful disorientation so chronic in Western man, lifted. The Three Sorrows would now be mere trifles. Nothing really bad could ever happen to me again.

Upen Maharaj and I finally left. We gave some money to the boy who had kept our shoes, noticing from the good pile in front of him that his unique business methods had won him more trade than all the other consessionaires put together. As we bargained with a rickshaw man and set off toward Calcutta, what I had understood was strong in my heart.

CHAPTER III

THE WELL-MANNERED SADHU
AT HOME

On a hilltop just outside Florence there is a famous Carthusian monastery founded in 1342. It is a most handsome structure, with a cloister adorned with Della Robbia medallions, a well believed to have been designed by Michelangelo himself, a guest apartment of magnificence reserved for the Pope, and a church as lush as a rococo palace. 'Doors around the cloister,' explains the guidebook, 'admit to the quarters of the fathers, each of whom has a small apartment of two or three rooms to himself, and a tiny garden. One of these apartments is kept empty for the inspection of the visitor who can thus imagine the life of strict privation to which members of the Order have vowed themselves. One then goes to the refectory where the monks take their meals together on festal days, though at other times each has his food brought to him by a lay brother in his own cell.'

Privation? No, I should think paradise. To have the luxury of privacy! To not have to be nice when you don't feel like it! For short periods, at least, I'm quite sure that seclusion must be easier to adjust to than that ghastly sociality which seems to be the rule in Indian monasticism. The lack of privacy, the absence of respect for my 'rights' of aloofness and secrecy, vexed me exceedingly during the first years of my life as a novice at Hollywood. In India the situation is even exaggerated. You probably won't even have your own room there but will just bed down in a group. From the cradle up most Hindus live a most throbbingly intimate collective life. This mode is carried on into monasticism, so that these communities are like a permanent family reunion or a boisterous gathering of the clan that just goes on and on and on forever.

I suppose the purpose of seclusion must be to develop personal discipline and chasten the ego. I do not know how well this works. But for the average aspirant, I wager that solitude cannot compare in effectiveness with living in a group. In the free-for-all of community life you cannot get away with anything: hypocrisy, self-delusion, posing, silence and retreat, which are such balms to the ego. You are pressed into being authentic, into being outwardly the person you are inwardly, continually driven back to the expression of exactly what you are. All masks and veils and window trimmings are ripped off you, and you must work your way up and out from there. Whatever virtue you finally attain, it is virtue you possess all the way through.

This training is accomplished through teasing, through gentle ridicule, through uninhibited give and take, through massive frankness. Mere external goodness has little chance to appear, or to remain. There is too much humour, too much good hilarity. Nor can ingrowing jealousies, dislikes, or resentments take hold. You are taught to 'spit it out'—express what is bothering you and so have done with it. Make a fool of yourself. Lose your temper. How much more preferable than to preserve a placid exterior while dark thoughts may fatten inside you and suck away all love for man and God. Through this form of discipline only those able to face truthfulness and achieve genuine self-acceptance can survive.

One of his most effective ego-reducers is the Indian's habit of asking direct personal questions. If there is any experience that makes the Anglo-Saxon wilt, this is it. It is a fundamental plank in his code that every man may enjoy the illusion that he is pulling the wool over other people's eyes. And straight, intimate inquiries make this most difficult.

One of the most shattering is the question: How old are you? This is generally directed to you by someone at the far end of the dining hall during the first meal at a new ashrama. By the sudden fall of silence you can see that this is something everybody has been eager to know since you arrived. Since twenty is considered the tag end of youth and thirty well inside the portal to middle age—and a point by which many have taken their final vows of sannyas—if you are in your late thirties and still a monastic probationer, you hesitate to answer.

But an experience one day taught me to give a prompt and unvarnished answer to this question of age. I was in a bad mood anyway when the young swami made the old, tiresome query. I thought I just couldn't go through it again, that I would put him off. "Oh, come now,' I replied, 'that is a question never asked of a Westerner.'

'But,' he responded, thoroughly hurt, 'I was not thinking of you as a Westerner. I was thinking of you as a brother.'

They will ask you all sorts of details about your family, what the original cost was of possessions you have, the state of your digestive tract. But there is nothing insinuating in any of this. The questions are put without guile, innocently as a child would do. You cannot take offence.

Being a doctor's son, I was brought up in the belief that the mark of a gentleman is his ability to keep confidences. But very little is kept a secret by Indians. All news is common property, as in a home. You will find monastic personnel talking about intimate features of their own and other people's lives without the smallest touch of embarrassment. I suppose this is another evidence of their ingenuousness. The real reason the American is willing to keep the confidence of others is probably, I now perceive, that he may never know when he may want others to cover up for him. But the Indian's idea seems to be that if something is true, then what is the reason for not bringing it out into the open? I don't mean they would actively pry into your affairs, but they would generally read your postcards. (For that matter, so would most Westerners; the difference is that the Occidental would be careful to hide his knowledge of the contents.)

But at least once I had my revenge. One day a picture postcard came for me from a woman I had sat next to on the plane from Rome to Karachi. She was one of those hearty Democratic types, who had correctly predicted the outcome of the 1952 Presidential Election, and was getting in a government-paid trip to Hong Kong while her party still had the authority to send her. She had left the plane for a stopover in the capital of Pakistan and had written from there. This is what she had scrawled on the back of her postcard: 'What a jumping-off place this is. For my money, they can give it back to the Indians.' From the curious way they regarded me for some time afterwards, I knew the Math office staff had not only read the card, but—still upset over the Partition—were seeking to grasp the implications of its deep and curious political, coded message.

One query that bothers you at first but later turns out to be perhaps the most innocent of all is the greeting everybody gives you in the morning: 'Well, have you had your bath?' Your natural reaction is to take offence and respond: 'Yes I have, but isn't that a personal matter?' But soon you see that the question does not mean exactly what it seems to. What they are asking has little to do with any evaluation of your bodily purity, but is rather a form of well-wishing, something comparable to our saying: 'Hi there. All set for a big day?' For yesterday has ended and today genuinely begun with the conclusion of your ablutions.

I don't remember when I first encountered the word 'tank', but anyway, for years it had mystified me. Indian writing is full of references to tanks, but what are they? In a Bengali translation I once edited I changed 'tank' to reservoir everywhere it appeared, thinking thus to have provided an equivalent. But this does not explain what is meant, either. Nor is 'artificial lake' or 'swimming pool' accurate. Perhaps 'water hole' is nearest. A tank is a tank—a unique thing, peculiarly Indian. One must visualize what it is if you would gain much of a picture of the inner life of that land. For a tank is also much more than a mere water hole. It is the locale of several important phases of the daily ritual of living.

Think of the manifold uses man has for water—for bathing, for laundry, for doing worship, for cooking and drinking, for washing dishes, for cleansing the house and furnishings, for irrigating plants, for providing drink for animals. In Western cities and towns today the source of all this is the central waterworks and more immediately the faucet. Previously it was the well and bucket. But consider a country which is hot and which moreover follows a most intense purity code. Central waterworks and piping are even now uncommon, and the well and bucket are simply inadequate to the requirements. What is a people to do? The answer—in India, at least—is that they construct tanks.

A tank is at once a bathtub, a swimming pool, a laundry tub, a kitchen sink, a storage basin for water, and an irrigation reservoir. Tanks are to be found everywhere: in the back and front yards of homes, in fields, in every village common, even hit and miss throughout the fully built-up areas of big cities. And of course—unless it is built on a river-bank—every important temple has a tank before it, for personal cleanliness is the first observance in any approach to God.

This desire for and delight in water is one of the most noticeable and interesting features of India. Outside the temples in the south the pools are enormous—as big as a city block—usually fed by underground springs, but otherwise all man-made, lined on the four sides with stone steps. Sometimes these lakes have island pavilions in the centre, where the deity is taken for his pleasure on warm days. At Puri one of the great festive times is the occasion when Lord Jagannath makes the circuit of one of the tanks in his personal barge, accompanied by a flotilla of cheering admirers. But mostly tanks serve important utilitarian purposes, making life for everybody more comfortable. It is not surprising that to construct a tank for the public has always been considered a deed of deep merit, worthy of a king.

Bengalis must be the most water-loving people in the world. Tanks are everywhere, and riverbanks seem always crowded. I can still see the young men coming to the well in front of Holy Mother's temple at Jayrambati. Bucketful after bucketful of water would be pulled up laboriously, not to be used systematically for washing the person but to be turned upside down above the head in one grand splash, time after time. Fortunately water is easy of access in Bengal state. The ground is largely alluvial, with water only a few feet beneath the surface. Indeed, the tank provides a great demonstration of the principle of economy of effort. You want to build a house, so you dig out a hole to get soil for the earthen walls. The hole fills with water, and this gives you a water supply source for the finished house and a washing place right in your back yard. To keep the tank fresh and clean you introduce fish. And then, of course, as you wish to do so you can catch and eat the fish!

I found the rite of going to the tank one of the pleasantest of the day. If you can afford soap you take a bar of soap with you, and a towel.

You go to the ghat, or platform, of your choice, putting on the towel and taking off your dhoti. I am under the impression that different parts of the same tank are used for different purposes—one part for bathing and another for scrubbing pots, for example—and that persons of different social levels may use different ghats or perhaps different tanks. Dressed in your towel, you now descend to the water, immerse your dohti in it, and proceed to soap it thoroughly. In Bengal you will kneel and pummel and knead the cloth on the stone steps, slowly adding water as the soap is flushed away. In the south you will stand up and bring the cloth down sharply like a whip against a stone pillar, driving out the soap and dirt thereby. (I fear that this plan of beating clothes on rocks shortens their life considerably. But when I once described the modern American automatic washing machine and spoke of the good work it could do and the vast labours it would save in a monastery where every man has to do a small washing every day, the response I drew was not enthusiastic. I now see that washing one's clothes is part of an immemorial pattern and has a kind of cabalistic importance.)

One of your first impressions in India is that many of the people are wearing dirty clothes. Later you realize that this is not the case at all. Putting on a freshly washed cloth every day is practically the universal rule. But it may never be sparkling white. The tattletale grey is a result of poverty; many possess no more than one cloth, and are unable to afford soap.

If you have more than one dhoti and have brought a clean one with you, you will now rub yourself with oil and proceed to take your bath, leaving the washed cloth to be taken home and dried there. If you have only one dhoti you will spread it out on the steps or rig it to a pole like a sail, to dry by the time you have finished bathing.

I used to love to watch the organic unity of this daily routine. I often felt it to be more like a stately rondeau than a chore in personal cleanliness. At a big tank or a river you will see hundreds of people in various conditions of nakedness, but without any look of immodesty. Women bathe separately from men, and both have an astonishing facility for slipping clothes off and on without ever seeming at any point actually to be undressed. They pray as they enter the water and think of the bath as also washing their sins away. Then the putting on of the fresh garment is something to admire. A bit of fullness here, a coil and a knot there, and behold: Grecian drapery at its finest. And now you twist and twist your red towel to make it dry and comfortable to carry home, perhaps on your head, and suddenly feel close to Sri Ramakrishna who on occasion compared the twisting of a wet towel to the state of his compassionate heart.

It is soon borne in upon you that a comprehensive purity code is operating and that you must adapt yourself to it. This code, stemming from awareness of the science of subtle vibrations, affects all personal and social observances, and largely legislates etiquette and the day's activities. The Indian's social order is determined by his anxiety to avoid self-contamination and unhelpful influences from others and at the same time to try to introject the finest subtle matter that he can.

The purity code of the Hindu is entirely different from that of Western man. Certain of his practices seem dirty to us, and many of ours must seem equally dirty to him, simply because two non-comparable theories of what cleanliness is are operating. Western cleanliness is aseptic. The object is to avoid all demonstrable, laboratory-identifiable germs which might adversely affect the body. Indian cleanliness is ceremonial, or it could be called psychological. Its purpose is to forestall influences detrimental to the mind or spirit. It has been said laughingly that to the American it doesn't matter whether something is pure, just so that it is clean; whereas to the Indian if something is pure that makes it clean.

I have seen monks do their daily washing by simply slopping their clothes up and down several times in a pail of cold water. We would say, not clean from our standpoint; they would say, clean from theirs. Eating off a leaky leaf plate placed directly on the floor seems unsanitary in our view, but not in theirs. The plate is always brand-new and has been rinsed in water, and the floor is sluiced with water before each use, with no one stepping on the eating area afterwards. Who is to say that a new leaf plate, although perhaps not strictly sterile, may have a worse influence on the essential you than a paper plate made of nobody knows whose discards, even though rendered absolutely germ-proof? And is a 'table' that may have been walked on or sat on during the time of food preparation necessarily any more detrimental than a tablecloth that has passed through a laundry in common with the personal relics of who knows whom? What about genuine mental hygiene? Is the effect of your own hand on your plate more noxious than rubbing the lips with a napkin which, although surpassingly antiseptic, has already touched the mouths of any number of unselected users? I should say that the way dishes are washed in an American restaurant would repel the Indian. Although the water may be hot, the soap plentiful, and everything scalded before drying, placing everyone's dishes indiscriminately in the same water is to mix up dharma hopelessly, an effect which is worsened by then rubbing them all with the same towel.

That such an obsession with purity should be practised in kitchens which seem so unhygienic is one of the paradoxes of the Indian scene. Because cooking is over open fires which have no hood above them or chimney, most Indian kitchens are smoke-filled caverns. The stoves are made of mud—just open cones with a small wood, charcoal, or dehydrated cow-dung fire inside, given draught through a hole near the bottom. Each is comparable to one burner on a stove, for each holds just one pot. The smoke simply rises to the ceiling and drifts out through vents there—through the porous thatch of the roof—while those cooking work in the fresher air near the floor. There are no tables or work-height counters. Food preparation is all done in a kneeling or squatting position directly on the ground, and because the walls are so blackened, usually in half-twilight. Buckets or serving trays of food ready to be carried into the dining room are simply lined up on the floor. Pots, utensils, and the permanent plates are washed by rubbing them with ash or sand, rinsing them in cold water, and turning them upside down on the floor to dry. After the meal, leaf plates are usually just thrown out, where hungry animals or birds will rush up to fight each other for any remains of food still clinging to them.

In the monasteries I visited I wanted to get to know my brothers as intimately as possible. I reasoned that sharing in their work would be a good way of doing so. Yet there seemed to be so little that I could do. I was inexperienced in the Indian approaches to so-called white-collar work, and never stayed in any one place long enough to undertake any real job. And as regards the various manual activities that occurred to me, the fear of running foul of obscure purity and caste codes was always present in my mind. But one area in which I did find volunteer labour welcomed was in food-preparation activities. Vegetables had to be cut up every day—twice a day—for curries. I saw that almost anybody could share in this work.

So one morning early in my stay at Belur Math I presented myself at the door of the cool, dim corridor which at mealtimes is the dining room, declaring that I wanted to help with vegetable cutting. Vikash Maharaj was head of the kitchens at Belur Math and an efficient director of the monastic assistants and hired cooks who worked there. At mealtimes he always took his seat on an unlighted firepot at the door of the dining hall, watching everything that went on, calling out orders to the servers, joking with the seniors at the head of the lines.

I must have been unconsciously intolerant of the Indian brand of purity, for when Vikash Maharaj received me with a rough question as to my fitness for vegetable cutting I was quite miffed; for what he was concerned about was my cleanliness. How could this barefooted, unshaven administrator of such primitive quarters question *my* physical purity? It was then that I learned, with a sharpness I am not likely to forget, a major point in the Indian code of personal hygiene. Indians are careful to bathe and put on completely fresh clothing daily, after the bowel movement, and they know—I suppose from having seen them wearing the same garments day in and day out—that this may not be the observance of Westerners. At Belur Math, as in most monasteries of the Order, the food is all 'cooked for the Lord'—that is, prepared for offering in the shrine first and eaten as prasad afterward. Thus it is that here even the usual strict cleanliness rules are intensified in food preparation. Fortunately I had happened to hit upon the approved sequence that morning, and upon my assurances that I had, I was invited to take my place upon the floor with the others, before the scythe-like blades rising vertically from chunky wooden bases.

But of course I was not allowed to enter the inner kitchens or partici-pate in any actual cooking. Most cooking is done by brahmin professionals who would find an amateur in the way, even if the fact that he was a sahib did not insult their purity code.

I still remember with much affection the orthodox brahmin cook at Madras. His name was Narayan, a young married man who worked for forty rupees, less than ten dollars, a month. He stayed in one of the little cottages on the monastery grounds except now and then when he had an evening's leave and could go home to visit his wife and children. He was tall, thin, and terribly intense, with rolling eyes, now tragic, now humorous, now adoring, like John Barrymore's. To him at first the post of cook at the monastery had been merely a job; but gradually he became a devotee. While I was there, President Sankarananda made a visit to the south and initiated many into religious life. Narayan had heard that Sri Ramakrishna had had a disciple who was a cook. He applied to President Maharaj and was granted his initiation. His efforts after that to please the Lord, the President, and the swamis and brahmacharis kept him in a frenzy.

Narayan dressed in the orthodox manner; in no wise were his clothes cut, stitched, or sewed. He served us bare-footed and dressed only in a gleaming white dhoti turned up above the knees. Diagonally across his bare chest hung the sacred thread. He used to rinse his hands in a can of water conveniently placed beside the door every time he went back into the kitchen from the dining room, an operation performed many, many times during a meal. Food is always dropped on to the plate so that there is no contact between diner and server. I remember how horrified Narayan was once when, in an abstract moment, I reached up to take the proferred chapatti from his hand. He pulled back just in time. If this connection had been made, he would have considered himself contamin-ated and might not have returned to his kitchen until he had bathed.

Once, early in my stay at Belur Math, I decided to spend the day in Calcutta, shopping for some of the many Indian goods friends had asked me to buy for them. As Hindu food had already begun to pall exceedingly, I also looked upon this excursion alone as a thrilling oppor-tunity to have a Western-style lunch. But when it was known that I was thinking of going to the city, a good deal of anxiety was expressed. Would I be able to find my way? Would I fall a prey to pickpockets? Would I know how to manage the currency and language problems? To all this I was able to answer that I was an experienced traveller, had already reached India safely, and felt sure I could cope with Calcutta. Then came the problem they were actually concerned about: Where would I 'take my meal'?

'Oh, I'll go to some hotel,' I answered. (Through devious inquiry I had already made up my mind which it would be—at the Grand Hotel.) 'Wouldn't it be better to let the Advaita Ashrama people know, and go there?' one swami urged. 'I will just ring them up.' He was referring to the downtown office of one of the Order's publishing departments, where half a dozen swamis and brahmacharis worked and lived.

I felt trapped. Couldn't they see I was longing for a room with tables and chairs and a rug on the floor; tasteful service; gleaming china, silver, and linen; and foods that were distinct and recognizable and cooked in a way I was used to?

Then the point emerged: eating in hotels and restaurants is rarely done by monastics because of the unhelpful influences likely to reside in the food. Food not prepared with devotion, not prepared with the idea that it is to be offered in the shrine—but just devised impersonally for making money by people with their minds full of gross thoughts—can adversely influence your spiritual growth. In fact, I have heard that Swami Vivekananda once stated that no one can attain God who eats in restaurants all the time. And Sri Ramakrishna could not even keep on the storage shelf in his room food gifts brought by visitors who were lustful, avaricious, or hopeful of getting some advantage as a result of their devotions.

I imagine I lunched at the Grand Hotel that day anyway; I do not remember for sure. But in any case a new idea was established in my mind which has not diminished with the passing of time. Judging by a difference I have noticed in myself since, I am sure there is something to it. As a consequence, I ate in public places in India perhaps not more than six or eight times all told, and then only when I felt my health was suffering for lack of familiar or protein diet. Since I have returned to America I have been glad enough to give up what was once one of my greatest delights—dining out nicely.

This concept also gave me a more acceptable rationale for the practice of cooking for the Lord. Previously this fundamental act of Hinduism had not appealed to me at all. It had seemed too dualistic. How could one think of immutable Spirit as making any possible use of material rations? Now I saw that, if looked at from this standpoint, one could find much value in the practice. If food is fashioned with the idea that it is to be offered to God, that food will be given the most beneficial attention. Only devotees will produce it, and such will take pains to select the best ingredients, to carry on the work with the highest attitude, to pour in dedication, to stir with love. So by all means let us feed the Lord, not because he needs anything but—for perfectly selfish reasons—because doing so guarantees a pragmatic benefit to those who consume the prasad. This is explained further on pages 186 and 187.

All this concern over cleanliness and defilement may seem out of place in an Order which preaches such a liberal religious creed. Perhaps it is overdone, although in fairness one must remember that social customs—like one's language for example—come down as a part of tradition, to be followed without much critical evaluation. Swamiji railed against India's 'religion of the cooking pot'. Already, I am told, many relaxations are to be seen in it, with the Ramakrishna Order being looked upon by conservatives as wildly progressive. I guess St. Francis's ecstasies were no less real because, like everyone else in his time, he changed his tunic but infrequently. Our religious efforts in Hollywood cannot be ruled out because we lie in our own bathwater and reach down to pet the cat while at the dining table—two procedures which would seem filthy to the Indian. On the other hand, our war against germs cannot make us spiritual, any more than the orthodox brahmin's constant ablutions can make him.

Yet I am sure there is something true in this system of ritualistic cleanliness—just as there is in germicidal cleanliness. Both viewpoints have virtue. The physical diseases of India could probably be reduced if there were more knowledge of and respect for aseptic cleanliness. On the contrary, if Occidental man were more discriminating in the influences he permitted to reach his consciousness, he might be able to reduce the frantic and scattered condition which characterizes him. The development that is indicated is an acceptance and harmonious blending of what is valid in both conceptions.

The cleanliness cycle is twenty-four hours in duration. It starts with yesterday's bath and concludes with today's bowel movement, shaving, and clothes washing, all of which are considered defiling acts. One's immaculacy is re-established for the new day by the bath, which follows completion of these others. Since it is not considered proper to enter the shrine, prepare food, eat, or in fact do much of anything in a transitional or impure condition, it is necessary to give careful attention to the timing of one's functions. In the monasteries I visited I would say there are two times preferred as termination points. Some monks arose very early —around 4.00 a.m.—to tend to everything before going to the temple for the usual 5.00 a.m. matins. Others awoke, went directly to the shrine, and completed breakfast and perhaps their morning's work before ending the cycle. This was the more popular plan, with the offices closing and the peak rush for the bathrooms and tanks centring on 11.00-11.30, just before the midday meal. Then the lines in the yards would be crowded with ochre and white cloths, like the sails of an armada of old-fashioned ships.

In a place where going in and out of doors is possible and convenient all the year, the basic plan of sanitation is likely to be simply recourse to the fields and woods. This is the case in India. In times past, as in rural places now, one merely went out, away from the house, and squatted, camper-style. When sanitation became more formalized, it was of course natural that familiar usages should be carried over into the new conditions. Hence the latrine of today is basically a small room with a slit in the floor, located as far from the living quarters as possible.

I had no trouble in adjusting myself to the indigenous facilities. I think the Indian's anxiety about this—invariably mentioned on my arrival at a new monastery—is uncalled for. Actually the scarcity of hot water, the absence of mirrors and the customary dimness of bathroom lighting were a good deal more of a bother. But these can be compensated for through various devices. I soon learned to carry an electric rod for heating the daily cup of shaving water—or it can be had by putting in an advance request at the kitchen. A hand mirror found its way into my medicine kit. Sufficient illumination can be obtained by doing one's shaving in broad daylight, in some spot other than the generally shadowy bathroom.

Even these troubles could have been avoided if I had found it within myself to go Indian all the way. A bath in cool water is the rule and is considered properly austere and moreover exhilarating. Absence of hair to comb and the periodic visitations of a common barber eliminate all need for mirrors and good visibility. I used to call it the execution block —the outdoor stone seat where the shaving would take place. Every week on a certain day the barber would come—often a devotee who would contribute his services. The men would line up, to have the face and underarm shaved, and sometimes the entire head. The monastic custom is that one should be completely shaved, or long-haired and bearded. One is to be clean but is not to pay any particular attention to his personal appearance. In practice, many men shave the face weekly but the head perhaps monthly or bimonthly, maintaining a short and attractive crew cut in between times.

I would like to make a few more remarks on the subject of taking the dust of the feet.

You see, there is no problem about doing this on well arranged occasions when you are formally presented to unquestioned seniors. There is something appropriate and satisfactory about the gesture then. But the uncertainty enters—and with uncertainty, the fear of disgracing yourself and insulting others—when the situation is, for one reason or another, obscure or set in an unfamiliar pattern. I am afraid, too, that pride was also a factor in making me draw back from this gesture of humility and obedience.

Within minutes of my 2.30 a.m. arrival at Belur Math a man wandered into my quarters and said hello. Blind with fatigue, anxious only to get to bed, and assuming that the caller was perhaps the custodian, I grumbled a short reply and continued to unpack. The next day when I was taken to be introduced to him I realized that what I had responded to with such gaucheness was a flattering welcome call by one of the more

senior men of the Order. Or you are walking on the Math grounds and
some unknown swami comes up and starts to walk along beside you,
wishing to get acquainted. Are you supposed to stop, stop him, and make
your pranams right there, with the danger of confusion and mishap?
What about it when you are taken into an office and introduced to about
five swamis all seated around a big table? Are you supposed to take the
dust of their feet? But they are sitting, as Indians usually do when they
sit on chairs, with their legs folded up in their laps. This actually happened
to me. A terrible moment of panic when I saw myself crawling around
under the table vainly hunting for ten feet! What about what I called
the baby swamis, the youngsters ten years my junior in age? Bow
before them? Did I do wrong in the case of the teen-ager I was introduced to at Kamarpukur—Sri Ramakrishna's great-grandnephew? I
only namaskared him. Should I have prostrated?

I finally concluded that the safest way to cope with this question of
etiquette is: when in doubt—do. Apparently there is no danger of making
the gesture too much. You won't trip seniors if you prostrate while they
are walking; they are experienced in pausing so as to permit you to
carry out your part of the introduction. As to the men around the table,
one could do nothing there; but if you go to a senior and he has his feet
under him, the correct thing to do is just to reach in their general
direction, then touch your forehead; that is enough. Yes, it isn't age but
monastic seniority which dictates pranams; you should offer to pranam
men younger than yourself if they have achieved a higher status, although
they probably won't actually allow it. And you should have bowed
before Ramakrishna's nephew. The relatives of the guru are to be
considered as the guru. The logic of this is that the only souls who will
achieve birth in the family of a great saint probably are only those much
advanced already.

In taking the dust of the feet it is implied that one is asking for a
blessing. The senior to whom the gesture is directed equally has an
obligation, of bestowing a blessing. Thus it is interesting to observe the
various external responses of those on the receiving end. Some will make
a gesture of shooing you away, as though to protest that they are unworthy of anyone's esteem. Some will stand quietly with downcast eyes
and their hands folded in the namaskar salutation while allowing you to
do what you wish. President Maharaj, who has to accept this mark of
reverence for hours every day, sits quietly with an indrawn expression,
permitting the act as a part of his job and hoping, I believe, that doing so
will help those making it. Some glance away in apparent unconcern
while accepting pranams. But the most amusing spectacle is that seen on
big occasions when numbers of sadhus gather and vie to take the dust of
each other's feet simultaneously. What a scene of retreats, bumping
heads, and colliding backsides then!

To my terror, this mark of respect was directed at me several times.

When little children were presented, they would often bow. This did not seem so bad. In fact it seemed sweet and polite. But when the women of a household at Udipi, where Swami Adidevananda and several others of us were entertained, included me in the deep and reverential prostrations made at our departure, I was abashed and hung in a corner. At Lucknow a fine brahmachari saw me off on a train for the Himalayas. He was so emotionally touched by that supposed goodness Indians were always imputing to me that he made a fast pranam before I knew what was coming. I was so surprised that I returned the compliment, which I now know to have been just the right thing to do.

The worst experience was at Belur Math in the spring, on the great celebration day of Sri Ramakrishna's birth. A gentle old man came out of the dense crowd and addressed me in a courteous tone: 'Sir, may I take the dust of your feet?'

'No,' I shouted, backing away. 'No, no, no,' and fled.

Who could it have been? A humble adorer of anyone wearing the cloth of the sadhu, who must have thought by my refusal that I felt his touch would defile me? Was he a buffoon, a comedian, someone not quite right in the head, trying to be funny? On the other hand, he might have been a saint. One of the characteristics of the saint is that—in contradistinction to the outlook of most of us—he imputes 'too much' worthiness to other people. Maybe it was God himself, in disguise, whose intent was to expose the hauteur, bow the stiff neck, through a demonstration of humility. Perhaps if my heart had been right I should have been able to see this and could have rushed to bow before him. Now I shall never know.

In this chapter I have touched upon some of the features of the daily life of the Ramakrishna sadhu. But I see I have not defined the word 'sadhu' itself. Just what does this expression mean, besides being a general Indian term for monastic?

A sadhu is someone who lives and moves and has his being in God. There is very little man left in him. To become a real sadhu, as is shown in Chapter X, is the one objective of the swamis and brahmacharis of the Ramakrishna Order.

Not having attained the condition of being a real sadhu oneself, one cannot perhaps know what it feels like to be a sadhu. But then again, one can tell how the sadhu affects him and so can perhaps gain a partial idea of what it would be like to have reached his state.

A real sadhu makes you feel good, merely being in his presence. It is easy to approach him. Pretence is not necessary in his company, and shame may be abandoned. To him you can open your heart. The acquaintance of a sadhu makes you feel as though it is not only desirable to be religious; it is also beneficial and easy. Because of his positive influences on others—this is why it is said that the holy man—although he may not 'do' anything—is the earth's most valuable inhabitant.

One quality that has never ceased to surprise me in the real sadhus I have met is how *considerate* they are. They seem interested in me, even though I am not worth such attention. But then, they are this same way with everybody. They invite you, as it were, to take advantage of them. This virtue stems, it must be, from an absence of concern about their own motives and a genuine identification with the needs of others— which is, of course, pure love.

In a word, to call a man a real sadhu is to say everything at once. For holiness is the bond of all the perfections, and the heart of all life's satisfactions. To be absorbed in God makes a man sensible, alert, far-seeing, understanding, wise, courageous, compassionate, joyous, welcomed, and a universal idol. Sadhuism is sufficient unto itself; and it only makes a man worth loving in life, and in death worth remembering.

CHAPTER IV

'A BAND OF STROLLING
PLAYERS'

SRI RAMAKRISHNA lived at Dakshineswar until 1885. Holy Mother attended him, while crowds of the curious, the troubled, the spiritually hungry came to him, to be taught according to their need and capacity. Then, as his throat cancer grew worse, the Master permitted his anxious devotees to engage a house for him in Calcutta, near good doctors, and later a home in Cossipore, a northern suburb, which was still convenient to the city but where the air was thought better. Here he completed the training of the inner circle of young men who were to remain in the world as teachers, passed his power on to them, with Narendra in charge, and died in August 1886.

After a period of development, the members of the new Order began to work together in an organized way, occupying a succession of temporary headquarters, until the establishment of Belur Math in 1899. Holy Mother, in the meantime, left Calcutta, spending some years in Kamarpukur and Jayrambati and in making pilgrimages to various holy places. For her this was a period of obscurity and even of hardship. In 1902 Swami Vivekananda died and Swami Brahmananda became leader of the Order. Branches began to be opened in the major cities of India. In 1909 Holy Mother moved to an ashrama specially prepared for her in Calcutta, dying there in 1920. Growth continued to accelerate, so that at present there are more than a hundred establishments of the Ramakrishna Math and Mission in India, with other centres in south-eastern Asia, Europe, and North and South America.

Once Sri Ramakrishna understood that the proprietor of the Dakshineswar temple was angry with him and wanted him to leave. Completely detached, the Master picked up his only personal possession, a towel, and headed for the gate. Then the proprietor changed his mind and begged him to return. As adaptable to the new twist of fate as he had been to the previous one, Sri Ramakrishna turned around, marched back to his room, put away the towel and went on as before. As a response to such self-abandonment a religious and public service organization of great power is functioning. In answer to such poverty, wealth is accumulating to make possible the preaching of the Master's revelation.

Since he did not possess a formal knowledge of letters we must class Ramakrishna as illiterate. He could hardly read or write his own Bengali. And in an era when an acquaintance with English was essential to any Indian hoping to get on in the world, Ramakrishna never learned to speak more than perhaps a dozen words of that language. Even then he used 'pencil', for example, when he meant 'pension'. Yet today orphanages and hostels, grade and high schools, and technical institutions and colleges are flourishing in his memory. Adult education classes, library services, the output of several publishing houses, and eight or nine magazines in as many languages add to the public's knowledge of Vedanta.

Today the life expectancy in India is about thirty years, contrasted to that of over sixty-five in the United States. Formerly the figure was perhaps even more distressing. The Master suffered from bad health all his life, experiencing the usual continuous and enervating tropical diseases, and dying at fifty. Today a dozen maternity, tuberculosis, and general hospitals are serving the people of India in his name, with many free dispensaries treating over two million out-patients a year.

While he lived Ramakrishna was known to very few. Sometimes at Dakshineswar he was taken for a temple caretaker and ordered about by visitors. He was so without ostentation and so absorbed in God that much of the time he hardly knew whether he was dressed or not and had to be reminded of the proprieties when receiving visitors. Yet the utterances of this incomprehensible being are now studied and meditated upon by many of the most thoughtful persons of five continents as today's words of eternal life.

A new mood is gripping people. In a world where the barriers of distance have vanished, how can the barriers of prejudice remain? Everywhere men and women are learning good things, human things, about other men and women. Exclusiveness, born purely of ignorance, is being replaced by curiosity, even respect. It is dawning on many that ideological isolationism in today's world has become untenable. If a person pursues this line of thinking—if he pushes hard against the walls of the old conditioning—he stands a good chance, sooner or later, of stumbling upon Ramakrishna and Vedanta.

I had experienced Dakshineswar. The next place to go in my attempt to draw closer to Sri Ramakrishna through enjoying scenes and relics of his life was Balaram Bose's Calcutta townhouse. You have only to read the Master's Gospel to see how often and marvellously his grace was expressed there. In leaving his temple garden and spending a day or two now and then with dharma-dedicated families like Balaram's, Rama-krishna showed his respect for the householder state. Besides, these periodic appearances in the city gave some persons who could not easily make the trip to Dakshineswar a chance to have contact with the Master.

On these visitations to Calcutta, the Master often revealed his intensely human side and at the same time showed how the mundane can be enjoyed as divine by a purified mind. His delight in theatrical perform-ances was extreme. They reminded him of the way people speculate about God until they see him, then talk no more but enjoy his vision. When the curtain goes up, he said, the audience stops chattering and watches the play. His joy in philosophical discussions and even in ordinary small talk was great—providing such were spirited and witty and free from hypocrisy. He sometimes even told naughty jokes himself, explaining, 'I don't give the youngsters a pure vegetarian diet; now and then I give them a little water smelling of fish. Otherwise, why should they come?'

Nobody knows exactly why people drink, but those who do are often drawn to alcohol because they find some apparent reflection of divine bliss or knowledge in inebriation. On at least one occasion, this similarity was recognized by Ramakrishna. Passing a tavern and witnessing the jollification within, he called from his carriage 'Make merry, make merry!' The sight of the drinkers' transports drove his mind to a God-intoxicated state. Or what could have been more human than this direction to a woman at Balaram's: 'Now go into the inner apartments and cook some curry for me. Put some spicy seasoning into it so that I can get the smell from here.'

Balaram Bose's house is in the northern end of Calcutta, which in Ramakrishna's time seems to have been a quiet residential section occupied by upper-class families. Girish Ghosh's old home is just a block away. The design of Balaram's residence is the same as is used all over the world by builders who wish in the middle of a crowded section to have a safe and private domain. You could discover its exact plan in ancient Rome, in Florentine houses of the Renaissance, and in Spanish urban dwellings right down to the present day. It is a two-storied structure standing severely at the edge of the street, with no way of access except a large gate in the centre of the front. Inside is a courtyard, around which the house is built. Through this gate, in Balaram's time presided over by a servant, persons could come and go, and shipments of necessities for the big establishment could be wheeled in. The ground floor surrounding the courtyard was used for service purposes, with the great joint family living mostly on the upper story. As you go through the gate you turn left, taking a stairway to the balcony above. At the head of the stairs is a small room which in turn opens into the main salon that runs across the front of the house, with long windows overlooking the

street, and doors opening inward onto the balcony. On his visits Ramakrishna slept in the little chamber. He was the guest of honour before
large assemblages in the salon, lounging Indian-style against a bolster
on the sheet-covered floor.

On the balcony which runs around the four sides of the courtyard the
Master enacted his classic play as God and God's inamorata. It is July
14, 1885, the day of the Jagannath car festival at Puri, three hundred
miles to the south. Balaram's family members are Vaishnavites; thus it
is that the family deity quite naturally happens to be that aspect of
Vishnu known as Jagannath. It is on this day that the images of the Lord
of the Universe and of his sister Subhadra and brother Balaram are taken
once a year from their guarded shrine in the Jagannath temple and drawn
through the streets of Puri on a great chariot so that any and all may have
darshan. The scene is being copied in Balaram's house with his household deities and a small car. Sri Ramakrishna has come for the
occasion.

The Master has been up since before dawn, singing and chanting the
name of God. All morning devotees have been arriving, to sit with the
Master in the drawing room, talking with him on spiritual matters.
Throughout the afternoon the excitement has been increasing. It is now
evening. A throng fills the house. The images of Jagannath, Balaram,
and Subhadra, wearing rich dresses and jewellery, and adorned by the
household priest with sandal paste and garlands, are brought out from
the family shrineroom. On the balcony stands the miniature temple car
all decorated with flags and bunting. The deities are placed on it. Now
the sound of the orchestra grows loud and fast. Drumbeats resound up
and down the street, attracting more and more people so that the courtyard is crowded. The Master catches hold of the rope and begins to
pull the chariot as exulting thousands are doing just now at Puri. Around
the four sides of the balcony it moves, with Ramakrishna dancing before
it in rapture. The voices of the singers swell:

> Beautiful Chaitanya,
> Youthful dancer,
> Fair as molten gold . . .

Who is dancing before the car? The crowd watches enchanted. Is it
Sri Chaitanya, Krishna's devotee and in some part a reincarnation of the
great Lord? Is it Krishna himself, returned to play this time, not on the
grassy downs of Brindaban, but in a modern townhouse in this Asian
capital of a Western power?

Not until midnight is it all over. Girish Ghosh has brought an
Anglicized friend with him who has been looking upon these scenes
from out of his own culture with a certain disdain. Now the visitor has
left. Ramakrishna remarks—his capacity for practicality as great as that
for bliss: 'I say this to you and to everyone: Please do not force any-

body to come here [to me]. Nothing happens except at the right time.' This counsel is followed as policy by the Order of his name.

After Ramakrishna died his relics were kept at Balaram's house for a time. Holy Mother stayed there, as did Swamiji and others of the inner group. Some of the early organization meetings of the Ramakrishna Order were held at Balaram's, and in 1922 Swami Brahmananda died there.

Well, the old house is quiet now. It is under the care of the Ramakrishna Order, which keeps up the empty front rooms as a shrine to the memory of all that transpired in them, while Balaram's descendants continue to live on in other parts of the building. But no one did I see anywhere, except a blind old man sitting on that historic balcony taking the sun.

'Forever isolated from those high days,' I mourned. 'How do you make contact with dead heroes? So strong it is, the mere passage of time, to cut you off, shut you out.' In referring to the appearance on earth of the avatar and his apostles, Ramakrishna himself once gave this description: 'A band of minstrels suddenly appear before a house. They sing and dance and go away as suddenly as they came; nobody knows them!'

Then I learned that the oblivious elderly gentleman at the railing was the brother of one of Sri Ramakrishna's direct disciples, Swami Premananda. Their sister had been Balaram's wife. And this old man had in his youth actually gazed upon Sri Ramakrishna! It was a living link—one of two I was blessed to meet, the other being Swami Ambikananda whom I shall describe a little later. Those strolling players hadn't quite got away without being seen—and I had known two who had beheld them and their engrossing leader!

The area north of Calcutta and on the east side of the Ganges is now an industrial slum. Jute mills, brickworks, and iron foundries line the river, intermixed with living quarters. Plunging down through the middle of this sector is a main road choked with buses, bullock carts, man-propelled freight wagons, rickshaws, and swarms of people and animals. Along this avenue one sees the typical Indian shop of the smaller sort: really an elevated niche in which the proprietor squats, surrounded by his wares, like a human incongruously appearing on a marionette stage.

To the right as you go north is an iron gate that takes you in behind some stalls to a large plot of ground with a two-story house in the centre. This is what remains of the once attractive Cossipore garden house where Sri Ramakrishna died and where the new religious movement bearing his name commenced some seventy-five years ago. There was nothing remarkable about the place when I saw it except its look of dilapidation. Here and there were remains of several estate buildings—stables, gardeners' quarters, cookhouses. In the front, the ruins of a ghat showed where a tank had formerly been. The residence itself had the atmosphere of a badly battered lodging house. I was one of the last visitors to enter the original building. For in 1953 it was torn down as unsafe and a reproduction was begun in its place.

For many years the poor and struggling Order had not been able to gain possession of its site of origination. After Sri Ramakrishna died it was occupied by an English family and was also for a time used by an Armenian Christian for a business in pork canning. Things came to a head in the mid-1940s. A religious teacher appeared who, capitalizing on the rising popularity of Sri Ramakrishna, claimed to be the Master's reincarnation. He was able to purchase the Cossipore house as the seat of his activities. It was then that the Order realized it must do something positive about getting the site. But now the price had grown very large. Finally a state of emergency was declared. A campaign to raise money throughout India was carried out. Americans sent offerings, eight thousand dollars going from Hollywood alone. Finally efforts were successful and the place was obtained, to be set aside forever as an international shrine.

My attention naturally focused on the second-floor chamber where Sri Ramakrishna spent his last half-year in the body. There was nothing visibly significant about it—just a large room running east and west through the house. What unusual mark I expected might have remained, I do not know. It was from this room that the young disciples of the inner circle were sent out one spring day in 1886 to beg food, this being the symbolic first act of the monk. As the official biography of Vivekananda puts it in its quaint English: 'They consented immediately with enthusiasm; and with the name of the Lord upon their lips they went forth to beg in the neighbourhood. They had varied experiences; some were abused for neglecting their duties; the sight of others caused many mothers to shed tears.' The food which they collected in this manner was, in accordance with custom, cooked in the garden and offered to the guru, who took a grain of rice and said, 'Well done. This food is most pure.' A little later the Master gave to each boy with his own hand the gerrua robe of renunciation.

To the southwest of Ramakrishna's room is an open deck where the Master sometimes sunned himself and took the air. Standing there, as the boy later known as Swami Saradananda had done on January 1, 1886, I could see diagonally across the yard, halfway to the gate, the place where Sri Ramakrishna had become the kalpataru, or wish-fulfilling tree, that day. The remarkable happenings of that New Year's afternoon are well known. Since it was a holiday, some thirty devotees had come to be near the Master. They were just strolling around the grounds, talking to one another, their minds depressed because they realized that their guru was dangerously sick. It was about three o'clock. Suddenly Ramakrishna left his bedroom and appeared among them. And as the boy watched from the balcony, a fabulous scene was enacted on the lawn. As the disciples came crowding up to the Master he entered an ecstatic state, blessing them one by one that their spiritual unfoldment might occur at once. 'Awake', he murmured to each. And they did. Some moved apart, to sit in meditation, enjoying the contemplation of their chosen deities that now had become living and visible. Some ran about shouting in joy. One devotee gained such an intense consciousness of his Chosen Ideal that it would never leave his mind. Being a businessman, he finally had to pray that it might dim sufficiently to allow him to carry on his duties.

Swami Saradananda said later that he did not consider the designation 'kalpataru' to be quite correct in describing Ramakrishna's gesture that day. The legendary wish-fulfilling tree is something different. It is said to grant to those who stand beneath it whatever they may desire, bringing results bad for you as well as good. But what the Master did that winter afternoon of 1886 and of his life was something else. Swami Saradananda says: 'It was more reasonable, it seems to us, to call it "the self-revelation of the Master" or the "bestowal of freedom from fear on all devotees by revealing himself". He made clear through that event the fact of his being a God-man and of his bestowal of protection against and freedom from fear on all without the slightest discrimination.' In other words, God spoke openly on this occasion to say that he had come again to this distracted globe and is an easily available refuge to any who may wish to come to him. A renewal it was of those promises God ever makes when he appears: 'I will never leave thee nor forsake thee.' 'Peace I leave with you, my peace I give unto you.'

From Cossipore I followed the route the Master's body had taken on his death and funeral day of August 16, 1886. He had died at one o'clock that morning. After daylight the body had been brought down and placed on a cot on the lawn before the garden house wrapped in gerrua and adorned with sandal paste and flowers. Many came to pay their last respects, and some thirty of the closer devotees had a sad photograph taken grouped behind the body. Then a procession was formed, and to the sound of devotional music the Master's poor remains were carried to the little cremation ground at Baranagore on the Ganges bank down a few small streets not far away. A year or two before, when the crowds of spiritual seekers coming to him had grown so incessant as to prevent Ramakrishna's bathing, eating, and sleeping regularly, he had questioned the Divine Mother: 'It is only a drum and with holes in it. How long can it last if it is played on night and day?' Now the drum was rent and silent.

A stone marker, like a large tombstone, covers the place where the Master's body was burned. The young swami who was my guide the day I went there inclined and touched his forehead to its cool side. Nearby are slabs showing where three of the Master's outstanding disciples were cremated: Swami Abhedananda, M., the compiler of the Gospel, and Gauri-Ma. It was just sunset now. This was the first burning ground I had ever visited. It was a little eerie, as I had heard such places might be; it is still in daily use. No cremations were going on when I was there, but there were several pits of burned-out coals where cremations customarily occur, and on other days I often noticed from across the river smoke rising from the spot. Big dark trees stood in the centre of the ground, croaking birds sitting heavily on the branches. Looking straight across the Ganges I could see Belur Math—tangible, substantial—silhouetted against the dropping sun.

Cossipore was the original home of the Ramakrishna brotherhood. There were three others after that before the Order was to have its permanent headquarters. For the first six years the boy sannyasins made their home base in an old haunted house where the rent was cheap, near the cremation ground at Baranagore. There was no organization yet— merely days of song, study, and meditation—and hopes that somehow food for the next meal might turn up. I saw the spot: only a vacant lot now, with a mouldering pillar or two to show where the wonderful free-and-easy early hermitage had stood. For the next five years a building near Dakshineswar was used. Then, for a year or two the Order occupied a garden house across the Ganges from Baranagore and just south of the present Belur Math. Finally in 1899 the permanent Math at Belur was established.

Swamiji himself carried the relics of Sri Ramakrishna to and installed them in the new site. There wasn't much there then—an old building or two left from the boatworks, with jungle all around. But Swamiji could see the future. 'It is my wish to convert this Math into a chief centre of spiritual practice and the culture of knowledge. The power that will have its rise from here will flood the whole world, and turn the course of men's lives into different channels.'

During the first year two buildings were finished: a refectory with a chapel above, and a residential building to the east, right on the river. These structures are still there, still in heavy daily use, little changed. Of course the old eating area could not accommodate the number who live at the Math now; it has been turned into food storage rooms, a new dining hall having been built on. They say it was a sight in the first years to see the row of original disciples of Ramakrishna sitting there having their meal! And the chapel upstairs is about as it was, except that it does not contain the relics any more since the completion of the big new main temple a few years ago. The dormitory appears not to have been altered at all. That is where everyone lived at first. The old visitors' room on the ground floor is still in use; now it houses a collection of pictures of the old days, and is used in the evenings for bhajans, or song services. As you stand on the second-floor veranda looking down at the

Ganges, you can almost hear the flap, flap of Swami Brahmananda's slippers coming out from his room behind you. And the big bedroom in the south-east corner is Swamiji's, just as it was when he was alive.

To me, these two original buildings memorialize Swami Vivekananda. He had a gigantic spiritual experience in the one, and he died in the other. I grew breathless every time I entered either, because he had been so often in each room. Swamiji has always appealed to me, as I think he does to many Americans, because—well, because he was so ideal a man and saint and yet seems so human and somehow so Western. No jarring adjustment is felt in accepting him and using him as a bridge to the more alien features of an unfamiliar culture. You feel as though, having been to the West twice and having liked Westerners and told them how to turn their goodness into greatness, Swamiji is a kind of founding father of the new spiritual dispensation which the nations of the West should eventually experience.

I would go to meditate each morning outside the old shrineroom which had been the original temple of the Ramakrishna movement. It isn't particularly impressive—just a room perhaps fifteen by twenty, with a nice floor of black and white marble squares. At the far end is a large picture of Sri Ramakrishna. Along the south are big windows letting in the sun. But here the casket of the Master's relics was kept for the first forty years, and here the first apostles held their worship.

On the last day of his life, July 4, 1902, Swamiji entered this chamber after breakfast, bolted all the openings from inside and stayed three hours. What happened, nobody knows. But it is understood later that he had decided to give up his body that night and must have been, before the remains of his Master, making ready for the end. This day is celebrated annually at Hollywood now, at the monastery at Trabuco, with a big American-style picnic. How Swamiji would love it if he could come—which then again in one sense I think he surely does! What is commemorated of course, is not Swamiji's death, but his great love for the United States and his insistence that every man must struggle for outer and inner freedom. He must have chosen Independence Day for a reason, and I have sometimes wondered whether it might not have been to underline his approval of the young, brash spirit.

Downstairs they were growing worried. It was almost dinnertime and still he was locked in in the chapel above. Then they heard Swamiji begin a towering hymn in praise of Kali—Kali in whom creation and dissolution combine. He unlocked the door and came out. I used to think maybe he brushed against the frame. And I would touch it myself and think: Through this space he moved in his moment of triumph; through this opening he came out, one man who lived an absolutely victorious life all the way.

Swamiji's bedroom too is just a room. It is well fitted out with mahogany furniture of the Victorian period, with many relics on display of his travels and honours. Overlooking the Ganges, with windows to the east and south, it is wonderfully fresh and sunshiny during the day. But at night that peculiarly intense Indian moonlight, bearing down on everything, makes it most disturbing. Then the power of that room becomes felt. You sense it like silent electrical machinery turning, turning, in the white stillness. At the open door I always stood awe-struck. I never dared go in until the last hour of my last stay at Belur Math. When finally I stood reflected in the long mirror I thought: his image once came from this.

The inhuman casualness of Swamiji's leavetaking showed the composure of his mind and his mastery of both worlds. In its deliberateness it was like the Buddha's last noble act. Recall that and weep: how quietly the Blessed One prepared his bed, how he lay down upon it in the lion posture, resting on the right side, with one foot above the other, how he comforted his lamenting followers and even instructed a stranger in religion as he died.

Swamiji's death was as remarkable. He never revealed by any hint that afternoon the decision he had come to. He ate a good lunch in the company of his brothers, taught a Sanskrit class of brahmacharis, and took a walk with Swami Premananda to the Belur market place on the Grand Trunk Road, chatting about everyday matters all the while. Then at vesper-time he went to his room alone for meditation. After that he stretched out on his mat on the floor, calling one of the brothers to fan him. And a little while later, with a sigh such as a baby makes in a dream, he left his body.

A leading swami of the Order once made the following statement in my hearing: 'Swamiji did a great work in breaking the old lassitude, stirring up people to become active, getting Sri Ramakrishna's work organized and off to a good start. And again, without Swami Brahmananda, with his stress on spiritual practice, love, and self-direction, the movement might have deteriorated into a kind of good-works Protestantism by now.' Hence both expressed the will of the Divine. They championed different aspects, expressed different emphases, furnishing richness, variety, and balance.

As Swami Vivekananda was known as Swamiji, so Swami Brahmananda was usually called Maharaj. Maharaj was President for a year or two before Swamiji died and until his own death twenty years later. Many present seniors are his disciples. The expansion which took place during Maharaj's administration was remarkable. I visited dozens of these branches and could tell about them. But why should they especially interest a Western audience? The Ramakrishna Order conducts many health services; but compared to Western institutions of healing, these are often substandard and small. The Order supports public relief and disaster works, and educational enterprises of many kinds. But any day in the United States you can see similar efforts ever so much more numerous and far more impressive.

No, it is not the service activities of the Ramakrishna Order that challenge the Western observer. Good as these are, and striking as they may be in India, they are often fairly minor in comparison to what busy and rich Americans have built. What people from the West look to the Ramakrishna movement for is something different, something we don't know how to produce in our country—namely, living examples of advanced spirituality. This, as will be seen, the Order does produce.

Yet, in order to convey the flavour of the service efforts of the Order, I shall tell about some rural aid work and one medical institution it administers.

Nearly 80 per cent of the people of India live on the land. But the Ramakrishna movement does not involve itself in rural uplift much, since development of the 500,000 small country communities has been taken on as a major responsibility by the Government, with millions of dollars' worth of materials and expert help being furnished by the United States.

Some of the men of the industrial school at Belur Math, however, do take a particular interest in rural improvement. Spaces between the buildings of the Math have been turned into experimental plots where the values of fertilizers or special methods of planting are demonstrated. On occasion some of the brahmacharis board a van and go out to small villages where they show, with US Army surplus generators, projectors, and loudspeakers, movies both entertaining and educational. Such fundamental things are taught as these: the importance of crop diversification, how to construct a homemade fly-proof latrine, ways of getting more food from the land, how to make and maintain a pure drinking water supply, the value to health of varying the rice diet through growing and eating more vegetables. At the end of the show a coloured portrait of Sri Ramakrishna may be flashed on the screen, but that is about as far as the religious efforts go.

During the week prior to the great public celebration of Ramakrishna's birthday in the spring, the industrial school sponsored a conference for village agricultural workers, with aid on practical problems of living and earning in rural areas. The best feature of the conference in everyone's estimation was the simultaneous inception of nine demonstration machines, all of different designs, for making cooking gas from cowdung. The dung is added at one end of a big structure—the idea kept occurring to me that perhaps this might be what a uranium pile looked like —and by gravitation flows through, coming out three months later much modified, and useful further for speeding the breakdown of compost. In the process gas is produced, which is led into a storage tank, to be used as needed. It is non-explosive and non-poisonous, and very hot.

Swami Vimuktananda, the head of the industrial school, used to give us tea every afternoon prepared with boiling water heated on the burner he proudly kept in his office, supplied by one of the machines outside. To have a plant like this on a farm would be a simple thing to build and maintain, and think of the convenience—since otherwise everything must be heated over wood fires that must always be built and fed by hand.

I am sorry I was never able to go out on any of the village expeditions or really see at first hand what some of the swamis were doing in out-of-the-way places. The nearest I came was when I was at Khatra in rural Bengal. The head of a Ramakrishna Mission basic education school nearby arrived for a visit of a day or two, bringing a prize cabbage as a gift. He told me about the work he was doing in the village and the improvement that was occurring there in health and living standards. Wonderfully enthusiastic, he was exactly like an American county agent or Farm Bureau worker. You might find his like in any farm or ranch community in the United States—except of course that he was an Indian swami with a shaved head, bare-footed, and wearing an ochre dhoti!

The largest hospitals of the Order are at Benares and Kankhal in India and at Rangoon in Burma. Perhaps the fourth in size is the one at Brindaban. This town of twenty thousand is in that northwestern part of India which is so hot, dry, and Mohammedan. I had expected to find green fields and a limpid Jamuna. Anyone familiar with the Krishna legends naturally pictures Brindaban in that way. It must have been idyllic in Krishna's time. But when I was there—late March and full summer already—Brindaban was dusty and the Jamuna nothing but a trickle away out beyond some exposed sandbars. It was 105 degrees in the daytime and 85 at night, and the really hot weather had not as yet come on. One day there was a dust storm during which the air was full of drifting particles, exactly like a gentle blizzard, only brown. Seeing it brought to mind that wonderful touch in Louis Bromfield's *The Rains Came*. The wealthy English businessman and his professional beauty of a wife are travelling through an area like this in their private railway car. It is night and they are trying to get some sleep. Blocks of ice have been set in the vestibule with fans blowing over them, to cool the staterooms. But the moist air combines with the dust to produce, to the annoyance of the woman, a fine coating of actual mud on her expensive complexion.

No one was there to meet me at the railway station about three miles away when I arrived at Brindaban. So I took a tonga to the math. The tonga is a basket cart with two wheels, pulled by one horse. The passengers sit in the rear, facing backward, the driver in the front. Shafts go forward and are fastened into the harness of the horse. The tonga's design permits a frightening flexibility. When you step in, the rear sags alarmingly, and if more than one passenger attempts to ride, there is the danger of overbalancing the conveyance and lifting the horse right off the ground—a hazard forestalled by the driver's crawling well forward on the shafts to add his weight to that of the animal when taking a heavy load. In motion the tonga develops a sidewise jerking action that is most shattering.

This part of India, the United Provinces, is very orthodox. At the time I was there I heard it had not contributed a single member to the Order as yet. What a peculiar commentary on the action-reaction rhythm of nature! For it is those areas which became the most heavily materialized by the British—Madras and Bengal—which yet furnished the largest number of men to this non-materialistic movement. The Brindaban ashrama looked very run down in 1953, and for a reason. It was on low ground and was subject to inundation by the Jamuna at flood stage. In 1947 water stood in the buildings nearly up to the ceilings. So the whole institution was about to be reconstructed on a higher site. About twenty brahmacharis and swamis were stationed at Brindaban. Most of them could not speak much English, which cut us off from each other and made them seem unapproachable. Somehow, word of my intended arrival had failed to reach the place ahead of me, so that I feared, after dismissing the tonga and presenting myself to the office, that my presence was inconvenient. My first impression of Brindaban, hence, was unfavourable.

But next day I saw the work that was being done and how my attitude changed! There are what are known as the outdoor department and the indoor hospital. By outdoor department is meant a dispensary where people come for treatment and then return home. Nearly sixty dispensaries are operated by the Order. Basically the dispensary consists of a doctor—usually, because the Order does not have its own MDs as yet, a lay medical man whose services are hired—and a pharmacist and medical aide or two, the latter monastic members. Patients line up to see the doctor, men in one place and women in another. One by one they pass before him, describing their complaints. He may prescribe medicine, giving a prescription which the pharmacist fills immediately, or send the patient to the medical aides for whatever service they are capable of rendering: cleaning infections, bandaging, giving minor treatments of all kinds. This is medical service en masse. Three to four hundred pass through the dispensary at Brindaban every day, seven days a week.

The indoor hospital boasts about fifty beds—many of these, because of lack of space, placed practically outdoors, on verandas and porches. Eye infections are common in the United Provinces. Many eye operations are done at the Brindaban hospital, including cornea grafting, an eye bank actually being maintained for this purpose. Nursing is not provided, so that the patient is encouraged to bring a relative with him, who will probably camp on the grounds and act as his orderly. In some hospitals food is served to the patients from a central kitchen. In others, because of local caste dietary complications, the attending relative is given facilities and expected to cook for and feed the patient.

The old idea is that a sadhu should have no established place of residence and do no utilitarian work. The people around Brindaban cling to this traditional concept and look askance at the Ramakrishna hospital as an enterprise for monks. But they admire the work done there anyway and gladly come from long distances to add their names to the heavy waiting list. Everyone is served free, whatever his attitude may be and whether he is Hindu, Mohammedan, Christian, or any other. This is the policy of all Ramakrishna Order installations. In Benares, for example, the leading community hospital is limited to Hindus, so that the many Mohammedans of that region, if they are to receive hospitalization at all, must patronize the local Ramakrishna hospital. I used to watch those purdah ladies being admitted, in their mobile tents with gaping eye-holes, like Ku-Kluxers or Halloween masqueraders. Their attitude is one of absolute opposition to all religious outlooks but their own. Yet they were thankful to avail themselves of the Order's free medical care and were served conscientiously.

Affiliated with most Ramakrishna centres there are lay devotees, something like church members, who help support the work and for whom a programme of activities is maintained of music, meditation periods and public worship, lectures, celebrations on holy days. But not at Brindaban. Few people in the United Provinces have even heard of Ramakrishna or Vivekananda. Day after day the throngs that crowd in just want their bodies ministered to, not caring or interested in knowing about the auspices under which the benefits are given. How I revised my appraisal of the place when I saw the work being done! Treating such people is anything but rewarding. They are illiterate and crude. It is genuinely home missionary labour of the most basic kind: patch up the body in any case and calculate not whether the mind may open. This is real karma yoga. One young swami said to me: 'I was not very happy in this place and the work when I first came. I would dislike it now if I didn't meditate a good deal. By doing so, most of the time I can really feel I am worshipping the Lord in serving these people. Now I am thankful to be here, for their very unresponsiveness helps me to keep my mind in him.'

Widowhood is a particular status in India, with established obligations. The old custom dictates that, should a husband die, the wife must shave her head, put on a plain white sari, give up all her ornaments, and remain chaste and unmarried for the rest of her days. If practicable, she should retire to some holy place, living an austere, nun-like life, spending her time in religious contemplation. I saw such little women by the hundreds in and around the temples and along the Ganges at Benares and Hardwar.

As an orthodox brahmin lady of the old school, Holy Mother naturally intended to follow the tradition when Ramakrishna died, even though she was only thirty-two at the time. But what happened instead was that the task of bringing spirituality into the world and illumining men's hearts which Ramakrishna had done had now to be carried forward by her. Once at Cossipore the Master had asked, 'Well, won't you do anything? Am I to do all?'

She had replied, 'I am a woman. What can I do?'

To this the Master had answered, 'No, no. You have much to do.'

On the basis of the Vaishnava scriptural idea that 'anyone wedded to Krishna can never be a widow', Holy Mother did not go into customary retirement when Ramakrishna died. Rather, she became the Master's leading devotee and instrument until she in turn passed away in 1920 at the age of sixty-six. She became chief guru and unspoken head of the Ramakrishna movement. Although the average person would not have taken her for anything but a rustic matron, those able to look deeper saw not a Bengali widow at all, but Kali, Shakti, Brahman manifesting itself as dynamic power. Apparently the more spiritually advanced one was himself the more he saw in her. With her the stalwarts of the Order were like awed little children. Swamiji came into her presence only after agonies of self-purification; and Maharaj, at the end of a few moments near her, would begin to tremble and perspire noticeably.

It fell to Swami Saradananda, first Secretary of the Order, to be Mother's special provider. For the first two-thirds of her widowhood her life was very hard. Although she was coming to be nationally recognized as a great saint, in the country at Kamarpukur and Jayrambati she had to act as busy matriarch over squabbling relatives and in-laws. On her appearances in Calcutta, where people formed long waiting lines just to pranam her, some rented house would be her stopping place. But during the last dozen years of Mother's life, through writing a Bengali biography of Ramakrishna, called *Ramakrishna the Great Master*, and making other efforts, Saradananda managed to get together enough money to provide her with a comfortable house in her village and a headquarters in Calcutta called the Udbodhan Office.

I had lunch at Udbodhan one day and saw many relics of Mother's life, including the two gold bracelets Ramakrishna gave her and which she continued to wear, against custom, after he died, because she saw that he had not really gone away. These famous bangles were brought out of the safe, and Swami Atmabodhananda let me touch my forehead to them. Mother's room is in the front of the house on the second floor. It is the shrineroom too, and the interior veranda on which it opens has been extended above the courtyard so that people may sit there for meditation.

One of my happiest days in India was that of the big celebration in December of the ninety-ninth anniversary of Mother's birth. It was a fine event which I observed both at Belur Math and at Udbodhan. It started the day before when all was made ready. Tents were erected as shade for the many who would take prasad there, and another portable room was put up as a shoe-check depot. Holy Mother died at Udbodhan and was cremated at Belur Math, just on the spot where her temple now stands. All the evening around this temple there was excitement as devotees came to put up decorations under the direction of Deven Maharaj, the sweet elderly swami who had been Mother's worshipper there for so long. An electric light bulb was fastened to the top of a pole attached to the highest finial, and beneath this a red flag. Then garlands and mango-leaf streamers were hung around the eaves. One family had brought a good deal of food, which was distributed to the workers when the decorating was done. I shall never forget their little daughter who, all swaddled in a maroon shawl, sat against a pillar like a china doll, just her great black eyes moving, for hours during the whole proceeding.

In the morning the long mooing of conch shells woke us around 4.30, and arati was sung at both the main temple and at Mother's temple at 5.00. There was a festive feeling as the crowds began to come in. The visitors and the monks were carefully dressed, most of the latter having had their heads freshly shaved for the occasion. The sweeper boy had fastened a flower to the handle of his broom. Worship was performed in all the temples as usual, starting about 8.30 a.m., but the largest crowd collected around Holy Mother's. Many devotees brought offerings: saris, garlands, fruits. Often these arrived wrapped neatly in newspapers or large leaves.

At 11.00 in the morning there was a kirtan in the main temple. In the centre of the big hall a group of musicians gathered, about fifteen as I remember, wearing hats just alike, as band members often do in the West. Around them the crowd squeezed in. Slowly the leader, a vocalist, began to sing, tentatively feeling his way, building up the volume and the mood. The instrumentalists closed their eyes and began to sway a little, catching the influence of the melody. Gradually they began to play, and then faster and faster as the enchantment spread. There was something that reminded me of Russian folk music about this: plaintive singing with a rippling instrumental background. Often the voice, one voice, would come out alone; then there would be a chord or two of music, and then all would join in for a few phrases. It lifted me, made new emotions run through me, even though I couldn't understand a word.

The entire day seemed well organized and efficiently handled. About 1.00 p.m. lunch was served. I went through the kitchen just at this critical moment. There were vast preparations, but no frenzy. Forty-five hundred guests were fed, in four sittings, each sitting requiring about half an hour. Leaf plates were used, placed directly on the ground, plus disposable earthenware mugs. Students from the various Ramakrishna Order schools had been recruited as servers. It all went off without a hitch except that one woman slipped while washing her hands in the Ganges after lunch and sprained her ankle. As people finished, they strolled about the lawns and talked to one another, or took naps under the trees. Then at 4.00 a meeting was held. This was outdoors, of course, with loudspeakers. Two swamis spoke in Bengali about Holy Mother. This was finished at 5.00.

Then I had the special joy of going in the technical school's US army surplus jeep with some others—seven, I think it was—to Ubdodhan for vespers. This is the biggest day of the year there, and the whole area around that crowded part of Calcutta was in a turmoil because of the large numbers coming and going. I don't know how we ever got in, and getting in managed to wriggle up to the second floor. But as 'visiting brass' we not only did, but actually were able to enjoy arati in the shrine-room itself. During all this, and apparently for quite a time before, a kirtan had been in progress on the roof above. The tops of neighbouring houses must have been commandeered, too, for when we emerged into the tropical night I beheld with amazement a whole sea of people sitting up there in the dark, watching a band and some singers performing under a lighted leafy trellis. For those who could not be accommodated on the roof the music was broadcast by way of loudspeakers throughout the house and indeed into the whole quarter.

Holy Mother certainly fulfilled the highest ideals of monasticism, though she never took the formal vows of sannyas, as did a number of women associates who lived with and near her. In addition, at least three of the direct disciples of the Master gave monastic initiations to women, and the first four paragraphs of Swamiji's rule for the Order declare that a female section should be started. However, the Ramakrishna Order never established a women's branch officially but continued as a solely male organization for many years. But here and there women came together to join in some work in the name of Ramakrishna or Holy Mother, renounced the world, and lived as nuns, even without any settled status. The workers of the famous Sister Nivedita school in Calcutta are examples—an educational centre for Hindu women and girls, curiously enough established by the Irish Margaret Noble and carried on by a native of Germany who grew up in Detroit, Michigan, named Christine Greenstidel, both disciples of Vivekananda. Then a peculiar thing happened. A convent had been started in a most casual way at the Hollywood centre about 1940, and six or seven years later consent to the initiation into brahmacharya of several of its American girl members had been given by the Trustees at Belur Math. The women's work began to formalize itself in India, too. Finally on the widely celebrated centennial day of Holy Mother's birth in December 1953, a women's order was officially constituted there. It is a going proposition now with its own headquarters in an old mansion once occupied by Jawaharlal Nehru's father on the east bank of the Ganges a little north of Dakshineswar. In 1959 several of its members were given the vows of sannyas and made female swamis—a grace also administered to five senior brahmacharinis from Hollywood.

It is hard to carry on any work without organization: some programme, some base of operations, some financing, some leadership, some following. This is true of religion as of everything else. Without a structure for amassing the revelations of a God-man, putting them to the test, and handing them down, in one sense his travail, the demonstration of his life on earth, is wasted. On the other hand, as Ramakrishna so often said, everything divine becomes sullied passing through the lips of men. You cannot deal with revelation without somehow spoiling it a little. This presents a dilemma. All struggle is individual no doubt, but to inspire it, who does not need the assistance of some affiliation?

Too much institutionalism is not good. The Roman Catholic Church is a strong organization supposedly devoted to applying the revelation of Jesus. But is its primary purpose now that of making liberated saints —Christ-men—or conforming Catholics? One need only examine the recent, unassailable documentation on the subject to see that what this organization has become is really a natural dictatorship of international scope—a private cartel—using supernatural sanctions to secure its power. The avowed purpose of the Catholic Church is to turn the world into one gigantic theocracy on its own terms—in other words, to cause every man, woman, and child living to owe his final allegiance to the Pope and hierarchy. European history from the time of the Renaissance to the end of the Inquisition furnishes many examples of what situations prevail when religious institutionalism goes too far. Conditions in Tibet today, or at least before its conquest by the Chinese, must be rather like they were in Europe then and would be again if the Church were to obtain its full ends. In Tibet a clerical aristocracy runs the country. Its first objective quite naturally is to perpetuate its own power. And instead of clergy and people straining to reach upward to a highly set ideal, the ideal is frequently adjusted downward to the levels of human weakness.

On the other hand, the situation of the typical wandering 'holy man' of India is not always reassuring either. He is certainly not institutionalized, and he has no wealth or power. But in his freedom often he may be more of a tramp than a spiritual paragon. Living off the land, it is only the exceptional man who is not shiftless, whose mind is not concentrated on his hope of a handout—the next meal, that night's place to sleep. I saw hundreds of fakirs in India. I moved among them, 'begging' my own food, briefly at Rishikesh. I would not judge them. No less an authority than Maharaj declared there are great illumined souls who live as wandering sadhus. But I did witness this. At Tanakpur on the border of Nepal, one of the main entrances to the Himalayas, I was in the office of a devotee having tea. Bands of nearly naked or gerrua-clad sadhus were in the town, bearing tridents or big fire tongs, camping here and there. A pair of them came into the room, each carrying two small pails, and asked for one measure of water and one measure of flour each, very boldly. When the owner gave them only a copper—I was surprised to see him do that, considering their insolent manner—they spat their disgust and walked out indignantly. It is public knowledge that rascality and laziness sometimes characterize many such 'holy men'.

So the question becomes: How do you receive the revelation of a God-man, live it and share it—with appropriate esteem—without commencing something which in time may develop a spirit antagonistic to the purpose of its founder? This problem challenged Vivekananda. It was about 1895 when he began to consider it earnestly. After Ramakrishna's death the boy sannyasins had taken to the life of the wandering sadhu, appearing at their headquarters only periodically. Swamiji himself had spent five or six years in this manner, walking over almost every square foot of his country. But now he was in America, on his first trip to the West. He witnessed the strength in affiliation and organization. His letters reveal he had been urging his brothers to undertake service activities wherever they happened to be residing. But now he saw that this was not enough. Some real structure would have to be started to give his boys the decent conveniences of life, that they might pursue their salvation and demonstrate the revelation of Ramakrishna with efficiency. Thus, in 1896, he wrote to India outlining a provisional set of objectives, code of conduct, and form of government, and in 1897 he set down the full rule for a definite organization.

Religion in India has never been institutionalized. As Sister Nivedita wrote of Vivekananda's appearance at the World Parliament of Religions at the 1893 Columbian Exposition in Chicago: 'Nothing could be more typical of the unorganizedness of Hinduism itself than this going forth of its representative unannounced, and without any formal credentials, to enter the strongly guarded doors of the world's wealth and power.' Hinduism is simply an aggregate of autonomous observances having no connection with each other except a common ancestry in the Upanishads and the identical objective of attainment of God-knowledge. The means are left to individual taste and vary most astonishingly. Ramakrishna had confirmed not only the various paths in Hinduism, but also that those of other religions are likewise true and effectual and will lead one forward to the same Supreme if followed with sincerity.

What kind, then, of an organization did Vivekananda create? What did he develop to combine the advantages of self-determination with those of alliance? What was his approach in making a movement that would have the values of institutionalism without its usual drawbacks?

First, Swamiji confirmed freedom as the indispensable condition of religion. He ordained no creeds or dogmas. It is enough to be a sincere spiritual aspirant. One may seek God in the way most natural and appealing to him. A member does not even have to believe in the avatar-hood of Ramakrishna.

Second, Swamiji defined all work, including service to others, as valuable only as spiritual discipline, as worship of God, to bring one to God. Accomplishment can never be the end, but must be the vehicle of individual realization. As Maharaj put it later: 'Disinterested work is a means of attaining devotion'. This view emphasizes the presence of God in man, stresses the equality of man and man, improves the quality of the work done, systematically reduces the ego, and makes external success or failure secondary considerations.

Third, Swamiji established a scheme of government for the Order along modern democratic lines but in the same articles of incor-poration directed that a man's first loyalty must be to the ideal of God-attainment.

And so the Ramakrishna movement began. There came to be the Order itself, of monastic members. Associated with this are lay devotees who support the Order and benefit from the services of its monks. The eternal message of the Vedas is preached: the Vedanta, the highest common factor of all religion, the perennial philosophy. Alongside of this, Ramakrishna is preached too, but not as *the* saviour; rather as a recent incarnation whose life and realizations substantiate the others who have come before and prove that the great articles of religious faith are true. And never has it been said that real religion is available only through the Order. Its claim goes only this far, that it is an open and available channel through which spiritual power of a strong efficacious-ness is flowing.

To put it succinctly then, the Ramakrishna Order is a congregation of highly individualistic spiritual aspirants loosely federated.

This reliance upon self-discipline, then, has been the policy since the beginning. It was reinforced by Maharaj whenever a need arose to do so. Swami Prabhavananda tells how Maharaj did that on one occasion early in 1915. Swami was present at Belur Math and saw it happen.

Swami Dhirananda, a disciple of Vivekananda, was the Math manager. He came to Maharaj one day and said, 'Maharaj, we have to make some new rules for these new boys who have come, in order that they can be directed properly.'

Maharaj said, 'But didn't Swamiji make certain rules?'

'Yes,' replied Dhirananda, 'but they are so general. We have to make some new rules.'

Then Maharaj declared, 'No it is not that we need to have more rules. What we need, Krishnalal, is more love.'

The spirit of love was always conspicuous in the disciples of Rama-krishna and it comprises the principal plank in the unwritten constitution of the brotherhood. The following is a description of an occurrence which happened prior to one of its governing body's early board meetings. It took place at Belur Math about 1915 outside the two old buildings I have already described. The Trustees were present: Swami Brahmananda, the President; Swami Saradananda, the Secretary; and Swamis Shivananda, Turiyananda, and Subodhananda, all direct disciples of Ramakrishna. But it was noticed that Swami Premananda was missing.

Asked Saradananda, 'Where is Premananda?'

'Upstairs in the shrineroom,' someone informed him.

Saradananda climbed the stairs. In the hallway sat Swami Premananda, deep in meditation. Sarananda was a big, husky man. He tiptoed up behind the slight Premananda, lovingly picked him up, and carried him bodily downstairs, dropping him in the courtyard where the others were waiting. Premananda landed lightly on his feet with his arms raised and his fingers extended ecstatically. Suddenly these spiritual giants began to dance. With Maharaj in the centre they circled round and round. Maharaj improvised a song, which the others joined. It went on for several minutes, while the younger members of the brotherhood stood and watched in awe. One who was a witness told me: 'It was as if the whole world was shaking. The song was a call to all mankind to come and get liberation and the bliss of God.'

His response to one of the questions I put to the General Secretary, Swami Madhavananda, clearly shows the free play basic to the operation of the Order. It was about publishing. Was there any attempt, I inquired, to maintain some central supervision over writing and publishing by members of the Order, to prevent overlapping of output and to assure 'authorized' editions and translations?

Swami Madhavananda stated that entire freedom prevails regarding publishing.

'But what about the little adjustments, the personal interpretations already appearing in new renderings of the original data?' I asked. 'If that goes on, who can tell what the result may be in time?'

'If things get too much mixed up,' was the answer in good humour, 'a new avatar will come with a new message, to straighten things out again.'

One of the most characteristic and delightful examples of the Order's casualness is to be seen in its mode of sending the periodic news dispatches from headquarters to the heads of member centres. Since these treat of appointments, disciplinary actions, personnel changes, organization finances, and all manner of other such things, one would presume the contents to be confidential. However, they are sent through the mails in ordinary open envelopes with the flaps merely tucked in, to take advantage of the lower postal rates prevailing for unsealed mimeographed matter.

You don't have to worship God in any particular way to be an acceptable member of the Order. In fact, after you are established, you don't even have to be present. I met one middle-aged swami who habitually took leave from his math every year, to spend six months as a poor mendicant begging his food from door to door. He felt it helped him spiritually to do so. Having previously encountered him doing a job in one of our monasteries, I was astonished one day later on to run into him with kamandalu (a gourd waterpot traditionally carried by sadhus) and staff walking along the Ganges at Benares, one of hundreds of anonymous ascetics there. I know of one very senior swami who left the precincts of the Order for fourteen years, spending that time practising hard austerities by himself. He was still considered a member in good standing, and when he returned was greeted warmly and awarded the respect his seniority and spiritual status merited.

That swami was Swami Ambikananda, the second direct link with Ramakrishna I was privileged to encounter. I saw him often over a period of two weeks at the Benares ashrama. He died the following winter. He used to sit on his bed in the room that had previously been Swami Turiyananda's and play on a stringed instrument and sing. He also painted scenes from nature very nicely. His contact with Ramakrishna had been when he was a baby. His mother was a devotee and had carried him to Dakshineswar, to present him to the Master, like an offering. Ramakrishna had taken the boy in his arms, blessed him, and accepted him as his own. When he came of age, Ambikananda joined the Order.

Swami Ambikananda impressed me simply as a jolly, bearded old man, with a twinkle in the eye, a person who was unusually and continually lighthearted. I had been told that he was an advanced soul and that I should go and sit in his room at the time of meditation; I would feel something. I tried this once or twice, without the slightest result. Indeed, the Swami seemed amused to find me there; it was as though he sang and played at these times purposely to distract me. How ignorant I was! I learned much later that this 'jolly old man' was a person of wisdom, a real friend of God whose intercession I could have gained had I known enough to press him for grace and favour. How clear a demonstration this was of Vedanta's contention that one sees solely what his eye is open to and gains only what he is capable of containing.

And that, finally, is what is important. With all its permissiveness, its enlightened objectives and splendid methods, does the Ramakrishna Order produce superior men? What is the quality of the Ramakrishna Order sadhu?

I found that few members have ever been out of India, and some have not even travelled in India extensively. Many, having joined the Order in their teens or early twenties, have never known any people, work, or way of life other than those of the homes of their childhood and of the Order; hence are anything but what one could call cosmopolitan. And the level of formal education is often modest, although now high-school graduation or its equivalent is required of applicants.

How hard do they work? I am still a little unsure. The Indian day is so broken up as to make direct comparison with American productivity difficult. The men certainly put in good long hours and they carry on their duties seven days of the week, for months and sometimes years without any break or diversion. It is in the area of drive and carry-through that I felt something left to be desired. But this is nothing more than the result of the tempo of the tropics and the Indian temperament. Work is carried out with an absence of nervous tension which is remarkable, which perhaps more than compensates for its moderate pace.

As in any group, all types seem to be present. I should judge the general level of what in the West is called intelligence to be at least average, with individual abilities ranging from below average to far above average. What one would call fine personality characteristics appear in abundance. The sadhus impressed me as exceptionally ingenuous, goodhearted, and of excellent disposition. Resentment, complaining, hurt sensibilities, preoccupation with self, ungenerosity, and other manifestations of selfishness seemed to be almost totally absent. In short, neurosis seemed negligible and mental hygiene very high. The members have a great respect for age, seniority, eminence in others, and religious ideals. Although they show what looked to me at times as an excess of humility toward superiors, generally there seemed to be a good feeling of democracy and comradery between levels.

But what about high sanctity? How spiritually advanced are they? This is something I wanted to know, because if the Order does not produce men of God, then what good is it? To evaluate this quality is very difficult. One knows enough to understand this, that you cannot judge inner unfoldment by external signs—the mellifluous voice, the tender manner, the forbearing response. These can be assumed by anybody. Indeed, the genuine saint will probably hide himself inside a cloak of ordinariness.

So the question becomes: What spiritual experiences have they had? This would give the answer. But, because spiritual experience is subjective, the making of any evaluation on the basis of this is also difficult. Like the source and magnitude of one's income among the old British aristocracy, enlightenment-status is sometimes just not talked about. Any data one may gather, then, have to be picked out of accidental revelations and are consequently meagre.

The main stages of illumination are: absorption, ecstasy, vision of deity, lower samadhi, and higher samadhi. First of all, I know it is true that not all swamis have experienced samadhi. Of course all the disciples of Ramakrishna attained the non-dual illumination. I am not talking about them, but of the generation active now. I fear Western romanticism is unduly generous in the advancement it attributes to monastic status and would make sannyas and samadhi synonymous. I have heard two fairly senior swamis admit they have not experienced this state. On the contrary, while you will never hear a man of realization refer to his own attainment, the appreciation accorded him by other advanced individuals will give an indication of it. One can thus ascertain that some persons, active and functioning at present, have experienced at least the lower samadhi.

Absorption and ecstasy I understand to be fairly common. And I once heard it said on good authority that the vision of deity has been experienced by many.

No, it is not a band of finished saints. Samadhi is not a common occurrence. But the Order is a company of honest spiritual aspirants in various stages of growth. You will not find hypocrisy there, or crooked reasoning, or any adjustment of the ideal or equivocation about the goal. Not all have attained it, but you will not discover a man who is not perfectly clear as to what it is and in his own way is not pushing toward it.

CHAPTER V

THE 'MADRAS MAIL', SOUTHBOUND

AFTER I had been some weeks in and around Calcutta, the time came for me to move out into other parts of India. Thus, in mid-December, I left by train for the south, on the well-known 'Madras Mail'. The journey took two nights and nearly two days, the distance being something over a thousand miles. This rail trip gave me a chance to see new sides of the country and to make the acquaintance of several most interesting people. In my life, never before had there been, and never again could there ever be, a journey like this.

When I bought the second-class reservation at the Calcutta ticket office, I knew little of Indian train travel. Having in recent years at home enjoyed on overnight trips nothing less luxurious that a roomette, I took privacy, cleanliness, and personal comfort on rail journeys as a matter of course. That none of these exists on average Indian trains I soon found out. Experience I was to gain also showed that going on them can be actually risky—nearly as hazardous at times as making the overland journey to California in 1849—or so I sometimes felt! I spent several hours of terror on Indian trains. I also spent many long periods cursing the planners who had conceived such peculiarities of design. They literally seemed devised to make overnight travel as inconvenient as possible. And yet again, what magic carpets they were to the inner life of the people and of the country!

My Belur Math mentor, Mahavir Maharaj, helped me prepare for the trip. The major new requirement was a carry-all for bedding. Your mosquito net, sheets, blanket, pillow, and mattress are considered personal property. They are not furnished to the traveller or guest; he must provide them and take them with him, like his clothes. The carry-all is a canvas cover in which the bedding fits. At night opened out, it serves as an underlining. In the daytime, caught together with straps, the bedding roll resembles a bulging duffle bag. Not only do travellers transport their own beds, but on journeys of any duration, as I was to learn, experienced ones carry food, drinking water, and bathroom supplies as well. All these, added to the huge square tin trunks with their heavy padlocks that serve commonly as suitcases, mean that most rail passengers journey with an array of luggage which is enormous. On the trains this poses only the problem of squeezing everything into the compartments; I don't know how it is accomplished when people travel by air. I made only one air trip in India—from Madras six or seven hundred miles north to Bhubaneswar—but was already overweight with nothing but my lightweight American suitcase and typewriter. The bedding roll had to be sent by train, necessitating crating and drayage at one end, and my personal appearance at the baggage department and drayage at the other, and borrowing bedding for several days pending its arrival.

The industrial school jeep took us to the railroad station. The Howrah Station! How can I ever forget it? For in and around this once imposing, somehow Germanic-looking yellow and red structure were displayed the compounded miseries of a poor and struggling nation.

'Baksheesh, sahib. Baksheesh, sahib.' A hundred hands held out, a hundred imploring voices as we rolled up under the portico. Beggars of all ages and conditions pulling at you: unkempt little children; bedraggled women with babies at the hip; tottering old men; yes, and even young males in the bloom of youth, jobless, homeless. Sahib! How I hated that word. 'Master', it meant, and in my case, something worse—'white master'. The term always made me ashamed—ashamed for those who had impressed a distinction based on power and colour, sorry for those compelled to use it, disgraced myself, because of being of a stock to which it could be applied. I didn't want to be a sahib. I wanted to be one of them—a brahmachari of the Ramakrishna Order. Yet to those who used the word, what else could I be, for I fitted the stereotyped conception perfectly. I had reverted to Western dress for the trip, had arrived in a motor car, and held an upper-class reservation.

The rush of porters was frightening—trembling with anxiety to be selected: far too many for the amount of red-cap work there was to do. Thank goodness Mahavir Maharaj was there to deal with the crush. After some bargaining a porter was selected. He balanced everything on top of his head in a pile several feet high, and in through the waiting-room we started.

And here was a scene even more distressing. I recall it now with the first sick emotion. The great hall had been turned into a refugee camp. Pouring off the trains from East Bengal, now East Pakistan, families had simply settled down in the station, exhausted and bewildered, with what possessions they had been able to salvage, and had begun housekeeping right there. The room had been portioned off into small squares, and in each square lived a family, conducting the circuit of its life in full view of surrounding families and the travelling public. Here babies cried, were fed, and perhaps even born. Here the old slumbered in the din against the hard cement, and perhaps died. Here cooking was done, on open fires built directly on the station floor, and here fathers, mothers, and children enjoyed their food and now and then laughed together as they ate. Home, sweet home! Choking smoke hovered overhead, and the rest-rooms were, of course, overglutted with a crowd they had never been built to accommodate. Through all this multitude hucksters walked and cried their wares—tea, garish sweets, religious images, towels, clocks, combs, fruit—Asia's ever-present small entrepreneurs, existing off the little margin between their daily purchases and their daily sales.

Around the sides of this arena of tragedy the work of serving the travelling public went on. It was a railway station scene I was to see over and over again in India. Always the long lines of the poor with their manifold bundles before the third-class windows. A smaller queue to buy inter-class space. And hardly anyone at all at the second- and first-class windows. As in all stations, there were separate waiting-rooms for each class, the third- and inter-class rooms swirling with humanity, and the more commodious second- and first-class lounges barely occupied. There was a vegetarian dining-room and a non-vegetarian dining-room, each with its own kitchen. Some stations provide as many as four such alternatives: a refreshment room, European; a refreshment room, Muslim; a refreshment room, Hindu, vegetarian; and a refreshment room, Hindu, non-vegetarian. How I confused their staff on occasion by entering a European room in dhoti or a Hindu room in Western clothes! One can imagine how uneconomic it must be to maintain so many different establishments. The real money-maker of the Western restaurant business—the bar trade—exists almost nowhere, for very few of the better class of people drink in India, and some states actually maintain prohibition. Vestiges of a former elegance clung to the Howrah station dining-rooms. Before the door of the non-vegarian restaurant a headwaiter hopefully stood in an immaculate but worn white uniform with bright sash and turban, perhaps dreaming of vanished Europeans. Inside I could see tables, with white cloths and bud-vases, and oak sideboards, straight out of Victorian England. But business there was non-existent.

Through the gate and on to the platform. If possible, even more noise and turmoil there. Pedlars balancing trays of foodstuffs on their heads, porters running with towering loads, travellers crying to one another, others inside the cars throwing fruit peelings and used leaf plates out on to the platform, jets of red spit cascading from betel chewers. Most of the train was made up of third-class coaches—uncomplicated vans with benches along both sides and also running down the middle, with luggage shelves overhead. Here near-riots were occurring as people tried to get places. Baggage and children were being pushed in through windows, and there were explosive arguments over seats. Some people even now were sqatting or lying on the upper baggage racks.

We came to the car where I had my reservation. It contained a first-class 'coupé', two second-class compartments, one with four lower berths and four upper berths, the other with three lower and three upper berths, and a compartment for the servants of those riding in that car. There are no corridors in most Indian trains. All compartments are self-contained and open directly outside.

A swaggering Indian in uniform, accompanied by several subordinates swung into the first-class coupé, an obsequious adjutant administering the stowing of baggage. I always winced a little to see Indians wearing the trappings or manifesting the characteristics of the masters they had so recently overthrown. Neither fitted their basically gentle nature and appearance, somehow. Fortunately, you don't see much of this. In the larger second-class compartment were two or three babus and their sari-clad wives, with a bedlam of children and a massive, heterogeneous heap of baggage. O Lord, I thought, what if I had drawn space in there?

It was at this point that the basic motif of Indian train travel began to dawn on me, that it is a wild but absorbing game of chance. Not for the riders in the lower classes, of course. They know ahead of time that they are going to be uncomfortable and can consider themselves fortunate merely to get their luggage and their bodies inside a car. But the second-class passenger pays several times as much and naturally harbours hopes of a comfortable journey. Whether he has one or not, as I was to learn, depends almost solely on his luck.

With beating heart I peeped into my compartment. It was relatively empty. On the bench across the back, with boxes on both sides of him, sat a youngish man who was obviously a European. On the bench along one side, with boxes on both sides of *him*, sat another Western-looking man, older. The third couch, on the far side, proved to be my space. Above each was a padded hanging shelf, the upper berths. On the fourth wall of the compartment was a fixed console table, and a door leading to the washroom. The mahogany of the interior, although battered, still reflected something of its original richness, while fans whirled in the ceiling.

Mahavir Maharaj led me to my berth. We had the baggage placed beneath it, while he hurriedly directed me to undo my bedding roll and open it out flat to cover the entire seat. This I did, wondering, however, why such a step was necessary at only four-thirty in the afternoon. Then we stood at the door talking. Every minute or two a would-be passenger would stop, look into the compartment, hesitate for a minute, and then move on to find a place in some other part of the train. At the last moment two more people did get in with us: a small middle-aged Indian wearing brown duck pants and shirt and a canvas sun helmet, with no baggage at all; and a second Indian in spotless dhoti, young but fat and pompous-looking. He brought a terrible collection of boxes, baskets, and string bags.

With an excited sounding of whistles and waving of flags by railroad officials along the platform, the 'Madras Mail' made ready to move out on its long journey south. Shrieks and wails of passengers and their friends bidding them farewell. What a tenderhearted people! They will go to see each other off, and cry openly, where trips are involved of only a few miles and perhaps but a day or two. I quickly took the dust of the feet of Mahavir Maharaj, drawing startled stares from my four compartment mates as I did so. He got out. Doors were slammed all down the train, and we were off.

Silence reigned while everybody sized up everybody else. The late-comers stood in the middle of the floor. Then the little Indian in khaki edged himself on to the seat opposite mine, nudging the baggage inward toward the man already in possession of the bench.

'I have this upper berth here,' said the portly young man in a meaningful tone, pointing to the shelf above the couch running across the back of the compartment. He piled some of his goods up there, leaving most of them, however, in the middle of the floor. The occupant sulkily shifted the baggage somewhat, to make room on his seat. I edged on to my berth, folding back a corner of my exposed bedding to do so. *Clickety-clack, clickety-clack*, went the wheels, and the old car creaked and rolled and hammered. We sat in silence and regarded one another.

This seemed like a good time to inspect the car. The windows behind me were fascinating. Permanent iron bars went up and down over the openings, as in most domestic construction, to keep out prowlers when windows must be opened |fully |for ventilation. Inside were three sets of adjustable coverings: a glass window, a louvered shutter, and a screen almost opaque with caked soot and dust. These could be raised singly or in combination, or lowered into the socket below. The outside doors, one on either side of the compartment, bore gigantic bolts at top and bottom. These doors could be opened at any time, even when the train was in motion—and often were; it was a common sight to see people hanging out while the train was in full flight, especially if we were passing any interesting sight, crossing a bridge, or approaching a station. Doors could be opened from the outside at any time, too, unless the bolts were shot home.

I looked at the console, bemused. I saw the countless British mem-sahibs who in pride and aggravation had ridden here and poured tea at that table. I saw too the many bottles of good Scotch whisky that had rested upon it, while colonials mopped themselves and cursed the heat, and servants stood and served and dozed on their feet and watched without a word.

The washroom proved to be a small chamber containing a washbowl with a very uncertain trickle, a sloped area in the floor with perforations where one could take a makeshift shower, and an amusing, anomalous water closet conceived by someone who had tried to produce a tactful compromise between Western and Indian style. There were no mirrors, no hooks—only damage-evidence that there once had been and that they had been forcibly vandalized. When I returned from my inspection tour, I saw that my sheets had become littered with soot. It was pouring in the windows like a snowstorm. Indian trains are at the pre-air-conditioning stage where American ones were thirty or forty years ago. I felt around inside the collar of my white shirt. It was gritty, and already my nails were getting black. I wondered about the grey flannel suit. *Clickety-clack, clickety-clack* sounded in my ears, and we looked at each other wordlessly.

Then the European-looking man across from me stirred. He was tall, with thinning reddish-brown hair, and a noticeably sallow complexion. Dressed in a worn white linen suit, he was also, as I remember it, wearing rubber tennis shoes. His eyes were odd, rather yellowish, and he had a peculiar accent—cockney, yet not quite cockney, either.

'How fast do you think we're going?' he asked, of no one in particular.

The other European glanced out contemptuously. He was petulantly handsome; when he spoke his speech was refined and British. 'Not over forty-five,' he remarked.

"That's true,' returned the other. 'but we'll be going faster soon.'

Instead the train began to slow down. We were coming into a town. We ran past a crossing, with bullock carts waiting, and rickshaws waiting behind the gates, and many men and women waiting. We swung in against a platform. I could see a big old tree, and tongas nearby, the drivers standing in front of them, with their little piles of grass for the horses. Under the tree a carved stone Ganesha leaned crookedly, with vermilion smeared upon the forehead. Many people squatted on the platform, just staring at the train. Others were running along the cars, looking for friends, searching for space. Dust swirled.

'How fast do trains go in India?' I asked, over the setting of the brakes. I watched the pie-dogs tearing through the crowd, leaping down beneath the carriages to scavenge for food leavings. Beggars trailed supplicating hands along the windows, pleading, 'Babu, babu.'

'Sixty in a straight stretch,' the first man replied, rising and going to the door and flinging it open. 'You'll see.' He stood scarecrow-like and menacing, blocking the opening. This was a small city. There weren't any prospective second-class passengers here, apparently, or if there were they didn't try to make their way into our space, with him in the door. 'My name's Kennedy,' he said. Then proudly, 'I'm an engine driver from up north. Am on my way to Madras to fetch my girls home for the Christmas holiday from St. Margaret's school—the Church of England school, don't you know.'

The engine breathed up ahead. An excited crowd accompanied by an orchestra rushed down the platform: a wedding party seeing off a bride and groom. Then whistles and flags and *whoof, whoof, whoof.* Doors were slammed, and off we went again.

The Britisher on my right offered cigarettes. 'Name's Peter Harrison,' he said. 'Bound for Bangalore.' He looked bothered and unhappy. He made brushing movements against his clothes. 'Damn this cheap coal they're using now,' he complained. 'Lord, what a country!'

Across the way the little Indian in khaki spoke. His English was sibilant and his manner hesitant. He smiled. 'And I, gentleman, am Gokul Chandra Das, and I am an Orissa state police official.'

The fifth passenger, the portly Indian on my right, said nothing. Squatting on the seat, fat and soft, he rocked with the motion of the train, a secret smile on his lips.

'And you?' asked Das politely, looking at me. 'An American, I think?'

I told him I was and gave my name.

'But there was a swamiji here with you . . . ?'

Everyone looked at me.

'Yes,' I answered. 'I am from Hollywood——'

'So—Hollywood,' he hissed happily.

'——a brahmachari of the Ramakrishna Order there.'

A kind of sigh went up from everybody. There was a considerable silence.

'Do you know Sanskrit?' asked Das at last.

'No,' I shook my head.

'Our Sanskrit is a wonderful language,' he went on. 'You should learn it. I have many books in Sanskrit which I love to read. I'm a busy man and have to travel continually on official duty. I have no opportunity to be religious, and that makes me despairing sometimes. But would you believe, I chant at least one chapter of the Gita in Sanskrit every morning of my life, and have for many years, no matter where I am or what I am doing. Yes, that is true. I've known it all by heart, and many other scriptures, too, since I was a boy.'

'We don't go in much for the technical side of Vedanta,' I explained. 'We merely believe in its main principles and try to practise them.'

'Now, just what do you do?' asked Das. 'What do you believe in—there in your Hollywood?'

'The law of karma,' I said. 'We think it is logical.'

'Indeed?'

'Reincarnation, also, of course. That explains so many things.'

'You do?' he grinned. Kennedy and Harrison were looking at me unbelievingly. The mystery man on my right rocked and smiled.

G

'But mainly we try to uncover the divinity within, by practising detachment and meditation.'

'Yes,' murmured Das. 'Yes, yes, yes'—sadly—'that is right.'

Then I stopped. What am I trying to do, promoting Indian religion to Indians in India? I could feel my face getting red with embarrassment.

'Ever ride in an engine cab?' Kennedy asked, staring at me. He rose and walked up and down the compartment restlessly in his rubber shoes.

'No,' I answered, adding to myself, 'and I wouldn't want to.' In the short while I had been in India I had read several news stories of spectacular railroad accidents: trains pitching off bridges, wooden cars splintering and burning, engines crashing head-on, two or three derailments. I knew that since the English had left, there had been much controversy about efficiency and maintenance. And the Indian temperament: well, it was not altogether comforting to think of a people who seemed to be more emotional than practical administering a railroad system.

As though reading my thoughts Kennedy said, 'Oh, it's perfectly safe. I've been a driver twenty-eight years and never been in a nervy spot yet.' Then, clenching and opening his fingers as though they were even then managing controls in a cab, he told us all about trains. And I could see that India is in the midst of a great era of railroading such as was experienced in the United States a generation ago. I learned about blocking and signalling systems, the way the key is caught, carried, and thrown out later on single-track sections, and much more. In fact, Kennedy proved conclusively that accidents on Indian railroads are incapable of occurring!

'Yes,' said Harrison, and laughed. 'Right now the bigger danger is from another quarter—that is, for those of us in the upper classes.'

'Yes,' sighed Das.

Even the mystery man perked up and nodded, wetting his lips. Everyone looked at everyone else covertly.

'What do you mean?' I asked.

'Haven't you heard about train robbers?' asked Harrison. 'Oh, they've come quite to the fore during the past few years——'

'——as a result of the poverty we inherited from two centuries of British rule,' finished Das.

'One of those devils will do anything for a few rupees,' Harrison continued. 'Sometimes he'll dress decently and ride for a while in first or second, then when everybody is asleep, rob them—anything they've got: watches, wallet, clothes, jewellery—escaping at his leisure. And if anybody tries to stop him, well, a knife at the throat, that's all. For a ring on a finger hands have been chopped off. People have been murdered for nothing but a pair of shoes. Or maybe he'll ride on the roof and crawl in when the train is in motion, to do his dirty work between stations.'

'How do they get in?' I asked, staring at the bars at the windows and the bolts in the doors.

'Mostly through the latrine window,' Harrison replied. 'They're putting stronger latches on them now. But always lock the washroom door from this side at night, and wedge it; and of course bolt the outside doors.' He got up and shot the bolts home right then, although it was now hardly dusk.

'They're very clever,' added Das. 'Train robbers manage to work without ever being seen and sometimes without anyone later ever being able to determine how they got in and out.' Then darkly: 'Sometimes even bolts don't stop them. They have ways.'

I was getting a creepy feeling. I thought of my bag under the seat with all the necessities for a long trip. My precious typewriter. The wallet in the breast pocket of my coat, with my passport, my ticket home, and hundreds of dollars in travellers' cheques, plus five hundred rupees in cash. Could any one of these men be not quite what he seemed? Could some of them even be working together?

The stranger on my right made me jump by suddenly speaking to me. 'Allow me to introduce myself,' he said, handing me a business card. 'I am Lakshmi Narayan Marwari from the city of Bombay, en route to Waltair on business. We are just coming to the station now where it is necessary to send word to the restaurant car if one is to have dinner on this train. Kindly eat with me, as my guest.'

I *had* been looking forward to two days of Western food, together with table, silver, and chinaware. A station or two later we left our goods in charge of Kennedy, Harrison, and Das—a person has to trust others sometimes—and left the compartment, walking along the outside of the train till we came to the restaurant car. An eager steward greeted us and led us to a table. It was a fine old car, similar to American diners, and had obviously been through many years of service. But it was practically empty and soot had been entering in here too. The tablecloths were smeared with it, and it had to be emptied out of dishes and wiped off utensils before they could be used. The steward interested me immensely. He wore a fancy headgear and a formal uniform—but no shoes. In his pierced ears were jewelled earrings—a sight new to me then, but to become very common as we got farther south. Marwari had the vegetarian meal, I the non-vegetarian. The cook had apparently attempted to copy European cooking but the result missed the mark just enough to be of no recognizable culinary style whatsoever. Across the aisle I watched a young Indian, perhaps a clerk or college boy, obviously essaying his first use of knife and fork. I'm afraid I took fiendish delight in this sight of his awkwardness with silverware, remembering my own struggles to learn to eat without it.

Marwari began to talk. He lost his condescending manner and became quite simple and eager to please. He inquired in detail about the United States. He told me he was a Jain and asked me if I had visited the famous Jain temple in Calcutta. (Eventually I did and found it rather like a tempting display in a confectioner's window, a little like the Buddhist temples in Bangkok, all made out of coloured curlicues.) He said he was interested in religion but was unable because of his position to give it much attention. His father having died recently, he was now at twenty-four (he seemed forty) the mainstay of a great joint family and had to devote himself fully to maintaining the hereditary fortune. At moments I wondered if I did not detect the same sadness in him as possessed the rich young ruler of the Gospel story. I don't know much of the Jain religion except that, like Buddhism, it stresses non-violence and dispassion. The founder was Mahavir, who was a contemporary of Buddha. As was the case of Buddhism, Jainism was a reform movement within Hinduism. But at present a Buddhist is not considered a Hindu while, for some reason, a Jain is.

Later I learned something of the Marwaris. They are of the third or merchant caste, Vaishyas, and originally came from Rajputana in the northwest. They used to control internal trade and finance in India and are still influential in it. They were the big financiers as well as the small village bankers; before the formalization of banking a note from a well-known Marwari financial house would be honoured anywhere in India, and even abroad. The Marwaris still represent big finance in India, but have added industry to it now. My friend, I believe, owned jute mills.

Eventually I was to meet a brahmachari of our order from the Marwari clan. As eldest son he had been sent to the United States to college. A prosperous life was in prospect for him; but he had felt a yearning for monasticism and had spurned college and the family's hopes, to join the Ramakrishna Order. I met his mother and sister when they visited Belur Math. Their characteristic dress interested me very much. Their saries bore great colourful designs, and much handsome gold jewellery adorned nose, ears, forehead, and toes. In this conformist age, how good to see such uninhibited splendour!

At the next station stop we walked back to our car. After we had knocked authoritatively and identified ourselves, the bolted door was opened. It was perhaps 8.30. The same three were there, but I detected a strained feeling amongst them. Kennedy and Harrison sat in their places glowering, and Das had shrunk into himself, looking abashed. It finally came out. Madras was at the end of the line, the second morning from now. Bangalore was an eight-hour trip beyond that. And we reached Waltair around noon tomorrow. But Das was getting out at the station where one changes for Puri, which we would reach about 1.00 a.m. He had just made the fact known. This meant that someone would have to stay up until that time, not only, I suppose, to be sure that he got out as baggage-less as he came in, but to see that the fortress was secured again after his departure.

So another piece of my education in Indian train travel was added. In second and first class, passengers are not supposed to be disturbed from nine in the evening until six in the morning. No one is allowed to enter between these two hours unless he has a definite reservation, or to leave unless willing to face the wrath of everyone else in the compartment. But this rule is impossible to enforce. When I went to the north I myself had to get out at Gaya once at 5.30 a.m., which also meant stumbling about the compartment in the dark for half an hour before that, trying to wash, dress, and pack. Of course I disturbed the other passengers in that cabin. On that same trip the man in the berth above me got off at 2.30 a.m. I didn't wake fully to the fact until I sensed movement through the compartment. The departing passenger had left the door wide open and people were using the compartment as a passage, coming in one door and going out the other, in order to cross the track without crawling under the train or going around the end of it. I rose in panic to secure the bolts and inventory my possessions. After getting back to bed again I heard creaking above me. Apparently some new occupant had found his way into the abandoned berth before I had awakened. Who was he? Almost certainly a stowaway. It can be imagined how securely I slept from then on. But I was never to know.

Hence the strategy of train travel, if you are a full overnight passenger, is to hope for compartment mates making the full overnight trip too, and to try to discourage riders from entering who may be making shorter runs. I now saw why Kennedy had blocked the door with his presence at so many station stops and why at other times Harrison had kept it bolted. You don't have to respond even to knocking after nine o'clock, for after that it is only the imperious order of the stationmaster conducting someone with a berth reservation, that need make you open up. I now realized also why Mahavir Maharaj had instructed me to unfold the bedding roll. This was not only to help control the number entering but to make it possible for me to retire at any time I wanted to. It is considered bad manners to sit on another's bedding, so no one would share my seat, to keep me from lying full length upon it whenever I should want to go to sleep.

Later we started talking again. Das told a most interesting experience about some hatha-yogi who had come to his town to put on a demonstration of his powers. The man proposed to have himself buried alive for seven days. The police force was asked to supervise the show: to stand guard over the tomb, to control the expected mobs, to be on hand to vouch for the authenticity of the demonstration. There had been, Das said, a quarrel among the civil authorities as to whether the feat was even possible and, if so, whether they should lend their support to it. In doing so, might they not be contributing to suicide or murder? But by then so much excitement had been built up among the townspeople that it was felt the matter had to be handled officially. Das himself supervised the entire event. When the yogi had taken a lying position and composed himself, the disciple who served him covered his face and body with a cloth. He was lowered into the pit. Policemen shovelled in dirt, six or seven feet of it, and packed down the earth solidly on top. Officers patrolled the spot every minute of the time, day and night, to guard against flimflammery. Bonfires burned, tradesmen set up shops, and holiday crowds gathered. As the seventh day dawned the assemblage became enormous. Then the policemen dug out the dirt. Das went down into the hole with the disciple, to see for himself that the demonstration had actually been what it seemed. The last portion of soil was removed and the cloth lifted back. The yogi was cold and of a deathly grey appearance. Thus he was raised to the surface. But in a few minutes he began to stir. And soon he sat up and before long seemed perfectly normal again.

Das told the story with incredulity in every syllable. Although the occurrence had come under his personal jurisdiction he seemed unable even so to believe it. This surprised me—and that is why I relate the incident—since I had long been led to believe that such curiosities are practically everyday events in India. But this worldly police officer sounded just as awed, and the others in the compartment listened with as much astonishment, as if the occurrence were being described in an airliner crossing the United States.

'So you never rode in a locomotive?' Kennedy asked again. He seemed obsessed with the topic. He lowered his voice. 'Would you like to, on this very train, tonight?'

This was carrying hospitality to a foreign visitor too far. 'Oh, no, I don't think so, thank you,' I answered.

'It's exciting at night, up there in the cab,' Kennedy went on. 'The headlight shines down the track. Sometimes a bullock cart gets across just in time. It jumps up in front of you and oh, you think you're going to hit it for certain sure. Sometimes you do. Sometimes you hit the animals that stray on to the tracks. Sometimes even people. I was coming round a curve at sixty, and there she stood, a woman, stock-still in the middle of the tracks, staring into my headlight with such a look on her face. Of course I applied the brakes full power. But what could anybody do? Blood and flesh all over the boiler and oh, even into the cab and on me. It was hundreds of yards before I could bring the train to a standstill. You can burn up the wheels and tear up the track if you do it too quick. She was just a country woman, we found out, crazed by the death of a baby son. Then sometimes you see jungle animals in the headlight: deer, tigers, their eyes shining at you like anything.'

Clickety, clickety, clickety. We were running fast now. The car swayed and banged. Was the roadbed being kept up at all nowadays? At this rate what could keep us from running off the track? A newspaper item crossed my mind, that spikes were now being welded to the rails they held in place, because of a recent spate of loosening spikes and fishplates to set a rail over a bit and cause accidents.

'So get ready now,' Kennedy ordered excitedly. 'Everything is arranged, at the next station. It's entirely against regulations, of course, and the driver could be sacked for allowing us. So could I for taking you. But this is a lonely stretch. There'll be no supervisors along here tonight.'

Could he really mean it? Did I have to? But it had been my policy from the first to open myself up to all experiences in India, to yield willingly to anything asked of me, so as not to censor out any understanding that might come my way, that might help me to know India.

At the next station we walked ahead to where the locomotive stood panting, drawing in water. Up the iron ladder. An engineer there, rather European-looking, with grimy overalls and gauntlets and a bandana on his head. Beside him an Indian in soiled turned-up dhoti, barefooted, with shovel in his hand. He was painfully thin; his ribs showed; sweat glittered all over him. The fireman. But he had the face of a smudgy angel and gave us an intense, beautiful smile.

Kennedy picked up a handful of dasootie and wiped off the steel jump seat that hung from the front of the tender. I sat. What would my clothes be like at the end of this journey? How would I look when making my entrance among new people at the math at Madras? The firebox door clanged open. Inside, a long tunnel of flame. Shovelful after shovelful of coal cannonaded in by the fireman, avalanches of it rumbling down inside the tender behind me. Whistles and bells and the signal in position. A great sighing in the monster, and we began to lumber ahead. A little and a little. I thought of the string of cars behind us and all the people we were pulling. Back there somewhere were my bag and my typewriter and my bed. The monster crouched low. Its snout hugged the rails, searching from side to side, spying out the way. We gathered speed. Buildings wafted past, seen in the light for a moment, then gone. How hard the beast rode! My seat was on the tender, but my feet were on the footplate of the locomotive. The tender heaved one way and the locomotive another. It jarred my spine, snapped my back. Kennedy knew how. He was riding easily, absorbing movement like a show rider on a horse.

It wasn't the banging up and down, but the swinging from side to side that shot the terror into me most. Surely we must run off the track. Once we came right up behind the dark bulk of stationary freight vans. This is the end, I thought. What an anticlimax, to come all the way to India to die in a train wreck! What was I doing in a locomotive cab anyway, Swami Prabhavananda would want to know. It would be a mystery never solved, puzzled over ever afterwards by my monastic associates. But we hit the points and the monster swung to a new track and the bogies flashed past and behind.

It was an hour before we came to the next station and the torture could come to an end. I held on and tried to keep clean and prayed most of the time. Shielding my eyes from the terrible brightness of the firebox I watched for wild beasts, but I never saw any. We just pounded and jerked, and it was finally a matter of endurance. Until at last it was all over. We coasted in to a clanking stop. A nod from the driver, another dazzling smile from the little fireman, and lamely backwards down the iron ladder I climbed. Would bed ever feel good!

No further worries about soot in the sheets or Mr. Das's late departure bothered me that night. Whole bands of dacoits could have slithered in and out without my caring. I awoke in the morning with the delicious smell of tea in my nostrils. Kennedy had opened his trunk of dishes and cooking utensils and was making a steaming pot of it with boiling water he had got from somewhere. Harrison was awake, but Marwari was still slumbering in his upper berth.

How exquisite mornings can be in India! A coolness and a warmth mingle, while spectacular colours paint the eastern sky. I lounged in a luxury of contentment and enjoyed the passing sights of country life. Not a whiff of air stirred. We ran alongside tiny villages with their mud huts and playing naked children, and I saw the smoke from breakfast fires hanging above each cottage like a big halo fastened there. Palms rose like silhouettes cut out of school construction paper. Men toiled in the wet paddy fields. At windlasses bullocks pulled slopping leather bags of water up from wells; a splash while the bag emptied and the water ran out into irrigation ditches. Then backwards the bullocks marched, with the bag plunging down for refilling.

'I suppose you prefer coffee,' said Kennedy. 'But we like tea. It is our national drink at home—England, don't you know.'

Harrison made a disgusted sound.

'Have some,' Kennedy offered. Bananas also appeared from the kit. They tasted good too.

Kennedy told about his girls at St. Margaret's in Madras. There were three of them. They sang popular songs very well and had once appeared on the All-India Radio. Perhaps they would become famous as they grew up—maybe even cinema stars. They would make lots of money. Then they and Kennedy and their mother would go home—to England, don't you know.

We pulled into a good-sized town. Passengers from the third-class cars raced for the drinking-water hydrants along the platform to make their morning ablutions. Kennedy stepped out. Some people were there on the platform to meet him: a man and a woman. They talked as old friends. They were like him: European, yet somehow not quite European, either.

'La de da,' spat Harrison. 'All that rot about home. He's never been to England and he'll never go there as long as he lives. And he knows it, the fool cheechee.'

'Cheechee? What is that?'

"Cheechee, half-caste, blacky-white—you probably call them Eurasians. Or Anglo-Indians is the word favoured now, I believe. There are whole communities of them in India—didn't you know that? When we ran this country we looked down on them, but we used them too, of course—among other things, for running the railroads. Now the native is top dog, so *he* looks down on them. As for them, they've always pretended to be British and considered Indians an inferior race, and they still do. But it's become a rather pointless game now since Independence. This effort to seem superior of course is only a pitiful cover-up for the Anglo-Indian's unfortunate antecedents—usually indiscriminate British army lads and equally thoughtless native women. No girl of good Indian family would have thought of touching a Britisher in those days, although in all fairness I have to admit it didn't always work the other way round.'

I looked out at Kennedy and his friends, and I could see it now. Suddenly a mystery cleared up for me. I had noticed dusky-skinned people here and there wearing European clothes and following European manners. The lighter-skinned of them I had supposed to be Westerners somehow modified by the climate and food. But they were Anglo-Indians. Those who looked more thoroughly Indian I had supposed to be native Christians—Hindus who had been converted. They may have been in some cases, for the old silk dresses, rusty coats, and little hand-me-down suits may have come out of missionary barrels. But generally these too were probably Anglo-Indians.

What an insecure life they must lead; yet they are not willing to let themselves become assimilated. Eventually I was to read a wonderfully sympathetic and informative book about this minority group, John Master's *Bhowani Junction*. I myself observed a second such person at close range at one of our ashramas. He must have been about twenty, and each day he came to do the most menial work, stooping and sweeping the ground with a handleless broom—yes, a real bunch of faggots such as you read about. I would like to have known his story. Anglo-Indians usually try to get into clerical or semi-professional fields, but he was doing the work of an outcaste. Bent over, he was a labourer; but when he raised himself up it was a shock to see the perfect head and face of a Scots highlander: green eyes and a north-country look.

Swami Prabhavananda tells a good story about Anglo-Indians. He was in India in 1950, accompanied by three American brahmacharinis.

They were going somewhere on the train when a group of Anglo-Indian girls got in. They were wearing loud Western clothes and heavy make-up right out of a fan magazine. They chattered on and on in out-land-ishly over-genteel English. But they were too brown to have fooled anybody. Then they began to sing American jazz tunes which they had no doubt picked up from seeing Hollywood movies.

'Start Ram Nam,' whispered Swami. Ram Nam is an immemorial Hindu hymn to the glories of Rama. It is sung regularly in Hollywood.

Our brahmacharinis did. And the sight of these white girls knowing so appreciatively music of a religion that, as Anglo-Indians, they had previously thought worthy only of contempt had produced first astonish-ment and then shame.

The pea-whistle blew, Kennedy got back in, and we were off again. Kennedy said he had heard there was trouble up ahead. We were now approaching Madras state. While this was mainly a Tamil-speaking area, there was a large Telugu language minority between us and Madras city which was agitating for a separate Telugu state, to be called Andhra. A patriot in Madras named Sriramulu had started a fast some weeks before to put pressure on the national government to allow secession. And in the area itself, through which we were to pass during the late afternoon and early evening, unrest was growing and demonstrations becoming frequent.

Well, we would face this when we came to it. In the meantime I asked Kennedy where he had got the hot water for the tea.

'Up front,' he answered. 'From the boiler.'

I guess I looked surprised.

'No,' Harrison grinned, 'that's quite a common thing here. Anybody can go up and tap the locomotive for a little steaming *pani* for his *cha*. It is one of the delightful services provided by Indian railroads for the comfort of the travelling public. And,' he finished, 'one of the many examples you will encounter of the steady assimilation by the tropics of incompatible machine-age invasions.'

I couldn't help but laugh. Employing a locomotive as a hot-water heater! How frustrating for the locomotive. Imagine, every time you got ready to move your heavy string of cars, to have your virtue dissipated into hundreds of pails and little cups thrust forward by people in search of a warm drink!

Marwari was up and packing by now. He had reverted to being remote again. Yet at the next station without a word he bought us a ridiculously huge quantity of oranges, which we were to go on eating for the next twenty-four hours, all the way to Madras. It was beginning to feel like a picnic. I had packed my suit and put on an old pair of trousers and a T-shirt. I just settled back and had fun. At Waltair around noon Marwari left us, and we were sorry to see him go. And here were more

Anglo-Indian friends on the platform for a visit with Kennedy. Apparently he was an influential man among his group and had acquaintances everywhere. The friends had brought a tiffin-carrier—a kind of tubular four-story lunch pail—full of hot food. When Kennedy got back in he shared the contents, with Harrison also offering food from his kit. All thought of the dining car left my mind. It was a real outing and I was having a good time. We lounged around barefoot and napped and ate whenever we felt like it, like children of nature, for the rest of the trip. The bedding roll had long since been folded up and put away.

And that is the third lesson I learned about Indian train travel, that you must treat it as a camping expedition. Relax and don't try to preserve dignity or neatness. Take what comes and forget about comfort. Then you can get along quite well. If you don't take this attitude you will just wear yourself out boiling over with exasperation all the time.

In the afternoon Harrison told me a little about himself. He was an unhappy man, with a peculiar mixture of attachment and aversion toward India. He had been born in Calcutta, the son of a British colonial official. His father had died about the time World War II came on; his mother had remained. He had served in Burma and Malay, and on a furlough had married a girl he had known for years in the British community. When Independence came his mother had gone to England with all the other returning British. But he had stayed on, as a supervisor in a government-operated heavy machinery plant in Bihar. His life had been good; he had adored his wife, and a boy and girl had been born to them.

Then the wife died. It was a tropical disease—something she would never have caught if they had not lived in India, and something that even then might not have taken her life if there had been better medical services at hand. He had put his children in a school in Bangalore—this trip was to spend Christmas with them—and was going on in Bihar, but life now had no meaning for him.

There were plenty of Anglo-Indians in the place where Harrison lived, but, as he expressed it, he was the only one hundred per cent white man for miles around. He loathed Anglo-Indians. He had some acquaintances among the Indians, but no real friends. The old-fashioned type of Hindu he found incomprehensible, and the Westernized variety offended him as much as did Anglo-Indians. With trembling voice he told about his lonely evenings, how upsetting the weather was in the monsoon season, how he had never been able to resign himself to mosquitoes, and how this country had torn away the one person he had ever loved. And yet the thought of trying now to make a life for himself in England terrified him. 'I'm the one who ought to be talking about going home,' he said. 'But maybe I couldn't make a go of it there. I guess I'm afraid to take my chances alongside any average man. I've been a sahib too long. I've gotten too used to having poor people around me, that I can order about and yell at in my fluent Hindi, so as to assure myself that I am competent.'

As we pulled into a station in mid-afternoon I beheld a sight which made my eyes pop. On the platform stood a tall young couple, both very blond, wearing typical American summer clothes. They were what might be called the ideal type of American young person—big, handsome, clean-cut, clear-eyed. The man looked into our compartment and said that his wife was going to a town a few stops down the line, and could she ride with us ? She came in and sat next to me. He too mentioned the Andhra state trouble on ahead and said he was relieved that his wife would be getting off before reaching the most troublesome spot.

It turned out that Mrs. Scherer and her husband were Lutheran missionaries from Minnesota. Along here was the area in which they worked. She told me how hard they had had to study to learn the language—eight hours a day, I think she said, for four years. She told about the problems they had to face daily of acceptance, of maintaining their health, of getting proper food, of combating lethargy back home and keeping the people who supported them sympathetic to their situation. You could see that these young Americans were most idealistic, service-dedicated, non-self-seeking. They genuinely were willing to sacrifice their youth, their health, and all hope of a normal life among their own type of person, to serve God as they understood him.

I questioned Mrs. Scherer as to exactly what she and her husband did. If it was educational or medical or social service work, this indeed was commendable. I never heard any Indian express anything but the warmest appreciation for missionary activities along these lines. But this was not the case. Mrs. Scherer soon launched into a regular revivalist harangue about the evils of Hinduism and the need for saving souls for Christ. Naturally she regarded me, as well as those other examples of Christian perfection, Kennedy and Harrison, as confederates in the war of enlightenment against heathenism.

Anger rose in me, but I decided not to say anything. I felt like a traitor, and I saw Kennedy and Harrison watching to see if I would challenge her. For of course she was talking against all I believed and the completely opposite knowledge I had of Indian religion. But I did not contradict this well-meaning fellow countryman, since I could never have convinced her, or even if I had, would have succeeded only in making her unhappy.

As the 'Madras Mail' continued on its southbound way and it began to grow dark, evidence of trouble mounted. At every town crowds stood around the railroad depot queerly silent. Then the announcement came that we would make no more station stops until further notice, so as to pass through the most agitated area without pause. We bolted the doors and pulled up the screens and shutters, but left the windows down for fear of flying glass, and turned out the lights. We scooted on for about two hours. At one point the thud of a hurled stone or chunk of coal sounded against the side of the car, and we heard shouting. Through the chinks in the shutters we could detect a flaring glow—probably a bogie on fire. By bedtime we seemed to have passed the danger spot, and the three of us settled down to sleep.

But I was lucky. Ours was one of the last trains to get through. I kept up on developments daily for some time afterwards in the paper at the Madras math. As Potti Sriramulu's fast passed the fiftieth day and approached the sixtieth, riots broke out everywhere in the Andhra district. The 'Madras Mail' failed to come through for a week. Nehru sent word to Sriramulu to stop his fast, that 'this method of fasting to achieve administrative or political changes will put an end to democratic government', and that the matter of forming a Telugu state would be considered on its merits in due course. Emissaries from New Delhi even flew to Sriramulu's bedside to reason with him. But he would not yield for less than an ironclad guarantee that the Andhra state would be formed at once. And thus, on the sixtieth day of his fast, the longest fast but one in recent history, he died. Later Andhra was constituted, but Nehru gave fair warning that no further fracturing of the young republic could be countenanced.

Well, that's about all. We are only a little late as we approach Madras city the next morning. I clean up as best I can, making a mental note to carry soap, towel, and mirror on train trips from now on. Kennedy is so excited at the thought of seeing his daughters again that he is fairly jumping up and down in his tennis shoes. Harrison is sitting morosely, resigned to the wait he will have before the time for his train to leave for Bangalore.

Slower now. All down the train, doors opening, heads thrusting out. We are coming into the station. Porters every few feet way out here, each squatting in the dust, his badge of office in his hand—the little length of cloth he will roll up to make a cushion on his head for the food lockers, water jars, bedding rolls, and great tin trunks we are bringing. *Whoof, whoof, whoof* in a descending rhythm. Up ahead I watch as the platform swings out to meet our buffer beam, misses, and slides by.

Who are my kin in this far land? I puzzle. Who are my kin now anywhere? An American from a state just neighbour to the place of my birth is foreign to me. Unreachable is an Englishman, my proper brother. And a person I should favour for his passionate adoration of the bloodline I share, I find instead pitiable. Do I not feel closer to Das and Marwari? For I am trying to be cured of the materialist disease, in which one lineage and religion is seen as superior to another, in which one believes that wealth will give peace, that expression can yield fullness. Marwari and Das understand the direction from which wholeness must come and how it can be had. They are devotees, or trying to be, as I am. Kinship I see to be not in nationality or colour, but in becoming children together of the one God. A police official from Orissa and a merchant from Bombay hence can be, with a Hollywood Yankee, of one confraternity.

We are clanging down the platform. The brakes set up a low, quiet scream. People are running past the windows and shouting. How are my friends in the cab, the other Anglo-Indian engine driver and his intense little assistant? Oh no; of course they will have finished their shift far back up the line, with others having taken their places long ago. Was it only the night before last that I was with them? Almost stopped now. Well, the shattering footplate for a little while at least will be still. Stopped now. Up in front steam rises in a tall straight column from the safety valve. Smoke gathers in a grey pall above the boiler. The 'Madras Mail' has finished another run.

I catch the flash of gerrua in the surging crowd. A porter catapults into the compartment, wanting to take my baggage. 'Sahib?' he questions, reaching forward. 'All right,' I nod. Yes, I may look like a sahib. The gerrua sees me, comes to the door. But things are changing and old demarcations losing their validity. The gerrua and I exchange hellos. For I'm related here, and this is my kinsman, come to meet me and take me home.

CHAPTER VI

IN INDIA'S DEEP
SOUTH

IT is often argued that the European nations went to the Orient to do social service to a backward people; and that the cause of India's present economic distress is her headstrong interest in religion. The Europeans went East because there was a great deal of wealth there and good opportunities for helping themselves to some of it. And a basic cause of India's current poverty is that they were so successful in their enterprises and carried so much of their gains away with them.

I have first-hand evidence about this. For an uncle of mine ten generations back was a Far East trader. He was the well-known Elihu Yale after whom, because of a bequest he gave to it, Yale University was afterwards named. He went to India in 1670 as a worker for the British East India Company. By 1687 he had risen to the governorship of Fort St. George, around which Madras was to develop. Five years later Uncle was removed because of financial scandals concerning his administration. In those twenty years, during which his actual salary probably never reached more than a hundred pounds annually, Elihu Yale managed to amass and take to England with him a fortune which would now be reckoned at five million dollars. The company for which he worked was able at times to issue a one hundred per cent stock dividend and a twenty per cent cash dividend yearly.

Madras city is a thousand miles south of Calcutta, just thirteen degrees above the equator. It shows its comparative newness in the spaciousness it displays. Although its population stands at more than a million, most of Madras is not congested. Streets are wide, and large houses rest graciously in big tree-shaded yards. Yes, it is deeply tropical, hot, and sultry there, but a helpful sea breeze rises in the afternoon. The city runs for eight or ten miles along the glittering sandy edge of the Bay of Bengal, from the harbour on the north to Adyar on the south, where the Theosophical Society has its impressive international headquarters.

Close to the harbour is Fort St. George. Within its fortifications for many years the British were able to carry on a great commerce and to defend themselves against sallies of Indian chieftains from inland, and menacing forces of contending European nations approaching by sea. Even in this pioneer fortress social protocol was observed, with the governor in the role of local princeling. An old traveller named Dr Fryer, who visited Madras in the late 1600s, described the governor's magnificence: his personal guard of three or four hundred natives; his flamboyant appearances in the streets of the fort heralded by fifes, trumpets, and a flag, himself borne in a gorgeous palanquin, shaded by an ostrich-feather fan.

Now, a kinsman of a nabob whose only interest in India was in what he could get out of her had come as a hopeful religious student. The grandnephew of one who had scorned the idea of self-naughting had arrived to try to practise it. Well, this is a reversal which bids fair to become a trend. With animal gusto whole continents of Western men scrambled for centuries after material satisfactions, their churches generously adjusting the ideal to the parishioners' strong engrossments. And Western men gained their object. They became masters of the physical realm. But fulfilment still eluded them. They controlled their environment and could adapt it to the delight of their senses; but now their minds gave way. And thus it has begun to happen that a man here and a woman there comes to see through the swindle, and turns for help to a tradition which has never forgotten that we are not fed by bread alone.

On the beach halfway between Fort St. George and Adyar in the community of Mylapore is San Thome, an important Catholic centre. Just four or five blocks inland is the leading math in south India of the Ramakrishna Mission. I lived in the latter while in Madras and often on my walks to the seashore passed by or stopped at the former.

While I was there, the nineteen-hundredth anniversary of the supposed arrival in India of Jesus' disciple Thomas was being celebrated. Much of the observance centred around the old cathedral of San Thome where, in a lower room just before the altar, is a much revered crypt regarded as his burial place. Whether the Doubting Disciple actually brought the gospel to the Orient is not known for sure, but there is a verified history of Christianity in south India from the third century onward. In 883 King Alfred the Great sent an English bishop to make an offering in his name at St. Thomas' shrine. Marco Polo visited Mylapore in 1293. Vasco da Gama stopped in south India in 1498, and later came St. Francis Xavier.

Naturally, Indian Christianity had grown up without any connection with the hierarchy at Rome and knew little or nothing of the dogmas developed there, which by this time were regarded by the Church as

4 Swami Vivekananda

Swamiji at Greenacre, Maine in the summer of 1894

Swami Brahamananda

Sri Ramakrishna's great-grand-nephew, Kanai Ghoshal

5 Group photo taken at Madras

Swami Atulananda

divine verities. In its isolation Indian Christianity had progressed in a somewhat different direction, a situation which so scandalized priestly visitors from Europe when such eventually arrived as to leave them no alternative but to decree Indian Christianity schismatic and heretical. Xavier even supported the introduction there of the Inquisition. Efforts were made to pull this errant offspring over to the 'true' path and into the Roman fold with—even to this day—uneven success.

It was always a pleasant experience to go to San Thome's. The grounds were airy and good-looking, and the cathedral gave off a feeling of home, having the aspect of a European or American church. But the similarity was only partial. Outside on the steps at the sand's edge in front of the bishop's palace there was always a cluster of old brahmin gentlemen who found this a comfortable place to meet and take the air. They were quite unconscious of the alien growth behind them—dhoti-clad, bare chests crossed with the sacred thread, long hair done up in a bun like a woman's—sitting and chatting while openly telling their beads. Inside, the incense smelled familiar, yet with something new and exotic added as it burned there beside the tropical sea. The vestments were usual, but worn by Indians gave an altogether unaccustomed look. The Mass spun forth in its customary Latin; yet it didn't sound the same. The genuflections, the gestures of the sign of the cross—all perfectly correct, but when made by a sari-clad Indian, somehow eccentric-looking. I was surprised to see that the Western custom of wearing shoes into the church and indeed up to the altar was followed here; this must have appeared as unseemly to many of the worshippers as it did to me; for removal of footwear when approaching any holy place in India becomes second nature. At Christmastime the cathedral and administration buildings which surround it were strung with coloured electric lights and looked for all the world like the scene of a gay carnival, as probably they were meant to. The enthusiasm outside and the reverence inside were as strong, it seemed to me, as generally expressed at Hindu temples.

The Moslem conquests which smashed Hindu temples for hundreds of years, beginning around A.D. 1000, occurred mostly in the north. Southern India was not so seriously affected. You will hardly find a shrine in the north whose present structure dates back more than two or three centuries. In the south very old shrines remain. Vedic culture in its more ancient form was able to continue on there with less interruption, so that at present the most traditional Indian society is found in the south. To witness the most beautiful white silk turbans, the most dedicated vegetarianism, the closest attention to Sanskrit, the preservation of the old brahmin hair-do and other antique forms, the greatest pride of caste, and the most aristocratic languor, look to the south.

Swami Vivekananda's trip to the West in 1893 had the support of many in Madras, and he was enthusiastically welcomed back there on his return some four years later. But the fact remained that Rama-krishna Vedanta was seen as an upstart movement—and a Bengali upstart movement at that!—by many elements. So in sending a brother disciple to begin the Master's work in India's deep south, Swamiji promised: 'I shall send you one who is more orthodox than your most orthodox men of the south, and who is at the same time unique and unsurpassed in his worship and meditation of God.' It was Swami Ramakrishnananda who was sent and who in the next dozen years was to foster the southern development.

The work was begun in rented places until the present site in Mylapore was obtained. As you go to the math now you must pass the Kapalees-war temple. Actually, the Madras monastery sits in a corner of land which was once part of the big banana grove which supplies some of the income of this temple and even at present hugs the math buildings. The Kapaleeswar temple is typical of the architecture commonly seen in the south, with a block-square tank and a towering gateway loaded with coloured figures, the whole place enclosed in the usual charming pink and white candy-stripe walls. When at the math you are forever aware of the nearness of this big old worship place just around the corner. Multitudes flock to it all the time, and early in the morning and at night the booming of drums and blaring of wind instruments are loud in your ears, as the temple priests and an enthusiastic populace rouse the deity or see him off to bed. Noisy processions often go by in the dark, lighted by smoky flares or compressed air-gasoline lanterns as bright as acety-lene torches. One day I went through the temple. It is like a walled city. The main shrine honours Shiva, and lesser chapels set here and there in the enclosure do honour to other aspects of God. The thing I remember best is a twisted tree in a quiet quadrangle beneath which it is said Swami Brahmananda sometimes went to sit for meditation.

Mylapore is a particular section of a large city. It is also a village centring around a big old temple. Life there goes on beside the sanctuary as it does in countless other villages in India now and has since nobody knows when. (The atmosphere of the European town must have been quite like this during the springtime of Christianity.) You can gain a beautifully clear picture of this temple-shadowed life from Sister Deva-mata's *Days in an Indian Monastery*. This early American Vedantist resided for many months just here between the monastery and the Kapaleeswar temple during Swami Ramakrishnananda's time. She describes the feeling of the quarter well: 'In South India day and night are almost equal, the greatest difference in Madras being forty minutes. Twilight and dawn are brief. The sun rises and sets with tropical ab-ruptness. I watched it daily—the Temple garden wrapped in a deep blue haze, a filmy veil of white mist over the Temple tank, a rosy tipping of the Temple gate tower and the sun was up. At night there was a glow, a greyness and it was gone. . . . Along the streets moved bare-footed crowds with noiseless step, stirring a low ground haze of dust—men and women carrying heavy loads on their heads, young girls going alone to the Temple; a freshly clad Brahmin holding aloft a polished tray bearing grated cocoanut, sandalwood paste, fruits and coin, a special votive offering to the Lord; weary parents with a tired child on hip or shoulder and other tired little ones following after; cows and bullocks with small boys clinging to dragging ropes; a dull murmur of many voices, the rumble of a low-hooded bullock cart, and over all an intangible spell which wove itself around the mind and heart.'

To this immemorial pattern of village life something different has now been added. At its edge, and to some extent becoming a new centre, is the math of the Ramakrishna Mission. These two institutions—the old temple and the new math—are sharply dissimilar. A young devotee summed it up this way: 'My religion used to consist in going to the temple once in a while to break a coconut; but the Ramakrishna Mission gave me something to do.' That is, orthodox Hinduism has in many places become simply a matter of rigid outward observance. Worship often consists in a mere appearance at a sanctuary administered by priestly families who monopolize temple duties as money-making private preserves. One's observance may consist in little more than bringing an offering of flowers or fruit and money, standing a moment in the pilgrim's chamber to receive the deity's darshan while the priest presents one's offering and waves a wickful of light before the image, then leaving with a bit of prasad, a sip of holy water, or some grey ash for the forehead.

But Ramakrishna ashramas are busy community centres. They are conducted, not by a married and often limited hereditary priestcraft, but by well-educated monks who have freely chosen a life of renunciation and service. To some Indians, of course, Ramakrishna Vedanta seems as much of a heterodoxy as it does to many Americans. But to numbers of the more progressive elements it is a welcome focus for the religious impulse. A full round of worship and meditation is observed; and in addition there is a broad programme of classes and lectures, musical entertainments and festivals. And for the really ambitious devotee there is, best of all, a chance to participate in the life of the math, to help the monks with the math work and the public service jobs they may be doing. As Swami Vivekananda said, 'It is our privilege to be allowed to be charitable, for only so we can grow'. Besides, this is the most effective and attractive way for spirituality to be gained: through association with holy company. And this mode is directly in accordance with the great tradition of Vedic education.

The Madras math sits in a lush and productive garden, bordered by prolific papaya trees. The main building centres around a two-story open auditorium. Balconies line the four sides, the balcony opposite the entrance, approached by a double staircase, comprising the shrineroom, and those on the other sides serving as living space for the monks. Behind this building is a delightful backyard sheltered by coconut palms and banana trees. Here are found the kitchen, dining hall, bathrooms, outdoor sink where the Lord's beautiful metal dishes are scrubbed gleaming with tamarind each morning, and the coconut shell fire above which the drum of bathwater is set to heat. In a front corner of the property is the math's public clinic, and behind this is the free community library, and the office of the publication department which has for nearly fifty years been bringing out good material in English, Tamil, and Telugu.

The design of the main building results, in effect, in everyone's living in the same room. Swami Ramakrishnananda stressed the invariable appearance of all inmates in the shrineroom at morning and evening worship, and this tradition is strongly carried on by Swami Kailashananda, the present head. Thus at 4.30 a.m. when the alarm clock of Durga Chaitanya, the worship attendant, bellowed on the balcony opposite, I would be awakened and with the thumping of the great gong in the shrineroom a few feet away from my sleeping pad promptly at 5.00 a.m., I would find myself tumbling sleepy-headed from my balcony into the Lord's. Supper is at nine o'clock, with a 'night class'—a social-cultural gathering of math residents and perhaps a few intimate devotees—following. Thus it was difficult to get to bed early. Since also I could not get used to afternoon napping, I found myself building up quite a negative balance of sleep. I finally backslid, sought out a little abandoned space at the head of a stairwell in the dispensary out of earshot of the call to matins, and let myself sleep when necessary as late as 6.00 or 6.30 a.m.

Devotees arrive all day. Washing at the hydrant at the head of the path, they then come in to visit the swamis, to ask them for spiritual advice, or simply to sit in their presence. Some come to meditate in the shrineroom during the daily morning worship, and a great number appear for singing and meditation at arati time in the evening. Some bring food or other offerings, since custom dictates that a householder should not go to a monastery empty-handed; all in turn are given prasad—often a token piece of sanctified fruit or a sweetmeat—or asked to stay for lunch or supper. On special holy days a more elaborate worship is done, and bigger crowds come. At these times hundreds of devotees are fed, and sometimes thousands of indigent people, too; and there are musical programmes in the daytime and speeches at night.

It was the habit of many young men to appear regularly at the math in the evening. Some were still in school and through easy association with the monks were testing out the possibility of joining the Order.

Some had already married and looked upon the math activities for their cultural and social, as well as religious, value. Vireswar Chaitanya, the editor of *Vedanta Kesari*, had installed a game for the boys. They sat with him in a circle and went round and round, each giving some edifying verse or text in Sanskrit till his store was exhausted. Boy after boy would thus fall out and eventually there would be a winner. I happened on this group once without realizing what was required and was called upon to give a stanza. A moment of blankness, and then to our amusement I rose to the occasion with the one bit of Sanskrit I know—the chant from the fourth chapter of the Gita customarily said as a grace before meals at our table in Hollywood, and in Hindu monasteries everywhere.

The wearing of the brahmin hair-do by high school and college-age men never ceased to enchant me. The front part of the head is shaved back two or three inches beyond the natural hairline, producing a phenomenally high forehead. The hair on the rest of the head is kept long. In the shrineroom women sit on one side and men on the other. One evening at arati, while we were standing during the ringing of the bell, I saw ahead of me what seemed to be a young girl incorrectly in the men's section. It turned out to be a teen-age boy who was wearing his dhoti very long and his brahmin bun very low! My good friend from Bangalore, Raoji, told me how his parents wept when at sixteen or so he had gone and had his tresses cut short. The brahmin's appearance is most peculiar when the shaved hair has grown out a bit and there is a black stubble across the great brow. And the strangeness is even more awesome when the wearer needs a shave besides and has let his long hair down to dry after his bath, as well.

Feeding sadhus, like feeding guests, is considered one of the most meritorious acts an Indian householder can perform. Sometimes, as in the West, they 'invite the minister home' to a meal. Sometimes they give money outright so that the math cook can provide something special for the Lord and his children, and there is feasting at the math itself that day. There was a businessman who came to the Madras monastery for vespers regularly. It was genuinely touching, how eager he was to give me something to eat that would be a treat to me. He took me for supper one evening to the Cosmopolitan Club, of which he was a member, and where the menu included a few dishes of the Western sort. I was glad, also, to have a look at the inside of this place, which before Independence had been a famous sanctuary of the British sahib. The former owners had furnished it in an imposing Georgian manner. This had not been modified, except that the faces of colonial heroes had disappeared from the great picture frames lining the card room, with those of Indian leaders having taken their place. What an odd mixture of styles there was now, the new proprietors in their fresh cottons among all the dark elaborateness, sitting with feet tucked up on laps on the Chippendale furniture!

At the time of Swami Vivekananda's birthday a woman devotee presented every swami and brahmachari of the math with a new dhoti and chadar. We stood in a circle, with the donor modestly in the background, while Swami Suddhasatwananda, the math manager, handed out the clothes. There were only about twenty inmates at Madras, but this woman, it was said, had performed the same act at Belur Math a year or two before when she had gone there for her initiation—and there are regularly well over a hundred residents at Belur Math.

Another way in which devotees express their devotion is in their respect for the President of the Order. I was in one of the leading silk stores in Madras, talking to the owner. I told him that Swami Sankarananda was in town for a few days. He immediately ordered his car and chauffeur and went to the math in the mere hope of bowing at President Maharaj's feet. This reverence for spiritual eminence is something that always impressed me. At Madras, while the President was there, several hundred would come each evening for vespers and remain for darshan. Swami Sankarananda would come out, usually garlanded with someone's flower gift, and sit in a big chair. One by one, monks first, individuals would come up to take the dust of his feet, while he sat with downcast eyes. It would take more than an hour to go the rounds. If President Maharaj was not feeling up to this, Swami Suddhasatwananda would announce the fact, and he would then take his seat while everyone simply stared at him in utter silence with folded hands, until after ten minutes or so he got up and went back to his room. When Swami Sankarananda left Madras by train for the north, hundreds went to the station to see him off. He sat in his second-class compartment before the train started while crowds came to the door, bowing to the ground, and often handing in flower tributes or food for the trip. It must be a great sacrifice to subject oneself to being stared at and adoringly touched by the hour. Incidentally, it is the policy for sadhus to travel third class on trains, an austerity which anyone familiar with such matters will appreciate. Because of his age Swami Sankarananda travelled second class, in a compartment for two, an attendant riding with him. But as the train was pulling out that day, we caught sight of the President's second attendant and private secretary grinning from their third-class space where they would have to sit up amidst a most frantic pandemonium for the next two days to Bhubaneswar.

Some devotees move toward the monastic ideal in their later life. There was a retired doctor who seemed comparatively wealthy, actually owning a car in which he drove me to some of the Ramakrishna Mission schools and orphanages around Madras. He was a father and a grandfather and kindly took me to his spacious home to show me how some of the rooms were furnished in Western style, and some in the Indian manner. He introduced me to his wife, grown daughters-in-law, and grandchildren. Then he drove some distance away and stopped before a little cottage in a small grounds.

'And here is where I live,' he said.

'But,' I responded, somewhat confused, 'but you already——'

'No, no,' he said. 'That's my wife's and family's home. They have been provided for, and I am now enabled to follow the Vedic ideal of entering into the third stage of life, of retirement from the world and meditative existence alone.'

Something that delighted me from the first about the Ramakrishna monasteries is how very gay they are. I have never seen so much laughter anywhere as I have found in them. The monks actually do not have much in the way of exciting distractions or a great deal of an individual existence, but they certainly—pretty continuously—have a blithesome time. And as I have witnessed it, the Ramakrishna humour is of a superior kind: fragile, without cruelty, and delightfully mad. Perhaps as it seeks purification, the mind takes pleasure in subtler, more innocent things. I have known a few party people and some reputed wits and raconteurs; but I have never witnessed anything like the freshness, spontaneity, and originality that develops when you have a group of Ramakrishna sadhus together in a playful mood.

Teatime in the tin snack shed at Belur Math is often the setting for scenes of wild hilarity. As best I could understand the Bengali horseplay, a running pretence is maintained that the gatherings are actually business meetings in an exclusive club of august greybeards. Certain frequenters are the various 'officers' and other club characters; and impossible motions are proposed and voted upon with make-believe seriousness.

A most wonderfully funny person was the brahmachari who was in charge of the kitchen at Madras, Priti Chaitanya. Standing on the cook-house veranda, swooping his chadar about him in new and improbable drapings, he would keep the kitchen staff and the volunteer vegetable cutters convulsed. I am convinced he could be the Indian Danny Kaye or Cantinflas if he wanted to. If I recall his story correctly, Priti Chaitanya came from a small place up the coast and grew up always wanting to be a wandering sadhu. Finally, one day he started out, with no money or anything else but, for the protection of his head from the sun, one of those country umbrellas which cannot be let down. Now the boy, although as thin as a stick, loved to eat; and his begging was not very successful. Besides, he immediately came down with a fever. So after a career as itinerant mendicant of hardly more than a few days, Priti Chaitanya was taken to a nearby Ramakrishna Mission home of service for nursing. The cleanliness and order of the place—and the regularity and amplitude of the meals—convinced him that there was more than one way to be a holy man, and this way was better than any other. He joined the Order and eventually was assigned to Madras.

But a lingering love for the role of great ascetic still remained in Priti Chaitanya's mind. One of his funny acts was to blow himself up into an exalted sadhu, at which time he would grant darshan in a melodramatic manner. Ordained swamis wear gerrua, so that the undeniable mark of the probationer is his white cloth. But of this Priti Chaitanya made light. 'I am senior to many swamis,' he would say in joking boastfulness. 'I just happen to like white and find it more becoming, that is all.' One day he acted out a story he had heard from someone who in his boyhood had known Sri Ramakrishna at Dakshineswar. This child and some companions would go and sit in mock-seriousness in the Master's presence, like spiritual seekers. Ramakrishna would ask them if they had any petition, and they would close their eyes harder and appear to meditate more deeply. Sri Ramakrishna, knowing what was really in their minds, would then send for prasad sweetmeats, which he would give the boys, thus granting them the boons they were actually seeking.

Since it is the custom to give out offered food to devotees who come to the math, or invite them to stay for a meal, one of the 'family jokes' in any ashrama is that so-and-so, formerly a devotee, now a monk, had been 'caught' by the cooking. This apparently is what more or less actually happened in the case of Priti Chaitanya, and now that he was in charge of a kitchen he was a generous provider to all. I had to give lectures wherever I went, one on Swami Vivekananda's birthday at Madras to a good-sized crowd. After this, Priti Chaitanya remarked: 'Yes, a thousand were there; but of these not more than ten per cent came for your speechmaking. At least nine hundred attended for the sake of my prasad.'

I saw two Indian dramas in Madras—one on the life of Sri Krishna, and another, during the Christmas season, on the life of Jesus. I had been warned that Indian acting is very long drawn out, one visitor having stated that she had remained a couple of hours at a play before leaving exhausted, the leading character having not as yet been born. On the contrary, I was delighted with what I saw, and found the action fiery, fast-paced, prettily naïve, and performed with a sweeping joy. How the actors pranced and shouted with Shakespearean abandon! I wondered whether this type of drama did not resemble the miracle play, once so popular in medieval Europe, which also was made up of a series of episodes taken from the life of some saint or wonder-worker.

The Madras company was composed of more than two hundred. Performances were on a great stage outdoors at the Industrial Fair. Curtain time was at 6.30 p.m., and the action unfolded before thousands who sat on the ground in intense silence, except when they rose to boo Satan or cheer Jesus. There was no intermission, scene after scene racing past in breathless succession. All actors were male; that is, as in the Elizabethan theatre, women's parts were played by boys or men. This was done at Madras with consummate artistry; the women were completely believable, there being nothing of the smell of female impersonator in any of their portrayals. (I met one of these actors of women's parts at New Delhi. He was an earnest devotee, having been initiated in his early youth by one of the direct disciples of Sri Ramakrishna. A settled family man, he worked at his job of playing female characters with serious professionalism.)

The interpretation of the Christ story was, to put it mildly, colourful, with an entrancing succession of stage effects. There were numerous angels with wings, and whenever the principal angel made an exit a bright explosion occurred, presumably to indicate instantaneous disappearance. The dove which descended upon Christ at his baptism had an electric light bulb inside it. Satan, with the aid of a wire device, actually carried Jesus up to the top of the temple at Jerusalem, and at the Ascension angels, again on wires, descended from above to uphoist Jesus bodily into heaven. The speaking and singing were all in Tamil, but even from the action I could tell that more than a few liberties had been taken with the 'original script'. But whatever injustice had been done to orthodoxy, I'd avow that the spirit was preserved. I watched a party of Catholic Fathers, probably from San Thome, sitting in the front row. They may have found their facts fractured, but they certainly enjoyed the show. And I feel sure that Jesus would have been—and perhaps was—the most delighted spectator that night of all.

I made several sidetrips from Madras.

One of them took me to Conjeevaram, called the Benares of the south, about fifty miles inland in the Tamil back country. I went with a math devotee named Sathyamurthy, and on the bus with us were a dozen Bengali pilgrims, all of them old widows. They apparently had been going to holy places for months, as we were able to make out that they had already 'done' the north. The tradition is that there were 1,008 Shiva temples and 108 Vishnu temples in Conjeevaram in its hey-day, which appears to have been around A.D. 700. According to one description the city then contained many palaces set on wide streets and was a big centre of Vedic learning. Powerful people vied with one another to erect and endow fine temples. Conjeevaram is quite different now: a dusty, run-down village. But the most remarkable ruins are to be seen everywhere, and it could almost be said that every resident there has the remains of at least one once-imposing edifice right in his own backyard.

The two major temples that are still functioning at Conjeevaram are Ekamranatha and Varadaraja. One sees a number of those pointed pyramid gateways—gopurams—with hundreds of brightly coloured mythological figures crowding one another for space, tier after tier, like decorations on some fantastic wedding cake prepared for a giant. These entrance gates rise to two hundred feet and dwarf the shrine buildings, which are normally quite flat. At both of these temples the stone carvings, as usual, were phenomenal: forests of wonderfully sculptured pillars.

Ekamranatha is a Shiva temple, and its main feature is a very old mango tree, whose story is this: Long years ago, before the temple was built, the tree stood there, and a river ran beside it. Shiva sent his wife Parvati to earth to perform tapas, which she did just at this spot. One day a flood came. Careless of her own life, Parvati grasped the lingam she was worshipping, to save it from destruction. Seeing her devotion, Shiva gave Parvati the vision of himself. Later, the temple was built to commemorate this happening. The lingam in the shrine there is supposed to be the very one which Parvati saved; and the mango tree is said to be that under which she carried on her austerities. Like all other pilgrims, I too touched the mango tree, but considering its frail and twisted look resisted the urge to try to pluck a leaf as souvenir.

Varadaraja, a Vishnu temple, has a high wall around it like that of a medieval town in Europe. The seat of the main deity is approached in a different way from anything I saw anywhere else. It is on a second floor of a fortress building. You approach this building through a gate, then half encircle it to the rear, climb a stairway, and come back around to make a complete circle before the door to the sanctuary. Thus you are forced by the architecture to practise what many people consider the reverent way to approach a shrine, to encircle it, keeping it on one's right. As usual, the sanctuary was a dim closet deep, deep back in through a whole series of small openings with high thresholds. Vishnu was there in his aspect of boon-giver, bedecked with gold and jewellery. I was pleased to see our Bengali pilgrims carrying on an impassioned discussion with some priests in the anteroom outside the shrine. I imagined it to be a learned disputation on some obscure scriptural point. But Sathyamurthy guessed it was an argument concerning the amount of the honorarium they were to leave. I was overwhelmed by the vast size of the temple compound, with its great tank and many smaller temples, including a marriage hall for the god and his goddess, and I enjoyed making friends with the amiable temple elephant.

Another sidetrip took me to Mahabalipuram and Tirukalikundram, two communities also about fifty miles from Madras, this time south near the coast. My companion was a brahmachari named Ramamurty.

Mahabalipuram has been written about so much that I shall not describe it again. Now a sun-drenched relic on the sands beside the Bay of Bengal, it was from A.D. 300 to A.D. 800 a principal seaport of the Pallava kingdom, of which Conjeevaram was the capital. What remains now is a great quantity of religious architecture and statuary cut out of the living rock, providing what might be described as a remarkable outdoor museum of Hindu iconography.

Archaeologically, Tirukalikundram has no comparable importance.

But I am glad we went there, because doing so gave me a chance to experience what may have been a miracle—the one and only one I ever saw in a country supposed to be abounding with the supernatural. A steep hill topped by a Shiva temple, like a robber baron's castle on a Rhine-side crag, dominated the town. Nearby was a jut of rock where the famous phenomenon of the two eagles was supposed to occur. Every day for centuries, about noon, two very ancient eagles were reputed to fly in from the north, to take their dinner at this spot. There are said to be actual records certifying this, going back three hundred years. One of the legends explaining the appearance of these mysterious visitors was this: Once upon a time there lived two rishis, brothers, the elder devoted to Shiva and the younger to Vishnu. They fell into a quarrel as to the relative superiority of the particular aspect of God each cherished. Shiva himself appeared to tell them he and Vishnu were equal and co-ordinate and that they were wrong to fight over a question which should not even arise. But the brothers continued the feud. Shiva then became angry and cursed them to become dumb eagles forever; but on the rishis falling on their knees in repentance, Shiva reduced the sentence so that it should run only to the end of the Kaliyuga, the present 'iron age'. So the brothers now come daily to this hillside to adore Shiva. It is said that they roost in the Himalayas, take their morning bath in the Ganges at Benares, have lunch here at Tirukali-kundram, and go on down to Ceylon in the afternoon. No one explained about the fifteen-hundred-mile return trip, but I presumed they must make it nonstop in the evening to be on hand in time for the next morning's schedule. Incidentally, the warning was given that the birds do not put in their customary appearance whenever a nonbeliever is present.

I took all this as a pleasant fancy but climbed the several hundred steps to the top of the hill anyway. We were assailed by an enterprising priest who offered to furnish us a portion of the food leavings of the disguised rishis in return for ten rupees. I laughed him off, but Rama-murty, perhaps more devout than I or more ready to enter into the spirit of the occasion, bargained with the priest, finally getting the price down to one rupee, four annas. It was now about 11.00 a.m., and a crowd of perhaps fifty was already on hand, one man with a movie camera to record the mystery, should it occur, on undeniable celluloid.

While waiting, we visited the cave of a hillside fakir. Actually, it was no cave at all, but rather a cell constructed of cut stone. The occupant was cleanly dressed and had no possessions, save a large book from which he read serenely while we assembled. I got the feeling that the man didn't live there at all but rather had obtained something in the way of concession rights, probably residing elsewhere, and putting himself on display only when tourists were abroad. After a while the fakir put the book away and, turning to us with heavy placidity, gave a short talk in

Oxford English on the beauties of the religious life. He looked at us with piercing eyes, so that I sensed he had some hypnotic power and turned away. Some of the visitors, though, crowded forward to offer him money. This he disdainfully rejected, referring them, however, to a disciple who had now appeared nearby.

Ramamurty was young, direct, and smart. Suspecting, as I had, the man to be a fraud, he challenged him, asking him point-blank who his guru was, what spiritual experiences he had had, and what he thought of Ramakrishna. Thus questioned, the fakir revealed himself as one of those metaphysical romanticists, who believe a humun guru is not necessary, that it is possible to spiritualize the body—surely a contradiction in terms—and that sense experience 'properly' cultivated can impel one into genuine superconsciousness. Citing scriptures, Ramamurty backed the man down on point after point, making him look very bad indeed in the eyes of the pilgrims. Finally his tranquility vanished, and the fakir sprang forward shrilling angrily at Ramamurty, whom he called an upstart of such little understanding as to be unable to appreciate a state of development as high as his. Since a real saint is unlikely to have made such a claim, Ramamurty now made his departure most jauntily, his position having been confirmed by the actions of the man himself.

And now there was a stirring in the crowd as the priest took his place out on the rocky ledge, carrying an umbrella to ward off the hot sun. He performed a brief ritual and then set out two bowls of what looked like cream of wheat. The man with the camera cocked his machine. We waited. Perhaps there *was* a scoffer amongst us, which, if they did not come, would explain the eagles' nonappearance. But then to my thorough astonishment, up, up in the sky two specks became visible, winging down directly toward the ledge. The camera whirled and most of the pilgrims sank to their knees. There they were, not fifteen feet distant, two ancient eagles walking forward to their food. They ate in a dignified manner, looked coldly at their audience, and then flew away. I admit I was surprised that they actually appeared. When the priest came puffing up with the prasad, I was too thoughtful to partake of any, but Ramamurty consumed his portion with impish glee.

The third sidetrip was more extensive, taking me inland to Bangalore and Mysore, and on across the subcontinent to Mangalore on the west coast beside the Arabian Sea.

At Bangalore I spent Christmas, attending the special worship of Jesus performed there as in most other Ramakrishna maths at this season; and a lecture by Swami Yatiswarananda, its head, on 'Christ as Mystic'.

My stay in Mysore gave me a chance to see one of the last of the old princely states, where things are still done on the magnificent scale once common to now mostly vanished maharaja courts. The Mysore math is well known to the royal family, the grandfather of the present ruler, when he was maharaja, having been an early devotee of Swami Vivekananda. This ruling family—as was Buddha's—is of the second caste. In the West being king would automatically elevate one to topmost social status, but in India this is not the case. Technically, the Maharaja of Mysore cannot be visited or dined with by orthodox brahmins.

From Mysore you may go to three wonders of the Oriental world: the superb colossus of Sravanabelgola and the two ruined temples of Belur and Halebid. So on the last day of 1952 I hired a car and together with some of the math inmates made the three-hundred-mile round trip into the far countryside to visit them. Even still the memory of those marvels makes my heart turn over. Except for the magnificent temple of Konarak near Puri, Sravanabelgola, Belur, and Halebid gave me, I think, more aesthetic joy than any other structures ever seen in this whole world.

Out through the country we went, through many small communities built near tanks and little lakes. Old temples here and there, some tumbled down. Wonderful trees standing next to emerald-green paddy plots as small as rugs. Alongside sandalwood forests. Everywhere we met bullock carts lumbering along at their customary three miles per hour, the driver dozing, drawn into himself, wrapped in a bright cloth. In clouds of dust we went, honking, honking for the bullock carts to move over, often having to come to a dead stop until they did.

Having started before sun-up, we reached Sravanabelgola by 8.30 a.m. This Jain pilgrim spot consists of two hills with a village between. There are over twenty temples there, the most famous, where the colossus is, on top of the higher hill. We ascended on steps engraved in the living rock. It is like a polished dome, this hill—so smooth and rounded that if one lost his footing he could easily slip off and over. Six hundred steps bring you to the portal of the citadel-like temple. You enter and continue climbing. At last you are at the feet of Gomateswara, made of polished granite, nine hundred years old, standing nude, sixty feet tall, stiffly, with hands at the sides, looking away to the lakes and mountains, enjoying the puffs of sweet breeze from the sandalwood forests below. We had brought the usual temple offering: coconut and bananas. The shrine is the space between the immense feet. I don't know anything about the saint the colossus commemorates. But I do know that there is something about this spot that is special; an unearthly atmosphere has been built up there. The figure smiles an indrawn smile, with an expression benign and permissive. Sculptured vines entwine the legs and arms, to show how deep and still is his absorption; and sculptured anthills surround the feet.

The veil between the gross and the subtle grows thinner at times like this. A familiar dream of childhood, of sliding off the sheer face of some smooth hill, clutching with slipping fingers, and shooting horribly backward to be smashed below, returned with its old vividness. Was this the hill? Had I been here before?

Around noon we got to Belur. This twelfth-century masterpiece took a hundred years to build. Formerly there was a thriving capital here, but now the temple stands at the edge of a lost village. Halebid is twelve miles away, and its story is much the same: decaying glory out in the middle of nowhere. I will not detail the architectural features of these two temples. There are entire monographs on the subject: about the great stone blocks, hundreds of them, turned into living, dancing images surrounded by graceful lacework; about the wit and good humour and exuberance poured into every line. It made me giddy, thinking of the verve and toil that had gone into these sanctuaries. And I concluded: as this level of excellence becomes more generally known, must not authorities give the Indian temple a much higher place in world religious architecture than heretofore they have done?

Then we had our lunch at a government travellers' cottage and rested under a tree until the light grew slanting. We started back, stopping at twilight at the town of Hassan on the way, to see the big country fair in progress there. Rural bazaars must have been like this in Europe during the Middle Ages. There were acres of home-made wagons piled high with hay, forage for the beasts which rested on the ground nearby. At night the farmers would sleep in the hay. There was a cattle show, and along the road, lines and lines of booths with everything for sale. How exciting it all was: hot, dusty, noisy, jammed with holiday people chatting, seeing the sights, and eating indigestible things! After a while we started again, going on mile after mile, honking, honking through the dust and darkness until at last the lights of Mysore were around us. And that is how I spent New Year's Eve that year.

The next day I went to Mangalore. The 160-mile bus ride over the western mountains took twelve hours. The scenery was fine as we went up through coffee and rubber plantations and finally down into the lush tropical coastland on the other side. As usual, the overcrowding on the bus was indescribable. Nor was one inch of this road paved. You just sat squeezed in on a hammering wooden bench and tried not to inhale any more dust than necessary. At the end of the trip you simply scrubbed yourself from head to foot and put all your clothes in the wash. In Mangalore the streets were decorated, and bunting hung from many buildings. I learned that the Maharaja of Mysore was about to arrive for a state visit.

The Mangalore ashrama is housed in a sprawling bungalow encompassed by wide porches, built years ago by a European industrialist. Swami Adidevananda is the head, and he had three brahmacharis as helpers. An orphanage is maintained, for about thirty homeless boys. What a nice group they were, and how well they managed themselves!

They seemed to be fully self-disciplined. They studied quietly in the evening, went to sleep in good time on mats spread in two or three of the bigger rooms, and without prompting did much of the maintenance work of the place in the morning before going to school. They regarded all my baggage with fascination and were especially bemused with my shoetrees. I suppose to people who have never even had shoes, shoetrees do seem preposterous. The boys recited chapters of the Gita from memory in the morning and sang arati harmoniously before the shrine in the shadowy evening hour. My last memory of them is sad-sweet, of driving away, with them all standing on the porch making solemn namaskars.

As the western coast was at an early time easy of access to European colonization, Mangalore includes many Roman Catholics. Throughout the city you see fine churches and institutions established by them. The Ramakrishna Math in more recent years has attracted people, so that a band of good devotees has formed around it. By going out to villages surrounding Mangalore, like an old-fashioned American circuit-rider, Swami Adidevananda has spread the ideas of Ramakrishna into country places as well.

I arrived just at the time when one of these provincial visitations was about to occur. The Swami, transported by a member of a leading family of the city, was starting for Udipi, where a religious conference was to be held. I should, of course, go along. So in the evening we started off, in an English car, on a wild road along tropical bayous the sixty miles up the coast. At one far crossroads a travelling tent cinema had been set up, and for miles on either side we could see country people on their way to the show, carrying torches of flaming wood to light their path and ward off the tigers said to be frequent in the area.

It will be remembered that a reform movement in Hinduism started a dozen centuries after Buddha, fostered by Shankara, and continued by Ramanuja and Madhva. The last, who lived in the thirteenth century, stressed the dualistic standpoint and encouraged the ecstatic love of Krishna as an effective approach to God. This trend reached its high point with Sri Chaitanya in the sixteenth century. Udipi is famous as the headquarters of Madhva; he was born nearby, and he established a monastic order there and an important temple. The conference, thus, was a meeting of sadhus, scholars, and devotees interested in dvaita philosophy. Swami Adidevananda was going to Udipi to show the sympathy of the Ramakrishna Mission toward all authentic religious enterprises.

The conference was to open the next afternoon, with the abbot of the math and the Maharaja of Mysore, who was coming on from Mangalore, as co-chairmen. We did not reach Udipi and finish our supper until after midnight, and it was then that we went to the Madhva math headquarters. It was crowded with people making ready for the important events of the next day. A huge tent had been set up, as for a revival meeting in the United States, and immense food preparations were being made. (This math, incidentally, has given free meals to a thousand people every day for the past seven hundred years!) We stopped first at the temple. The shrine consisted of a kind of stone blockhouse with a number of images inside; one peeps through slits and sees them within. The most famous is a small black stone figure of Krishna, which was installed by Madhva himself. This, peculiarly, faces backwards, away from the entrance. Originally, it is said, it faced in the usual way, and the change of position came about for a very interesting reason. An earnest devotee of Krishna, but of a lower caste, came to worship before this image. He was denied entrance; but so anxious was he for the darshan of his beloved that he found a way of stealing in through the back. Krishna rewarded his devotion and proclaimed that all devotees are equal in the sight of God by turning around at his approach, and has remained facing in that direction ever since.

The math is headed by a swami who holds the office for two years. There are eight so qualified. At the end of his term of office the abbot must relinquish his post and devote his time to the practice of austerities while another takes over, and another and another until, should he then be able, his turn comes again after fourteen years. We were taken to have an audience with the present head. Up a wooden ladder we clambered to a bare second-floor chamber with only a tiger-skin for furnishings. To my astonishment the abbot turned out to be a mere child, perhaps fourteen or sixteen years old. Later I learned that these leaders are selected very early and educated for their future roles somewhat as is the Dalai Lama of Tibet. Brahmins are chosen at birth on the basis of horoscope indications and family religious distinction; and if all goes well they take their vows of sannyas at about the age of eight. The smiling boy abbot before me spoke no English, but I have never met a more charming or keen-looking youth—or anybody of any age, for that matter —more in command of himself and the situation. He was surrounded by capable pundits and the city fathers of Udipi, but his personality dominated the assemblage. He was said to be an excellent philosopher and a master of all the scriptures. The little swami just sat on his tigerskin and talked to me in a sweet, hospitable way through an interpreter, and I too became his admirer.

But it was now after 1.00 in the morning, and all I could think of was: 'This youngster had better get some sleep. He has to preside tomorrow, together with the Maharaja of Mysore, at the conference. We all ought to leave so that he can go to bed.'

I don't know how it turned out for the boy abbot. We ourselves actually did get to bed that night, although not for long. At five we were up for a busy day which included a trip to the beach, lunch on the way back to Mangalore at the home of a devotee who lived in a midway town,

6 Belur Math on Ramakrishna's birthday

Holy Mother's
native village
of Jayrambati

7 Ramakrishna's native homestead at Kamarpukur as it is today

Sri Ramakrishna's birthplace at Kamarpukur

with sightseeing there, a big afternoon dinner in Mangalore with many men of the community to show off Kanarese cooking at its best, and speeches by me at Udipi at 8.00 in the morning and at the Mangalore ashrama after vespers that night. I must say I felt like a Presidential Hopeful; and an old conclusion was again reinforced, that the indispensable requisite of the religious life is stamina! But it all went off remarkably well, except for the fact that our minds wandered considerably during the morning talk at Udipi to the rising enthusiasm outside as the whole city made ready to welcome the arrival of His Highness's entourage. Well, it isn't often that one is placed in the position of trying to compete for attention with a Maharaja!

Back in Madras, before returning to the north, I had to give a talk at the Sanskrit College. This is a stronghold of most orthodox South Indian brahminism; and since Indian brahminism is the oldest aristocracy there is, consequently at one of the most exclusive 'clubs' in the world. Such people do not change their traditions easily, and we felt it as a significant indication of respect for the progressive Ramakrishna movement and its American extension that a representative of both should be asked to speak there. I was received by several most distinguished-looking gentlemen wearing beautiful white handspun, handwoven cotton garments and white silk turbans, and led to the chair. This consisted of a place on the floor behind a low desk. I spoke sitting directly on the floor, and the audience listened in the same position.

My subject, as usual, was 'Vedanta in Southern California'. I told how Swami Vivekananda had come to the West Coast in 1899-1900 and how Sister Lalita had met him and later welcomed Swami Prabhavananda to her Hollywood home where the present work was begun in 1929. I described the struggle necessary to establish a foreign religion stressing renunciation in a nationalistic, materialistic place like ours. I showed how, on the contrary, some Americans have turned to this philosophy, and how in addition to having grown intellectually convinced, they have become devotees and taken to practising detachment and meditation. I told of their enlarging love for the old Indian mythology and the new body of chronicles growing up concerning Sri Ramakrishna and his disciples.

The persons before me were not necessarily admirers of Sri Ramakrishna, and some of them may even have held the old viewpoint that non-brahmins must not be trusted with higher truths. It was a cool audience, very difficult to make contact with. Although Sri Ramakrishna was not averse to the consumption of fish, meat, and poultry, out of respect for the strong vegetarianism of the south I had decided not to mention that one of the activities of the Hollywood Vedanta Society's Trabuco monastery is chicken raising. I managed to avoid reference to this when describing the work of the brahmacharis there, but was

I

shocked a moment later to hear myself describing the interior of Trabuco's half-spherical chapel as shaped like the inside of an egg! But finally, when I got to the part in my talk about how we are supported, and spoke of our income-producing orange grove and how the whole crop is contracted for in advance to a packing house, thus prohibiting us from picking our own oranges for our own table, the men before me loosened up. (Those mad Americans!) From then on things went well.

The question period, in fact, was free and exciting. Inquiry was made as to the attitude of Catholics and other Christians in the United States toward Vedanta. I had to say frankly that yes, there was a certain amount of opposition. This, it seemed, was based partially on ignorance of what Hinduism really stood for and partially on reports concerning abuses in it which traditionalism apparently had made little effort to correct.

One man asked whether the swamis of the Order working in America, when initiating devotees into religious life, employed 'real' Sanskrit mantras. I smilingly replied that |this was a subject on which none of us was able to speak with much knowledge, but that we certainly believed and hoped so.

A member of the audience inquired whether American people were attracted to the Indian puja and other rituals. When I answered yes, that many liked and participated in them, he said he was surprised and wondered why. The only answer I could think of, which seemed to satisfy him, was: 'The intellect is glad to be convinced; but the heart likes something to do.'

Then we got on to a subject on which Western Vedantists are bound to feel strongly. It is sometimes intimated that Americans are too worldly ever to take real religion seriously, and that the Ramakrishna Mission is unwisely throwing away good manpower in allowing its sannyasin teachers to go to the West. I have even heard it suggested that Swamiji's brief life was partly wasted because he worked so long in Europe and the United States. People are born, it is argued, in other lands to enjoy the delights of maya. Any soul finally ready for serious spiritual struggle will take a body in India.

This subject was opened at the Sanskrit College by this question: Are lives of Americans actually changing as a result of their acceptance of Vedanta? To this I was able to give a strong affirmative answer, something along these lines: 'Yes, I have seen extensive changes in many lives: several complete transformations, and any number of examples of remarkable advancement. The American is seeing the fraudulence of materialism and is disillusioned with it. He wants a faith to live by; but he is acutely practical and demands that it be sensible. As he tests the logicality and effectiveness of Vedanta, he may well become an enthusiast for it and plunge into its practice with Yankee fervour.

'As I understand it, this is the one prerequisite—recognition of need coupled with intense earnestness. Well, candour and industriousness are strong in the American temperament. Swamiji knew exactly what he was doing every step of the way. If he spent half his precious period of productivity in the West, then he did so for good reason. Ramakrishna recognized no spiritual elect. In fact, he saw in vision throngs of Occidental people making their way toward God through aid of his revelation. Of course his Order cannot do less than declare it and live it the whole world over. Wait a few years and see if recognition of Vedanta in the West does not become a considerable trend. Perhaps, even, in the ripeness of time, the next great wave of spirituality may rise there.'

Later I wondered whether I had spoken too evangelistically. But the session ended on a note of very good feeling, and when the chairman proposed a vote of thanks he actually admonished the members of that singular gathering to find as much value in, and to practise as diligently, their own tradition as the Westerners were now doing!

The thought of Uncle Elihu's astonishment at this scene, could he have witnessed it, filled me with high humour. Here on the very doorstep of his old dominion, in India's deep south, an established categorization had dissolved. It had been so clear 250 years ago who were the children of light and who were the heathen. But now everything had shifted round. The word pagan, it now appeared, could be applied to a man of any nationality; as equally could the term true believer. It all depended, it seemed, on the direction in which his love looked.

CHAPTER VII

GOD'S MOUNTAIN AND HIS
SECRET CAVE

————•◦•————

INDIA is a fat spearhead hanging from the gigantic land mass of Russian-Chinese Asia, pointing toward and nearly piercing the equator. It is a wedge separating Africa and the Near East from China, Japan, and the South Pacific. India is like a triangle, bounded on the north by the Himalayas, along the southwest side by the Arabian Sea, and toward the southeast by the Bay of Bengal.

I have just completed a two-months' stay down in the lower part of the country and am now moving northward along the triangle's eastern edge. I am in an old DC 3 operated by Airways India. This morning at nine we left Madras. Paralleling the shoreline of the Bay of Bengal seven hundred miles, we should be in Bhubaneswar at two this afternoon. On my right, over the horizon, lie Burma, Thailand, Malaya. Bhubaneswar is three hundred miles south of Calcutta and is the capital of Orissa state.

From the appearance of this plane the airline does not seem very flourishing. There are only four other passengers, and the door of the aircraft will not close properly, so that a frightening hissing noise fills the cabin. I think this machine must have seen heavy service in the War and by the looks of it may even have been one of those which strained so heroically over the Hump. Nevertheless, we are proceeding along comfortably in the brilliantly sunny weather, and the view of fields and swirling estuaries and of the very blue sea below is lovely.

I lean back and try to remember what I know of Orissa. The most thrilling fact is that it is the site, at Puri, thirty-five miles from Bhubaneswar, of the Jagannath temple, the world-famed seat of the Lord of the Universe. Puri is one of the four sacred destinations of India, a leading pilgrim centre. It has been a holy place for centuries. At present, the image of Jagannath is considered to be that of Vishnu or Krishna. Many historians are of the opinion, however, that Jagannath, originally

Hindu, became for a time a Buddhist temple, possibly the first depository of the sacred tooth relic of Buddha. When Buddhism declined, the temple fell under the influence of the followers of Shankara, and the worship of Shiva was probably carried on there. Still later, the Vaishnavas grew numerous, and Jagannath became the Vishnu sanctuary it is today. Something I have heard about Jagannath, but do not understand the significance of, is that its altar contains a lakh—a hundred thousand—of salagram stones. Puri is considered a special repository of spiritual force. There is a saying that Brahman's power is most manifestly present in earthly objects in the dust of Brindaban, the water of the Ganges, and the prasad of Jagannath. Sri Chaitanya spent his later life in Puri in a state of perpetual religious rapture, and many other saints of India have worshipped there. Sri Ramakrishna demurred from going to Puri because he realized that the intense spiritual atmosphere of the place would tempt him to give up his body. The attraction of so much bliss would make him merge fully into bliss.

Now we are coming in over Bhubaneswar. Bhubaneswar too is noted as a temple community. Ahead I can see the old town built around a lake, dominated by the great lingam-shaped tower of the famous Lingaraj temple there. A couple of miles away is the new town, the new state capital. Between them is the airport which we are now approaching. As the plane descends, I observe all around the jutting spires of other temples against the horizon. A terribly fast landing, and we are down. The twice-weekly plane from the south has arrived.

I am the only one to alight, as the others are going on to Calcutta. At the radio room, which is the airport's main accommodation, I am told that my transportation to town will soon be at hand. After a time this airport conveyance appears: a bicycle rickshaw slowly pedalled by an old man. I get in, holding on my knees my suitcase and typewriter. It is that one quiet hour of the day in India—siesta time—as we grind ahead over the rutted paths. Bhubaneswar is a little country place now, and those eyes which are not asleep watch with unwinking curiosity as we pass.

I see that Bhubaneswar is simply filled with small old temples. They are at every intersection, in every back yard, even standing out in the middle of paddy fields. Most are empty and unused. I was to find out later that they were built in A.D. 800-1300 when Bhubaneswar was the metropolis of this area, and that there are reputed to have been some seven thousand of them then. Their conception is elegant, the carving profuse, and the piled-up stone construction admirable. What a pang it gives one to see how tippy, how abandoned and rickety most of them are. Shades of William Randolph Hearst, as I speculate on the possibility of rescuing one of these orphaned sanctuaries, packing it up stone by stone, and taking it back to Hollywood! Set up there, it would be cherished as the marvel that it is.

Past the Grand Hotel, which looks like a hostelry in a Western movie, from which ear-splitting gramophone music is later to pour all evening, to the Ramakrishna ashrama. I am very anxious to see this place, since it was established by Swami Brahmananda in 1919 as a favourite retreat, and strongly reflects his influence. It turns out to be a settlement of attractive buildings made of the porous stone of the area, painted pink. There is a main building, a library, a guesthouse, a charitable dispensary, a small school, and several farm and service buildings. Surrounded by a high wall, and without electricity, the hermitage is shadowy and withdrawn in feeling, conducive to a meditative mood.

In the evening a brahmachari named Kalidas and I take a walk through the old town. I see several buildings with big signs proclaiming them to be sanitariums and express my puzzlement. Kalidas tells me that about a hundred thousand pilgrims come to Bhubaneswar every year to visit the Lingaraj temple. To cater to them are a number of lodging houses, and those taking special pains about cleanliness and nature's remedies proclaim the fact by terming themselves sanitariums. Old Bhubaneswar's centre, of course, is the market place before the temple. A few candles and kerosene wicks illumine those stalls where business is still being done, but beyond these circles of radiance the darkness is impenetrable. The look is like that found in remote Mexican villages after dark. We want to make a reservation for my trip to Konarak and we stumble through a jumble of alleys to the home of the bus owner. I cannot see a thing, but by the sounds I know there is intense life on both sides, only a few inches away behind the earthen walls.

The new town is as contemporary as the old town is antique. Under the British, the area headquarters was at Cuttack; but with Independence it was decided that the state capital of Orissa should return to its ancient site. Built up from scratch in the past few years, the residences and government buildings of new Bhubaneswar are all straight lines and raw concrete. The feeling is something like that of the new boom parts of Palm Springs, with walled villas built in the middle of stony plains and unfinished construction projects and piles of building materials all around.

Because of its geographical features, Orissa developed in isolation. It is a kind of self-contained pocket in India's side. It is barricaded round by hills, with rivers flowing downward across it from the heights to the sea. Before the coming of the railroads, travellers could not get into the pocket easily, nor once within it, cross it with convenience. The history of Jagannath contains painful chapters of pilgrims converging on Orissa from all quarters of India, at times to perish there. Many have drowned crossing the unbridged streams. Many, waiting to cross during flood times, have fallen prey to the pestilences which then flourish in the watery lowlands. Famine too has killed multitudes. In 1867, when the heavy floods remained on the fields throughout the rice-planting season, a million people in the state died of starvation. Yet pilgrims by the hundreds of thousands keep coming to the abode of the Lord of the Universe every year, and no doubt always will.

Even today Orissa has an aboriginal look. The women are often tattooed and wear enormous nose bangles and heavy anklets and wrist and upper arm bracelets. The state is a great centre for the growing of betel, most of the population—including women and children—appearing to chew it constantly, with consequent crimson mouths and blackened teeth. Villages are chaotic jumbles of primitive dwelling places, often unconnected by any through highway with the outside world. Walls and doors are frequently painted with folk designs. Considering all this, I remember how startled I was to see in one of these places alongside the road to Konarak a sign nicely lettered in English: 'In 1921, Edward, Prince of Wales, Stopped Here.'

Primitive as the present external appearance of the state may seem, a most thrilling type of temple developed in Orissa. If you give attention to the subject, you will find that the Orissa sanctuary has been studied and described with intense admiration by scholars from all over the world. Called the Indo-Aryan or nagara style of structure, this type of temple found its conception and reached its perfection at Bhubaneswar. The dozens of chapels still standing there demonstrate its origin around A.D. 800 and show the states of its development until it reached its fullest flower in the Lingaraj temple built about A.D. 1000. The present Jagannath temple at Puri is a replica of Lingaraj, merely bigger. It is believed to have been consecrated in 1118. The Konarak temple of about 1250 would probably have been the ultimate example of this style except that it was never quite completed. The grandness of its conception appears to have been beyond the powers of its builders to execute. When I went to Konarak I talked to some French scholars staying at the government travellers' bungalow there, studying the structure. When I asked them what they thought of it, their eyes filled with tears. '*Magnifique, magnifique,*' they breathed. They were just awe-struck. I was too.

As I sauntered about Bhubaneswar and went in and out of the many houses of God there, I could see that basically the Orissa temple consists of two parts: a tower and a hall. Both are made of piled-up stone, thickly carved on the outside, bare of ornament on the inside. The tower houses the shrine; from within, it is rather like a closed chimney, with the image of the deity installed in the centre under the soaring vault. From the outside the tower rises foursquare until about halfway up, then grows circular and rounding as the sides converge. The tower is capped with a flattened ball; there is a vase-shaped finial above; and at the very top is the metal trident of Shiva or wheel of Vishnu and a flag. The height of the tower is proportionate to the size of the temple, those of big temples such as Lingaraj and Jagannath rising approximately two hundred feet.

I found out later that the proportions of the tower are elaborately stipulated in old architectural 'scriptures'. In fact, every detail of temple construction, from the selection of the site to the final consecration, has been set down precisely in Indian sacred books. 'If the measurement of the temple is in every way perfect,' declares one, 'there will be perfection in the universe as well.'

The hall is merely an enclosed porch with a pyramidal roof. This is the place where the pilgrims assemble, to gaze through an opening into the tower, there to behold the deity. He is not to be seen easily. In the womb of the spire he dwells in the cool darkness, only clearly visible when one's offering of camphor flames before him. Windows are not common in the Hindu temple. The brilliant sunshine is reflected into the interior through the doorway without any need for windows—the object being to restrain this searching light, not to encourage it, and to promote that half-darkness which gives its halls their religious solemnity. The Gothic builders, who were beginning at about the time the Orissans were finishing, strove for the other extreme. In the European cathedral one finds more void than substance, for light and more light was the architect's constant aim in a climate of low visibility.

But the Hindu temple, it dawned on me, is not regarded particularly as a building. Or, in characteristic Indian manner, it both is and is not. For it also stands for something else. The tower, with its shin, trunk, shoulder, neck, and head, some say, is but a microcosm of Prajapati, Cosmic Man. Some see the spire as no spire at all, but instead a locally available Kailas (which is the Himalayan abode of Shiva) or Mount Meru (the Olympus of the Hindus). The worshipper may, by having the mountain literally brought to him, gain the darshan and merit which would be his through an actual pilgrimage to the abodes of the gods. The temple thus is heaven on earth. The shrine is the secret cave inside this magic mountain, and it in turn is like the cave of one's heart, where one may behold God secretly and worship him in one's individual way, deep within.

All at once I had the answer to something that had bothered me about Indian temples up to that time—why the Lord, instead of being displayed for all to see, is instead 'kept in a closet'. The plan of tucking the deity deep into a dark vault where only a person or two at a time may go up and stand before him had puzzled me; I had missed the Christian plan of putting the object of veneration in centre stage, well lighted. But now I perceived that there is a masterly significance in the scheme. Realizing God is not a congregational matter. It is individualized, with each proceeding according to his own inclination. Temples are even built with the holy of holies within five enclosures, to symbolize the sheaths of the human constitution, and teach men that they must go deep within—beyond body, senses, mind, intellect, and ego—if they would reach the innermost sanctuary of God-union.

The Orissa temple tower, I also saw, has strong horizontal lines contrasting with its vertical thrust. Subsidiary turrets and projections
distract the eye, tease the attention to linger at lower levels. So also the
mind runs horizontally, outwardly, distractedly. Yet these members
cannot deter the upward sweep of God's spire; their opposing movement
only emphasizes its essential rising line. In their ultimate ascent and
meeting are symbolized for the worshipper his aspiration and his struggle
and the final absorption of all in Godhead.

As the Orissa temple developed, two additional halls were added
on ahead of the pilgrim shed, namely a dancing hall and a chamber
for food offerings. Doorways in a straight line permit the worshipper
to advance through the successive outer chambers to the portal of the
shrine. And the deity in his sanctuary can 'see' out through the
audience chamber into the hall of the dancing girls and on through it
to the offering room where food is brought to be 'prasaded' by his
gaze.

I know the offering of food goes on continually at Jagannath and in
vast quantities. I saw many bearers with baskets of eatables among the
multitudes going in and coming out of the Jagannath gate, and there are
tremendous kitchens within the compound. The prasad of Jagannath is,
one might almost say, the staple diet of Puri. To partake of it is one of the
main reasons pilgrims go there. And Jagannath prasad is also carried and
shipped all over India and is received everywhere as a most desirable
delicacy, somewhat as is the case in the United States with pralines from
New Orleans or maple syrup from Vermont, except that Jagannath food
is valued not for its good taste so much as for the spiritually efficacious
properties thought to have been infused into it.

As to the present function of the dancing hall, however, I am afraid
I don't have anything to report. I never saw a temple dancer that I
know of. Perhaps they belong to the golden age of the past, although I
have heard that in some temples performances by them still take place.
The idea of a corps de ballet in a cathedral seems curious at first until
you remember that the Lord is regarded in Hinduism as a specially
revered personage who presides from the shrine like a monarch from a
throne room, the temple being his royal palace. Why should not entertainments be put on for his pleasure? He is roused with singing, clothed
daily in rich garments, fed, fanned, taken for rides, and ceremoniously
put to bed again at night. Such attendance upon God in his concrete
representation in the image can be very helpful in concentrating one's
attention, channelling one's affection—useful in centring the errant mind.
From a more non-dualistic standpoint, of course, God is complete in
himself and needs no entertaining or anything else; he permits his
devotees to wait upon him for the help it gives them to do so. But until
a man has reached this realization, let him by all means dance for the
Lord and think he is doing so for God's benefit! In the Western tradi-

tion there is the example of how an offering of acrobatics was made and accepted, in the story of the juggler of Notre Dame.

Three objectives now lay before me: to go inside the Lingaraj temple at Bhubaneswar; to see Konarak; and to enter Jagannath when I should go to Puri. Jagannath most of all—so important to the Indian, so controversially reported on through all the rest of the world. Yes, Jagannath especially, whose power over the Indian mind even the British rulers had respected, whose gigantic assemblages—with the dangers they held of epidemics or political disorders—they had never dared oppose. (Those rulers, it is interesting to note, had often climbed to an upper room in a tall building across the street from Jagannath's lion gate to stare, like children coveting a forbidden party, into the precincts all their power could not earn them the invitation to enter.)

This temple tour did not start out auspiciously. On a walk through Bhubaneswar on my first day there I happened into a compound of a chapel I hadn't realized was still in use. Like a ferocious dog, a priest ran out, yelling and waving, to chase me away. I knew that non-Hindus and unsympathetic foreigners, are not allowed inside a few very orthodox Hindu temples. But I was shocked nevertheless, for I no longer classified myself as belonging to either of these categories. I had worshipped in many Hindu temples in India, having received a bad reception in only one—where I had presented myself in Western clothes and pretty much in the attitude of a sightseeing tourist. I think the denial I got was justified in that case. I never made the same mistake again. But brahmachari dress or no brahmachari dress, here at Bhubaneswar I was barred from this little temple, and that was that.

The same thing happened again on a grander scale the next morning when I tried to enter Lingaraj. Lingaraj is a very traditional shrine. The people at the ashrama feared that some question might be raised about my going inside it and so had done what they could by arranging in advance for a Lingaraj priest to escort me. But this precaution was not enough. When Kalidas and I arrived at the gate, although impeccably clad in dhoti, khadi shirt, chadar, and cap, I was turned away. The priest went inside to negotiate. We stood in the dust of the marketplace, nosed by animals and stared at by children, while seemingly every Tom, Dick, and Harry of the town went in and out of my unattainable destination with the utmost freedom. Quite a little time went by. A knot of people gathered to speculate on the outcome. I felt more and more mortified. I understand that the event produced a big squabble within the temple. Even the civil authorities were consulted to see what their attitude might be should I, if refused, make trouble. For the new Indian constitution stipulates that no one can be denied entrance to temples on the basis of social undesirability. Apparently the police decided not to get involved. Having their hands full with the more pressing problems of a new republic, in general they have not cared as yet to come to grips with the hereditary boards of trustees whose word has been law in such old temples for centuries. Finally after nearly an hour, the decision was rendered: I definitely might not enter. I left the marketplace humiliated before everyone, and very, very mad.

Later I was to understand and take a moderate view, but at the time I felt nothing but fury. The refusal, I reasoned, could not be because of fears of an unsympathetic attitude on my part toward the religion practised at Lingaraj. The authorities knew that, as a ward of the Rama-krishna Order, I subscribed to the Vedanta philosophy. The only reason, therefore, could be my unworthy social level—my castlessness—or my undesirable colour. What unjust prejudice! What unfair segregation! I raged and raged, causing much pain, I am sorry to say, to the swamis and brahmacharis of the math. They felt as embarrassed and helpless as an enlightened American would feel had a foreign guest been treated, say, to a Southern lynching bee.

Later we talked to a high state official, a devotee of the ashrama, who helped me toward the sensible attitude I finally gained concerning this act of discrimination. Basically, no people are more tolerant than Hindus. But due to many factors, social freedom has declined, so that rigidity and exclusiveness have taken a firm hold on Hindu society. In addition, for hundreds of years Moslems have taken delight in despoiling Hindu temples. They have demolished many. Or they have resorted to tricks to upset the Hindu, such as coming into a sanctuary covertly to cast a piece of bloody butchered beef on the deity. While not destroying a temple physically, such an act can put it out of commission until costly repurification ceremonies can be completed. Nor since the European ruler and the American missionary have been in India have difficulties subsided. Through the propagation by them of many grotesqueries about Hinduism, India has been done many disservices in world opinion.

Thus put on the defensive, naturally temple authorities have grown cautious and have made certain rules about the exclusion of people they do not know. I might be a ward of the Ramakrishna Order, but I was also an American and everybody in town knew it. Many had seen me coming in from the airport as a typical foreign tourist. Breaking the rule this time might not have bad consequences; but sooner or later it might be regretted that the ban had been relaxed.

The kind of thing that happened to me at Lingaraj will grow ever less frequent as the memories of India's invaders dissolve, as Indians regain control over their own affairs, and as the flexible doctrines of Ramakrishna spread. Indeed, in 1959 a party of American Vedantists was admitted officially into both Jagannath and Lingaraj. What happened hurt me; yet in a sense I am glad that I experienced it. I know now the unspeakable frustration a person feels when discriminated against simply because he is foreign, may come from an uncustomary religious heritage, or has a divergent skin hue. I grasp how a Jew feels when—both of them knowing it isn't true—a hotel desk clerk tells him every available room is taken; or what an Indian like Swami Prabhavananda experienced when he was turned away from a leading Portland theatre because of a prejudice against colour. It is very educational to be on the wrong end of Jim Crowism or an Asiatic Exclusion Act. You learn in one piercing moment how stupid and wrong segregation must be.

The state official also told me some interesting facts about the operation of big temples like Lingaraj and Jagannath. Lingaraj, for example, is the private domain of about four hundred local priestly families, who look to it as their one source of livelihood. In Puri it is estimated that about twenty thousand persons are employed in the service of the Jagannath temple directly, with practically everybody else in the town benefiting in one way or another from the rushing pilgrim trade. This reminded me of the way things are organized in Western tourist localities such as Taxco and Venice.

'Travelling salesmen' also are sent out to all corners of India to advertise the spiritual benefits to be derived from a trip to the shrine they represent, and to organize and shepherd parties of pilgrims. When arriving at Bhubaneswar or Puri, the pilgrims are turned over to appropriate temple guides, or pandas, who sell them housing and assistance with temple rites. The distribution of pilgrims to pandas is based upon historical evidence in the form of old registers which make up every panda family's most valuable professional accessory. These go back for generations, containing the name and place of origin of every pilgrim patronizing the family in the past. A new arrival is expected to give his custom to the descendants of the panda who guided his ancestor, and he in turn must leave his name so that the arrangement may be continued. When any pilgrim comes to town uncertain as to what panda he 'belongs' to, there is intense rivalry to 'get' him, the contest being settled on the basis of evidence from the old records supporting the solidest claim.

By contrast, going through Konarak was easy, for it is now a nationally treasured ruin, protected by the government, and no longer in use as a temple. It was getting to Konarak that was hard.

At the time I didn't know much about the Temple of the Sun except that it was called the Black Pagoda, a title given it by the skippers of the Indiamen who had used it as a landmark in steering for Calcutta. It was later that I discovered Konarak's fame as the great final achievement of the Orissa builders, and the international notoriety it enjoys for the eroticism portrayed in its exterior.

Konarak is on a lonely stretch of the Bay of Bengal seacoast, twenty miles northeast of Puri. One can get there by overnight bullock cart along the beach from Puri, or by a rural bus—during the dry winter season at least—from Bhubaneswar. I chose the latter assault, a swami who was visiting at the ashrama going with me. We started at 7.00 a.m. and it took four hours to go the forty miles there and nearly six hours returning. We went first class; that is, we had engaged the two places on the front seat beside the driver, our feet over the jet-hot engine. My feet burn and my spine still throbs whenever I think of Konarak! We roared and rolled over practically non-existent roads, forded streams, and ground through the final sands. We went through such primitive hamlets as it is hard to imagine. The reasons for the disproportionately slow return trip were several: the sickness of some passengers who had never been aboard motorized transport before; the loss of baggage periodically from the top because of the roughness and the need to stop and recover it; the extreme casualness of the driver regarding time, who permitted at least one passenger to get out after starting, to return home for something he had forgotten; and the driver's odd habit for the last two hours on the return journey of stopping to argue with would-be passengers that no more accommodations were available. One would have thought that the sight of the jammed interior, plus the presence of several people riding on fenders and hood, would have made this conclusion abundantly clear.

But it was worth it! Imagine this great stone structure on the sands facing east. The sands are yellow; above them twisted cypresses slant away from the wind, as they do along the Pacific at Monterey. Beyond is the Bay of Bengal, intensely blue. A wall encloses the temple yard, with imaginary beasts of heroic size guarding the gateways. The sanctuary tower is gone, only a stump of it remaining. But the pilgrim chamber still rises in its first glory. It is a square box a hundred feet on a side, with a big pyramid on the top. It rests upon a massive platform, along the sides of which are carved fourteen huge wheels. Lions crouching on elephants strain forward before it. The dazzling and original idea: an entire temple built to simulate a massive car being drawn towards the rising sun.

As we looked at this grand relic, I tried to think about the men who had built it. Who were they? Where have they gone? No one lives in this part of Orissa now but a few small farmers. Yet with enormous vigour and unmatched genius some sophisticated people erected this marvel to express a joy of life, an adoration of the divine potency of the sun. The builders at Greece and Rome could hardly match the work of the Orissans. Yet they are so well known, while these have disappeared and must be forever anonymous.

As such thoughts were going through my head, a pale young man and several thin children came up to us. In a respectful way they asked for money, explaining through a chart lettered in quaint English that there was no school round about, and they were collecting from the visitors to Konarak to get funds to start one. I found a rupee or two and watched the innocents making off, picking their way carefully among the fallen stones so as not, it seemed to me, to splinter their frail bones, and I meditated upon the obscure workings of a fate that had left nothing of the brimming race that had thrown up this monument to exalted spirits but these.

And now we began to look at Konarak closely and to marvel at the wonderful statuary which adorns it. Suddenly we perceived that many of the carvings portray highly explicit scenes of sexual intercourse, some according to modes which would generally be called perverse. As sculptures these are extremely good; but I confess I was startled to find the subject matter they picture ornamenting a temple. And apparently the good swami accompanying me had not been aware, ahead of time, of this feature of Konarak any more than I. As host to a foreign visitor he looked abashed and guilty, but confused rather than met the issue, it seemed to me, by stating that he would propose a Math rule prohibiting brahmacharis from visiting the Temple of the Sun thereafter!

In time I found out that Konarak is not the only Indian temple displaying erotic scenes. You will find some at the Jagannath temple, on Jagannath's so-called Aunt's House, and in other places. Various interpretations of their function are given. Such carvings have been described as graphic illustrations of the erotic recipes of the Kama Shastra, the so-called 'scripture' of love-making. Or these figures may be thought of as representations of what have been called 'auspicious pairs', which in less extreme forms have been used in Indian art from a very early period. Their embraces have been interpreted as typifying the idea of moksha, or union of the divine, the reachievement of that primordial unity broken at the time Purusha divided himself to create the world. 'As a man in the embrace of his loving wife knows nothing that is without, nothing that is within', the Brihadaranyaka Upanishad puts it, 'so man in union with the Self knows nothing that is without, nothing that is within, for in that state all desires are satisfied.'

I myself found satisfaction in a further interpretation given by Swami Jnanaswarupananda, who was my friend and guide at Puri. One must realize that these figures are always on the outside of the building, the inside being virginally bare. And they do not appear on the tower, not on God's mountain, so much as on the assembly hall. May they not then symbolize the world, the outer life of the senses? These masterpieces of relief composition with their feeling of movement and the marvellous suggestion they set forth of the participants melting with love, show us the 'very best' maya has to offer. Look frankly. Maya is—comparatively—real—and it does have its joys. Do not, in puritanical self-delusion, pretend that this is not so. A man with sex on his mind will see sex everywhere, even in church. If you want maya, have it. Look at the world steadily; look at the world whole. And when you are through, forget about it and come inside.

I like this interpretation. It shows a genius at work in temple conception that simply enchants you. What realism! What intelligent acceptance of man as he is! There is no hedging here, no fuzzy thinking, no mixing up of profane and divine. The symbolism of the Orissa temple grows. Built of stone, big, permanent, the centre of daily life, it gives every man, woman, and child a ready object lesson in life's design. The truths of man and God, of limitation and liberation, of the fleeting and the real, are all laid bare in God's mountain and his secret cave.

In the Katha Upanishad we read: 'The Self-Existent made the senses turn outward. Accordingly, man looks toward what is without, and sees not what is within. Rare is he who, longing for immortality, shuts his eyes to what is without and beholds the Self.' Two men went to Jagannath. One stood outside and stared at the carvings. The other went directly in, to look upon the face of the Lord.

The next day I said good-bye to Bhubaneswar to go by train the short way to Puri. I looked for the last time at the relics of my guru's guru: at the many things in Swami Brahmananda's room that he had used—the clothes, his lounge chair with extendable arms to hold the feet should one feel like stretching out, the hubble-bubble pipe Maharaj is shown smoking in one of the best pictures there is of him. I remember it was made of brass and is kept well polished. Then a final prostration at the shrine upstairs, and outside Ramakrishna's nearby ceremonial bedroom, where the Master is ritualistically put to rest each night and where there is a cradle for Maharaj, complete with two miniature bolsters, beside the big bed. I recalled that Maharaj was the Eternal Companion of God when the Lord came before as Krishna, and was regarded by Sri Ramakrishna in his last birth as his darling little son.

The train jogged along. I thought about the rebuff at Lingaraj and wondered whether I should be lucky enough to get inside Jagannath.

Then I recalled an incident which had happened in the life of Swami Atulananda, the Dutch-American who had emigrated to India early in the century, to become an ordained swami of the Order. The story is related by Swami Prabhavananda, who shared in the occurrence as a brahmachari in 1915, when it happened. The two of them had made the hard climb up to that one of the four sacred destinations of Hinduism which is in the Himalayas, namely Badri-Narayana. This is a most orthodox shrine, and there was a serious doubt whether the undeniably blond Gurudas Maharaj, even though in monastic dress, would be admitted. On the morning of their arrival the travellers were waiting, along with many other pilgrims, for the temple to open, wondering what might happen. Then a fine-looking young priest appeared and beckoned to Gurudas Maharaj and Swami to come inside with him, motioning to the other pilgrims to wait. They entered and had their darshan of the deity. They decided to stay on for some days in the locality and did so, growing to know the priests of the temple well. But they never saw their young guide again.

In the meantime, taking it for granted that Gurudas Maharaj might not go inside the temple, the kindly authorities made arrangements one day for the doors to be opened wide and strong beams of light to be directed upon the image, so that Gurudas, having come so far, should not miss obtaining darshan even though he might not enter. Thinking this curious, Swami and Gurudas inquired about the young priest of the first day. No one could recognize the description as belonging to any of those living at Badri-Narayana. Still puzzling over the incident, Gurudas and Swami asked Swami Turiyananda about it when they saw him upon reaching Almora. 'You fools,' was the great Swami's response. 'That was the Lord himself who came to let you in.'

Could that be so? Yet, if Swami Turiyananda said it, it must have been. But the adjusting of the 'lawful' flow of events is a miracle. So much the better. A miracle to affirm that all devotees are to the Lord his equivalent children, whatever may be the accidents of the cultural lag!

And now up ahead the famed tower of Jagannath stood out. God's most famous peak swam over Puri, on its small hillock above the beachy lowlands. 'I am coming,' I whispered. 'This pilgrim is coming. Maybe I reached Orissa by airplane and am entering Jagannath's capital by train. But I am making my way toward you with a big hope, just like the multitudes who for centuries have been walking from all over India to fulfil their life's aim of gaining the blessing of the Lord of the Universe.'

The Ramakrishna Math, Puri, sits on the edge of what must be one of the world's finest beaches. Resort hotels and the summer homes of maharajas surround it. Hundreds of feet of sand lead to the water's brink; and beneath the surf the slope is still so gradual that one must walk on another long way before finding water deep enough to swim in. I was given a small room on the roof, open to the sun and breeze on four sides. The view from the ashrama and the strong whiteness of the light brought to mind Florida in the winter season.

I must somehow, I thought, as I dallied in the warm waves or walked the hot beach watching the fishermen repair their primitive skiffs—I must somehow make contact with Sri Chaitanya while I am here. My memory went back to that New Year's Eve in 1948-49 when a deeply troubled mind saw the possibility of peace at last in the words of a poem chanted in a little white temple above the roar of a celebrating Hollywood:

A drowning man in this world's fearful ocean
Is Thy servant, Oh Sweet One.
In Thy mercy
Consider him as dust beneath Thy feet.

Ah, how I long for the day
When an instant's separation from Thee, Oh Govinda,

Will be as a thousand years,
When my heart burns away with its desire,
And the world, without Thee, is a heartless void.

Then I had not even known what Govinda meant or heard of the author of this ode, Sri Chaitanya. But at present I was in Chaitanya's town, and just there against the horizon was the roof of the house where Govinda had lived.

Who was Sri Chaitanya? Chaitanya is considered an incarnation of God, was born in a Ganges-side Bengal village in 1485, and died in Puri in 1533. His contribution was to show to a sensual society how the drive of love, focused on God, can win the mind away from the senses and lead it to God-vision. He popularized religious singing with instru-mental music, called bhajan, stressed kirtan and japam, and himself lived in an ecstasy of devotion to Krishna in his cowherd boy or Govinda phase.

Sri Chaitanya started a monastic order, and one evening in Madras some of us had gone calling at the Chaitanya math there. The monks were gracious to us and served us prasad fruit sitting down in their dining hall. They told us about their life, how they do not stress karma yoga as the Ramakrishna monks do, but give their days mostly to devo-tional activities, with the result that they do not earn much public support but must beg for all their wants. Some of the men wore bead-bags on strings hung from the neck, into which they would reach from time to time to do japam on their rosaries. At vespers we watched the monks perform their kirtan. Their shrine is a separate building in the courtyard, containing nearly full-size images of Radha and Krishna, accompanied by Sri Chaitanya. Around this they walked in rhythmic gait, as in a stately conga line, working in now and again an extra turn or a light dance step. Circling ever to the right around they marched, fingering their drums, booming the gongs they carried, singing out the poignant lyrics of the moving old idyll of Krishna as sportive prince of love, and of Radha, the incarnation of the hunger in all of us for God:

A loving youth is he, and he has jewellery on.
A lovely crest has he on his forehead.
At the sight of him my mind is plunged into a sea of loveliness.
Only by luck save I my life.

Friend, I saw him on the way, while walking all alone.
A weak woman am I, straightaway forgetting my duties.
His smiling glances were like arrows smiting my heart.
A thrill passed over my body, and my robes came off.
I forgot to fill the pitcher.

My sleep is not sound; it is full of dreams.
I dream the dream of this unspeakable love.

K

Chaitanya was not a bhakta at the beginning. A brahmin, he was born into one of the most rationalistic families of the day. He was an intellectual prodigy, becoming a noted professor of logic at an age when most men are barely beginning their careers. But he had a vision at Gaya, and his life was changed completely. He gave up his disputations, his role of pundit, took at twenty-four the vows of sannyas, and became one of the sublimest exemplars of bhakti the world has ever known. His friends called him Gauranga, the Golden One. Mad Gauranga, who rolled on the ground crying the glory of God's name: 'Hari bol.' Mad Gauranga, who for the final eighteen years of his life stood in samadhi morning after morning in the pilgrim chamber of Jagannath looking into the face of his Ideal.

Sri Ramakrishna said of him: 'Bhakti matured becomes bhava. Next is mahabhava, then prema, and last of all is the attainment of God. Gauranga experienced the states of mahabhava and prema. When prema is awakened, a devotee completely forgets the world; he also forgets his body, which is so dear to a man. Gauranga experienced prema. He jumped into the ocean, thinking it to be the Jamuna [on whose banks Govinda played]. The ordinary jiva [individual] does not experience mahabhava or prema. He goes only as far as bhava. But Gauranga experienced all three states. . . . In the inmost state he would remain in samadhi, unconscious of the outer world. In the semi-conscious state he could only dance. In the conscious state he chanted the name of God.'

Chaitanya's sweet mood rolled across the whole land of Bengal, splashing over into Bihar and Orissa. His love knew no bounds. The non-Hindu had a share in it. So did the spiritually dull. So did the immoralist. Everyone who heard the Gauranga story was cleansed by it, turned in God's direction. To this day the sect of Vaishnavism is the refuge of the poor, the down-trodden, the outcaste, the weak.

Sri Ramakrishna was a keen admirer of Chaitanya. Once he thought how nice it would be to witness one of the scenes of bliss from Chaitanya's life. His desire was fulfilled in a vision of a kirtan. The Master felt wonderful waves of devotional music coming toward him from the direction of the Panchavati. He saw the Golden One advancing, proceeding with a slow gait, absorbed in the love of God. A disciple was on either side, and a dense multitude followed. All were in a state of spiritual drunkenness, produced by Chaitanya's love. Some expressed the bliss they felt through losing outward consciousness, some by performing wild, ecstatic dances. Ramakrishna noticed some faces in the crowd which he later recognized among people coming to him, thus knowing that they had been companions of Sri Chaitanya in a previous birth.

There are many appealing parallels between the earthly play of Sri Chaitanya and that of St Francis of Assisi. Each came at a time when

the religious impulse had lost spontaneity; each lived in a continual
state of rapture; each scorned philosophizing in favour of unobstructed
love; each coupled with his bhakti deep humility in the service of others
without distinction. Chaitanya's story deserves to be as well known in
the West as is *The Little Flowers* of St Francis, and perhaps some day
will be. Children will delight in it, and the thorniest oldsters will weep
as they read of the experiences of the Golden One, and feel blessed.

As Swami Jnanaswarupananda and I walked around Puri the next
day, I tried to open my mind to Chaitanya's influence in the places
associated with him. Here was the wide avenue leading from the Jagannath temple the mile to Gundica temple, or Jagannath's Aunt's House.
Every June or July the Lord of the Universe emerges from his stone
residence to go for a week's stay at this country home. Jagannath makes
his journey on a great wooden float, inspiring the car festival, so un-
sympathetically reported these many years the world over. (When a
number of people were crushed in the crowd trying to get into Chicago's
Soldier Field to observe a Marian Year celebration, September 8, 1954,
I thought: What capital someone attempting to give Christianity a bad
name could make out of this!) Dancing before the car, Chaitanya re-
vived the forgotten meaning of the festival, which Swami Vivekananda
commented on in this wise: 'Know for certain,' he said, 'that there is
no greater holy spot than the body of man. Nowhere else is the Atman
so manifest as here. That car of Jagannath that you can see is but a
concrete symbol of this corporeal car. You have to behold the Atman in
this car of the body. The sight of the Atman is the real vision of Jagannath.' What a tremendous idea—a big enjoyable yearly celebration to
teach the hundreds of thousands who attend it a religious truth like
that!

Gundica temple is relatively simple and is almost abandoned except
during the annual visitation week. There was no question about my
getting in—no question from any human source at least. But one of the
features of Aunt's House is the herd of cows that cluster around the
entrance gate, butting every visitor, keeping him from approaching,
until he has bought and treated them to a few handfuls of grass. For this
nice touch one must not, of course, blame the cows. They are, like the
organ grinder's monkey, the tools of their trainers, in this case the grass
sellers. Inside, the place is empty, a vacant stage showing where the
deity stands during the time of his visit. Before the big week each year,
surrounded by hundreds of devotees, Chaitanya himself in ecstatic love
used to scrub away the dust and cobwebs of the temple of Gundica.
The disciples said, 'Thus he shows us how one's tarnished heart must
be cleansed before God can step in.'

We visited the room where Chaitanya lived the eighteen years he was
a resident of Puri. A Chaitanya Order monastery has been built around
it since. As we went in we saluted the abbot, who was sitting on a plat-

form at the entrance, smiling, greeting everybody, and telling openly the longest string of the biggest prayer beads you ever saw. No reaching into a bead-bag for him! The authorities let me touch Chaitanya's sandals, his waterpot, and a piece of clothing he had worn. As we went out, there was the abbot still at his post, watching everything, smiling, still working away at his japam.

It is said that when Sri Chaitanya passed away he just vanished, no trace of his body ever being found. There are three stories of how he died. One version is that he took his departure from Aunt's House. Another is that he merged with the image of Krishna at the Totagopinath temple, a neighbourhood chapel near the place where he lived. I saw the image there and bowed before it—a primitive little representation with an unexplained rent in one limb, reputed to be the place where Chaitanya entered. The third theory is that Chaitanya saw Krishna in the waves of the sea outside the famous bathing place of Svargadwar Ghat. Finding his beloved calling him, he pushed out toward him in the water in a rush of love, never to be seen again.

There are many other sites of interest to pilgrims in Puri: man-made sacred tanks as big as lakes, constructed for the public by estimable kings; historic hermitages like the Puri home of Balaram Bose, where Holy Mother and many of the disciples of Ramakrishna often stayed in the old days; and the Puri math of the Shankara Order. In the latter is a marble statue of Sri Shankara which is worshipped, a seat where the great preacher of non-dualistic Vedanta is supposed to have sat, and—in common with many other shrines throughout India—a salagram stone.

Here, then, was my chance to see, at close range, a salagram stone. I felt that Puri was the right place to investigate this mystery, since one of the features of Jagannath spoken of with deepest reverence was the cache said to be there, in a stone vault behind the deities, of a hundred thousand of them. I remembered too the story of how Khudiram, Rama-krishna's father, before the Master was born, found a salagram in a field and took it home, where it is now and has been for four generations, worshipped as the family deity.

A shrine attendant held it out toward me on its small cushioned throne as I knelt at the altar. It was just a smooth pebble about the size of a plum, black in colour, with a hole in it, and bearing some white markings. Salagrams are natural formations, and this one probably came, as most of them do, from the banks of the River Gandaki, a tributary of the Ganges.

It didn't look like much, and it was hard to see what significance such a thing could have. I didn't understand it then, and I don't yet; but one couldn't say the Indian's regard for the salagram is merely super-stition. 'A curious round stone is the emblem of Vishnu,' explains Swami Vivekananda in his *Inspired Talks*. 'Each morning a priest comes

in, offers sacrifice to the idol, waves incense before it, then puts it to
bed and apologizes to God for worshipping him in that way, because he
can only conceive of him through an image and by means of some
material object.' Sri Ramakrishna, remarking on the fact that the whole
world is nothing but materialized spirit, pointed out that God manifests
himself, however, more in certain things than in others. The salagram
is one of these. To the research-minded M. he said: 'Perhaps you do not
believe in the salagram. "Englishmen" do not believe in it. It doesn't
matter whether you believe in it or not. It can be worshipped as the
emblem of God.'

Several times that day we pass the great portal of Jagannath. It is indeed
the hub of Puri and probably of all Orissa. A veritable carnival surrounds it. Everything is for sale. Hawkers cry their wares. Holy men
address groups of people. Musicians perform and processions pass.
Rickshaw men arrive and depart with worshippers. Here stands a man
looking in through the doorway, up the steps toward where the image
must be, with hands in the namaskar position at his forehead, bowing
forward again and again. There is a steady traffic of people hurrying in
and out. Could I not just slip in, unnoticed in the throng? But I know
that guards wait just inside the entrance, inspecting everyone, especially
uncertain entrants not accompanied by pandas, and many temple police
patrol the grounds.

Swami Jnanaswarupananda reads my thoughts. 'I am trying to
make some arrangement,' he tells me. I feel like a child before Christmas morning. Will it come to pass? Will I get my wish? I feel I cannot
wait another minute to find out.

Here before the gate rises the splendid stone column which originally
adorned Konarak. Just here a Christian preacher once stood years ago,
as Swami Premananda was going in to worship. Pointing toward the
great temple, the missionary was violently condemning idolatry, de-
nouncing the veneration of gods of wood and stone, admonishing the
people in the market place to give up their heathenish ways, promoting
Jesus Christ as the true savior.

The ignorance of the man, and his insulting manner, made Swami
Premananda angry. He bethought himself of a means for driving him
away.

'Hari bol,' he shouted, above the man's raucousness.

'Hari bol,' answered a dozen voices.

'Hari bol again,' cried the Swami.

'*Hari bol!*' This time a thousand joined in. '*Hari bol, Hari bol, Hari
bol.*'

And thus the sermon of the missionary was drowned out completely
by the sound of chanting, and he had to leave.

But that night Sri Ramakrishna appeared to Swami Premananda in a vision and rebuked him. 'Why did you drive the man away?' he asked. 'Do you not know that he was also preaching my name?'

And Swami Premananda sought out the missionary the first thing the next morning, and went to him, and asked his pardon.

'Well, what *is* in there?' I ask Swami Jnanaswarupananda. 'Who *is* Jagannath? This is a Vishnu temple, so I know the image is not that of Shiva, or Kali. Is it Vishnu, or Rama, or Krishna, or who? Chaitanya worshipped Govinda. And anyway, if it is even an aspect of Krishna, how can it be called the total Lord, the Lord of the Universe?'

'Technically,' Swami Jnanaswarupananda answers, 'three images stand in the Jagannath sanctuary. They are crude in workmanship and made of wood from a design whose origin is not known. They are replaced every twelve years with new copies. While the images are thus always comparatively new, they do contain relics which come down from the immemorial past and which are each time transferred to the new copies. Nobody knows what these relics are, since the attendants who transfer them blindfold themselves when doing so.

'The images are, from left to right as the pilgrim approaches, Balaram, Subhadra, and Jagannath. Jagannath is dark and may be said to be Krishna, Balaram being his elder brother, and the little Subhadra in the middle their sister. But this is only one view. A blind man went to Jagannath. He passed the shrine holding out his stick. It rapped against the three images. Then he passed back the other way, but this time the staff touched nothing at all. For you see, God is also formless. There is something a little strange about Jagannath. There is the idea that the Lord in there appears different to everybody—is always what the worshipper wants him to be. He takes the form of the observer's Ideal. That is why he can be called rightly the Lord of the Universe.'

It is now sunset. The date is January 29, 1953. It is full moon tonight, and there is a partial eclipse. An auspicious evening. Everyone will be going to Jagannath. I wait in my upper room for my panda's assistant. Across the sand the water becomes scarlet and then purple, a clean breeze coming in across it. The sounds of twilight rise: a barking dog, the ringing of temple bells, someone chanting in rolling Sanskrit. I have taken a careful bath and put on my freshest brahmachari dress. In a few minutes I am starting for Jagannath. Several from the ashrama accompany me, including a brahmachari named Sunil.

By bicycle rickshaws we advance to the temple square. What a throng! The panda comes out to meet us, billed on the souvenir leaflet he gives me afterwards as: Ramakrishna Paramahamsa's Panda, late Brindaban Chandra Singhari Mahapatra's son, late Krishna Chandra Singhari Mahapatra's son Sri Vitachha Madhusudan Singhari Mahapatra. Sri Vita is only sixteen years old, but is a principal panda nevertheless, as he has inherited the position from his father, who has recently died.

We leave our shoes in the rickshaws and stand outside gathering our forces. Parades with bands march about. The setting is like the moment in a political convention when a Presidential candidate has been nominated.

I am very excited and rather frightened. We lock hands and drive in through the gate, fighting against the crowds coming out. Up the great flight of steps we race, and around to the left to push our way in through the side door of the pilgrims' entrance hall. Doormen there struggle to hold back the crowd, but we wriggle inside. Sri Vita and helper are as experienced at this sort of thing as New Yorkers are at a Macy's dollar day.

In the vast stone chamber there is simply bedlam. Everyone is yelling, gesturing, jumping up and down to catch a sight of the distant deities. There they are, far up ahead where the torches flare. Everyone is pushing in that direction. I feel I am in a cinema mob scene, very realistic, of epic proportions. But there are no cunning theatrics here. This *is* a mob, and the dangers of getting hurt are very real. And if I should be discovered for what I am, something really serious could develop. The temple policemen, I have been told, are ignorant and passionate fellows.

At one time like this Sri Chaitanya stood somewhere here. On that occasion too the crowd was enormous, with everyone straining to have his darshan. A respectable young lady was so eager to see the images that, unconscious of what she was doing, she climbed up on Chaitanya's back to get a fuller view. And the Golden One broke down and wept, because her devotion was so great and his was so small; he had not gotten up on anybody.

Now, with our party forming a closed circle, we make the assault straight ahead into the shrine. A heavy log like a telephone pole bars the way. It is meant to valve back the multitude. But we crawl under, pass down a step or two, and continue to fight forward. The heat and noise are intense. Very tall ushers, who stand head and shoulders above most of us, reach out with batons, to rap on the head everyone within reach. At the time I thought this was the Jagannath method for keeping the crowds moving. But afterwards I was told that this is a traditional act, symbolizing the driving away of ignorance.

Now they are right in front of us, three big figures on a stage: Balaram, Subhadra, Jagannath. The images have an unfinished look, as their limbs are of sticks and their heads are but engraved plaques painted with crude features. Except that they are larger, they are like dolls a child might fashion. Jagannath's face is dark, as was Krishna's; the faces of the others light. The figures are dressed in robes and laden with garlands. In the old stories, Balaram was Krishna's elder brother, Subhadra their sister. According to one of the many interpretations of the Jagannath figures, this is what they represent. Balaram is the 'matchmaker' who brings man to God and God to man. For man's good the incarnation always attends himself with such an intermediary. When God came as Rama, Lakshmana played the role of go-between. For Buddha, Ananda was intercessor; for Krishna, Balaram; for Ramakrishna, Vivekananda. Subhadra is Mahamaya, the cosmic Illusionist who spins, out of practically nothing, maya and bodies—the medium and the means for progressing toward our realization. And Jagannath is the divine Abstraction. Impute to him your aspiration, supply the details according to your need, and he will come true for you in that way.

What do I see at Jagannath? My revelation is not great, but it is something. I see the permissiveness, the total reciprocity of the Lord. He is not a difficult and absolute standard, like an iron shoe, into which everyone must force his soul. He is flexible, comfortable. I see that God allowed at Jagannath the therapeutic advantages of free association long before Freud; and that the much-maligned idols of the Hindus are his form of ink-blot test—into which you may read what is in your mind —available millennia before Rorschach. Except, of course, that every grade is a passing grade on his device. The Lord of Vedanta is as sensible as a good dietitian, who adjusts the nourishment to the needs of the constitution; or a modern teacher catering to individual differences, fitting the goal to the abilities of his children, and the assignment to their interests. I see this and I like it immensely. Now *there* is a God who really is a God!

Of course to get this idea takes but a moment. My main feeling is one of naked terror before incalculable power. God's mountain has turned into the hugest dam, and his cave has become the powerhouse in its depths where an awful generator whirls, that would suck me in and electrocute me. Yet the feeling is not unpleasant; it is delicious. Electrocute and see if I care! Delicious, like feeling yourself falling improbably, fatally in love.

To the left we move, and around to the right behind the images, through a narrow stone corridor. How wet the floor is—it always is wet in Hindu shrines because the offering of water is part of the ritualism— and how slippery the going is in there under my bare feet. The lofty interior of the tower fades up out of sight above me, and the wall of stone to the right is the rear of the vault that holds the lakh of salagrams. Back across the front again, to emerge through a side door. Around the temple compound on the run. No use straining the luck that has kept me from being noticed. Circling to the right we move, saluting at a few of the more than a hundred subsidiary chapels which surround the main temple like stupas in the yard of a Buddhist sanctuary. Before I know it we are back down on the street, breathless and joyful, standing at our rickshaws, feeding each other a rice pudding called payas Sri Vita has brought—the efficacious prasad of Jagannath which is the nearest thing on earth to Brahman. It feels as if a century has passed; yet the whole experience cannot have consumed five minutes.

I am all broken up. As Sunil and I ride home side by side in our rickshaw, I keep sighing and swallowing. I, a boy from Lansing, Michigan, have been through Jagannath. I have had about the biggest darshan there is. I have seen that which transfixed Shankara, Ramanuja, Madhva, Kabir, and my dear Chaitanya. I have made my pilgrimage to, and received the benediction of, the Lord of the Universe. How lucky can a person be!

The next day Sri Vita's aide comes to the ashrama. I pay him the honorarium of fifteen rupees and sign my Anglo-Saxon name to my panda's register. He gives me a strip of Jagannath's robe as a memento. That night I take the train for Calcutta, back to Belur Math.

But something had modified in me. First Ramakrishna's room at Dakshineswar, which made me an aspirant. Then Jagannath, which gave me a hint of how excellently much there is to aspire to. I sit here now, years later, with Jagannath's picture before me, that bit of orange robe adorning it, and I feel like a patient having undergone shock treatment. All the atoms of my mind were blown sky-high that night, like popping corn, never to settle down in quite the old design. A new conception of God has unfolded—that he must be very *tangible*. A real world, with its own constellations of experience and delight, must be just there, beneath this mountain, within this cave. With the guru as panda, one may enter his Jagannath, push ahead to its shrine, and light the torch of recognition before him.

CHAPTER VIII

THE NORTH AND
THE HIMALAYAS

I RETURNED from South India at the end of January and stayed at Belur Math through the great Ramakrishna birthday celebration of February 15-22, then went up through the north and left India by air from New Delhi in early April. While at Belur Math I made a side trip to up-country Bengal, where I visited Kamarpukur and Jayrambati, and the boyhood home of Swami Prabhavananda. I am going to vary the chronology in the chapters which follow, however, telling of the north and the Himalayas in the present one; about the countryside of Sri Ramakrishna's birth and childhood in Chapter IX; and last of all about the exciting Ramakrishna birthday time, with which final chapter I shall conclude the narrative.

The pilgrim destinations which remained to me were Gaya, Benares, and Brindaban in the north-central plains of India, and Hardwar and Rishikesh to the northwest at the Ganges gateway to the Himalayas. I also spent a week at the Advaita Ashrama in the Himalayas, which is not a pilgrim spot but is a place every member of the Order must find interesting because of the associations there with Swami Vivekananda and other early personalities of the work.

I have already written a great deal about the science of darshan and the value of pilgrimages in instilling some spiritual 'vibrations' into a person who goes on them. Sri Ramakrishna compared holy places to bodies of water. 'You may be sure,' he said, 'that there is God's manifestation in those spots where people have practised spiritual disciplines a great deal. The thought of God has become, so to speak, solidified there. Water is ever present, no doubt, and can be had by digging anywhere; but it is more accessibly present in wells and lakes.'

Yet from another standpoint Sri Ramakrishna made light of pilgrimages. He often said, 'One who has it here [in the heart] has it there; one who has it not here has it nowhere'. In other words, if devotion is unfolding, the process will be enhanced by association with holy places; but if it is not, no amount of traipsing about to temples and shrines will do much good. The Master used to laugh about those young men, experiencing a momentary enthusiasm for religion, who rush off to Benares or some other sacred spot to renounce the world; but who in a few weeks have settled down, opened a business, and are sending home money regularly to their parents. Of his own experience in Benares and Brindaban in 1868 he said, 'I thought I should find everyone in Benares merged in samadhi, in the meditation of Shiva all the twenty-four hours; and all in Brindaban beside themselves with devotion and divine love in the company of Krishna! But when I was there I found everything just the same as anywhere.'

But mainly the Master meant that everything can be found within one's own self. In 1886 Narendra experienced a rush of religious impatience and had gone briefly to Gaya, to the site of Buddha's enlightenment. Like Buddha, he apparently intended to remain beneath the Bodhi Tree, letting the body be sacrificed if need be, in the attempt to get his illumination. Everyone was upset at Narendra's absence except Sri Ramakrishna, who said, 'Why be anxious? Where will he go? Although you go to the far corners of the earth you will find no true spirituality there outside. Whatever there is, is here.' He indicated his own body, meaning, it seems probable, within himself—by taking refuge in God. One of Sri Ramakrishna's favourite songs, which you encounter again and again in his Gospel, is this:

> Why should I journey to the Ganges or Gaya,
> To Conjeevaram, Benares, or elsewhere,
> So long as I may have upon my lips
> The name of Mother till I die?

But since Sri Ramakrishna never did anything without there being a meaning in it, we must conclude that he went to Benares and Brindaban for a purpose. Swami Saradananda, in his *Sri Ramakrishna the Great Master*, suggests these as the reasons: to add the darshan of his own presence to the darshan already there—that is, to reinforce the spiritual atmosphere, as it were; and through independent verification, to confirm as true the pilgrim's faith in and beliefs about these places.

The spots of interest at Gaya are two—the site of the Bodhi Tree a few miles outside the city, and the Sri Gadadhar or Vishnu temple in Gaya proper. I went to both.

The place of Buddha's nirvana is marked by an old temple behind which is a pipal tree said to be a descendant of the very one which shaded Buddha; a stone slab marks the supposed exact spot where the

Enlightened One is believed to have taken his determined seat. An old text describes the scene: 'Here at Budh-gaya Gautama sat down in a cross-legged position, firm and immovable as if welded with a hundred thunderbolts; then the evil Mara came against him mounted on his elephant 250 leagues in height, and hurled at him great mountains. The mountains as they reached him turned into bouquets of heavenly flowers, and the mighty elephant itself fell down on its knees in worship. And so the Great One finally obtained enlightenment, at which lotus wreaths hung from the sky, and the great ocean itself became sweet down to its profoundest depths, and the rivers were stayed in their course.'

The area thereabouts is one of the few centres of Buddhism remaining in India, with Tibet, China, Japan, Ceylon, Burma, and other Buddhist countries having representatives and pilgrim hostels on the spot. The Tibetan monks interested me. These were big men with wide, flat, smiling faces. They walked around in rather tattered woollen garments of brown and orange, telling their beads openly, often while talking to one another. Some wore quilted snow boots. I went to their monastery and into their temple. One saw prayer wheels beautifully fashioned from coloured tinsel paper, made to revolve by the warm current rising from little lamps. The place held a marvellous accumulation of bright silks, brocades, jars, murals, and brass and silver vessels.

The other important spot at Gaya is Sri Gadadhar. This ancient shrine is one of the most important temples of Hinduism and was named, along with Vishwanath in Benares, as a place where one should certainly 'feel something'. Gadadhar, it will be remembered, was the temple to which Sri Ramakrishna's father, Khudiram, in 1835, as countless Indians had done before him and do to this day, travelled to discharge his duties to his departed ancestors by offering food and drink there in the name of Lord Vishnu. Even the prehistoric Rama is said to have performed at Gaya the obsequies of his parents. It was here that Khudiram had his vision that God would be born as a son to him; and it was for this reason that the baby who was to become Sri Ramakrishna was named Gadadhar.

Gadadhar temple is a cluster of buildings surrounded by a stout wall, running downhill to the edge of a now dried-up river. My experience at Lingaraj made me leery of attempting to enter any temple where there might be some problem as to my acceptability. But I felt it would be a shame to miss such an important holy place, and was assured by the local devotee who was my guide that we could manage if we were quick about it. I changed to dhoti and chadar, and since I was in Gaya only between trains without any place to leave it, or any pocket about me in which to place it, slid my big wallet containing passport, money, and traveller's cheques down inside my shirt.

There is a great variation in the plan of Hindu temples and especially in the deities enshrined. I thought I had seen everything, but when we entered the holy of holies at Sri Gadadhar to find the deity a yard-wide circular pit with people sitting on the floor and reaching into it, I was more than mystified. There was, however, no time to lose, so I knelt down and reached in, too, my fingers touching what I saw to be, somewhat obscured by water and rice offerings, a right footprint in the head of the massive rock on which the shrine appeared to be built. (The tradition is that Vishnu overpowered a demon here by placing his foot upon its head. The demon turned to stone and the footprint remains— veritably God's.) But it was all a blurr really, for at that moment I felt my wallet sliding upward, and the thought of what would happen should such an act of irreverence occur as allowing anything made of leather to touch a Vaishnava shrine almost made me faint. I remember clutching the bulge beneath my shirt, rising, and nearly bumping into a cow which was standing there right in the sanctuary serenely regarding everything; and having the funny thought that it all depends, whether it is profane or not, upon what form cowhide is in.

Benares proved to be all I had expected of it. It was different from any other large city I visited in India, in that no Westernization seems to have occurred there at all. For example, I was able to buy the airmail overseas edition of *Time* magazine easily everywhere else, but not in Benares. I went to the Benares Hindu University, to the Cantonment railway station, and even to that last remnant of the British occupation, Clark's Hotel; but not a copy was to be found anywhere. Yet again, the sight of a Westerner in brahmachari dress attracted less attention in Benares than anywhere else I went. Perhaps this was because the people are so used to variety there that they are beyond reacting to any new kind of freakishness. Dwarfs, women swamis, camels and elephants, sadhus in every state of nudity and ornamentation, the halt, the lame, and the blind, Moslem ladies in their ruffled mobile tents, persons in palanquins, dead bodies—all these and many more crowd the bazaars and ghats.

I bought a guidebook and map and was able to locate everything pretty well. Some of the time a brahmachari friend from Bangalore, Raoji, was with me. I avoided all the temples, however, especially the two main ones, Annapurna and Vishwanath, until such time as I could be properly conducted inside them; for Benares is not only most orthodox but has suffered perhaps more than any other place from the desecrations of outsiders. I spent hours along the ghats, going as early as 4.30 a.m. There may be some manufacturing in Benares and other kinds of secular activity, but I didn't see much. The main life of the city is concerned with religion and pilgrim activities and seems to be carried on at the ghats or near them, and in the temples which line the Ganges just behind and above the ghats.

The situation of Benares reminded me a little of that of Laguna Beach. It is mainly on a ridge of high ground stretching about three miles along a curving water's edge. It has been compared to the crescent moon above

Shiva's forehead. You can stand at either terminus of the city on the Ganges bank and see along the riverside clear up and down to the other end. They say that at times of high water the metropolis gives the illusion of floating. When I was there the water was low, so that at the bottom of some of the ghats and fortress-like riverside buildings there was dry ground.

With all this concentration of life on the north bank I was surprised to see that the area just across the narrowish stream is unpopulated—mere farm lands. The reason for this, it seems, is that a tradition exists to the effect that entering into Benares, like laying claim to the liberation which one may get by so doing, must be steadfastly undertaken. To be outside looking in—so near and yet so far—must be as hideous to a feeling man as Tantalus's condition, who was condemned to abide, famished and thirsting, in sight of food and drink forever just out of reach.

Even though there are no really old buildings in Benares, the ancient Hindu temples having been demolished by the Moslem invaders, the city looks most ancient. This is mainly true in the old section along the Ganges and particularly between the Vishwanath temple and the river. Much of the construction for thousands of years has been concentrated into this tiny space, so that there are things built on top of things, a picturesque and chaotic jumble, going down to the water. Flood tides and neglect have caused ruination at the river's bank, with hillsides, parts of buildings and walls, and in one case a complete small temple now slowly settling into the water. I happened to have a copy of Aldous Huxley's *Those Barren Leaves* with me and marked this passage, which he wrote to picture Perugia in Italy, and which could also describe the heart of Benares: '. . . they plunged into the labyrinth of steep alleys, of winding passage-ways and staircases behind the cathedral. Built confusedly on the hillside, the tall houses seemed to grow into one another, as though they were the component parts of one immense and fantastical building, in which the alleys served as corridors. The road would burrow through the houses in a long dark tunnel, to widen out into a little well-like courtyard, open to the sky.'

Much of the importance of Benares is based upon the belief that salvation is assured if you die there. And that salvation is granted by the great Lord Shiva whose seat is the Vishwanath temple. Hence Benares is filled with old people, chiefly—since women, it appears, outlive men in India as they do in the United States—widows. These can be seen, often with shaved heads and white saris, sitting along the ghats or climbing the steps to the temples, carrying brass pots filled with Ganges water to offer to the temple deities. The day of such a retired person—in accordance with the sanctions of the third stage of life of Hindu dharma—goes like this: a period of japam upon waking, a dawn bath in the Ganges, attendance upon a temple, a light meal at noon—the one meal of the day—siesta, japam in the afternoon, a return to the river toward sunset to hear the scriptures being read and explained, vespers at a temple, more japam, and bed.

One of the names of Benares is City of Gold. The treasure of all India has poured into Benares for so many ages, to build there temples and shrines to the glory of God, that indeed this name is an apt one. But Benares is a city of gold for yet another reason. So many of India's saints have journeyed there to walk in its streets and bathe from its ghats, there has been so much prayer and chanting and reading from the scriptures in Benares, and so much holy dying there, that the whole place is alight with faith. Buddha's first sermon, for example, was given at Sarnath, nearby. This quality at least Sri Ramakrishna was able to see in Benares; he spoke of the city as hardly material at all, but rather as composed of pure sattwa guna, of purity and truth. So tangible to him were these vibrations of luminosity that oftentimes during his stay, out of respect, he betook himself beyond the city limits when answering calls of nature.

The ghats presented a varied scene. There was an atmosphere of Muscle Beach, California, about them, in that some of the sadhus who made their residence in huts nearby were youthful and given to per-formances of body-building exercises. One caught as well the feeling of St. Petersburg, Florida's ocean front. Especially in the late afternoon one would see them, rows and rows of little old white figures, the widows, sitting quietly, facing someone giving a lecture or singing. And there was something of Coney Island about the ghats, too. Boat rides were obtainable; foods of all kinds were to be bought; you could have your fortune told; flower garlands were for sale; and if you wanted a guide for sightseeing, a mere look of uncertainty was enough to bring one to your side.

Muscle Beach, St. Petersburg, Coney Island—all are there. But in one regard Benares is Benares and cannot remind you of any other place in the world: the night-and-day business at the burning ghats, rendered all the more grandly sombre by the nearby noisy water antics of the youngsters of the town and all the merry commerce of the busy river.

It was my custom when the Indian cuisine grew too monotonous, to put on Western clothes and go to a European-style hotel to eat. In Benares it was Clark's. Clark's is also where American tourists alight for a brief moment to 'do Benares' en route from Delhi to Calcutta. I was there when one US couple arrived. The sleepy atmosphere quickened. The staff grew attentive. Several men who had been dozing in the garden moved forward to spread cloths on the ground and to arrange thereon souvenir wares of ivory, brass, embroidery. A snake-charmer opened his baskets to let two fat cobras slide out. In the Americans dashed, their loud voices, their well-clothed persons, the terrible assurance that years of substantial food and prosperity bring, as shocking in that atmosphere as a thunderclap on a still summer day. The Mohammedan guide who was to show the tourists the sights of Hinduism waited at his 1937 Ford sedan. The woman introduced herself to me; they were from Burbank, California, and were too thankful for words, she said, to see someone else from home. The husband was in the garden enthusiastically aiming his movie camera, shouting to the cobra trainer, 'No, higher, higher. They won't show up at all. Make them dance higher. Another rupee if you can make them dance higher.' Then a rush to the desk to send telegrams and airmail letters, a dash to the bar for refreshments, and a dart to the restaurant for a quick lunch; then off in the impossible 2.00 p.m. sun, to see the holy city of Benares before catching the evening plane.

Late that afternoon, back in dhoti and chadar, anonymous in the throng on the Ganges bank, I spied the Burbank friends majestically skirting the ghats in a tall river boat. Her eyes met mine. Oh no! She poked her husband and pointed. Oh no, it couldn't be. And yet? A last sight of them looking back, with puzzled frowns.

One day as I idle at the ghats I watch a group of youngsters operating an ingenious toll system at a principal ghat entrance. Over a wire stretched between the second-story windows of two facing houses they have thrown a string with a hook on it. Along comes a prosperous citizen, perhaps saying his prayers, unaware of anything except that he is approaching the sacred river. The boys lounge in attitudes of indifference. Then at the right moment the hook is lowered to catch the man's chadar and pull it from his shoulders. A quick jerk and it is up in the air, just beyond arm's reach. The innocents skip about in glee. The citizen sheds his dignity, rails and threatens, and makes futile little jumps in an attempt to pull down the chadar. The boys jeer and demand their price. Finally capitulation. A small ransom is paid and the cloth is lowered. The citizen settles the chadar around his shoulders with an abused shrug, tries to collect his thoughts again, and marches on toward the stream.

I never got inside Annapurna, the temple of the bountiful world Mother, but I did enter Vishwanath and actually touched the 'head' of Shiva there. This lingam is perhaps the most highly regarded deity in perhaps the most highly regarded temple of all India. Thus I have had that privilege which millions of Indians aspire to all their lives.

It happened on the evening of Holi, the springtime festival of colour when everyone flings at everyone else red powder or squirts of coloured water. The whole town was out that evening. People and animals looked as though they had been victimized by some unskilled tie-and-dye batik worker. And every living thing in Benares seemed to be trying to make his way through the tiny alley that leads to Vishwanath.

Several of the monks from the Math went with me. We pushed through the lane and into this most holy temple of Hinduism. Unlike the huge temples in the south, Vishwanath consists of nothing but a small pilgrim chamber and a shrineroom perhaps not more than twelve or fifteen feet square. The ages-old former Vishwanath temple was torn down long ago by Moslems and a mosque built of its material on the old site. The present temple is about two hundred years old and was squeezed into an inadequate plot as near the old spot as could be—just, in fact, in the shadow of the mosque. We crowded in through the outer hall, giving a good clang, as custom requires, on the row of bells that hang above the entrance. Then into the sanctuary. Thousands pass through this place daily, to pour water and place flowers on the lingam, and reverently to touch it. The deity is of black stone some eighteen inches high. A recess surrounds it about four feet square, enclosed with a railing of silver. The recess is usually, quite naturally, full of water in which the offered flowers float.

We watched arati from the temple gallery—actually a porch on the second floor of a house across the lane, a few feet away from the temple's famed gold roof. What a tremendous ritual! Half a dozen priests—long hair drawn back in the brahmin's knot, chests bare except for the diagonal sacred cord—seated themselves in the shrineroom while the excited, noisy crowd pressed close. Many offerings were made to the Reality represented by the lingam: a big bowlful of sandal paste, flower garland after flower garland, leaves, water, coconut water, ghee, yogurt, honey. A silver frame with erect silver cobras was fitted around the lingam, and it too was bedecked. Sanskrit mantras sounded, bells were rung; there was a drum beating and the waving of many lights. At the end all the priests threw handfuls of Holi powder up in the air, which filled the room with a vermilion mist, colouring them and the deity alike.

I have no idea what it all meant. I didn't understand and I didn't, unfortunately, even 'feel' anything. In his ignorance one might regard such a performance as a huge drollery. But there remained the undeniable fact of verification. Many had seen and had felt something. And I remembered Swami Vivekananda's remarks about the matter in his lecture called 'The Ideal of a Universal Religion': 'It is good for you to remember, in this country especially, that the world's great spiritual giants have all been produced only by those religious sects which have been in possession of very rich mythology and ritual. The greatest men I have seen in my life, the most wonderfully developed in spirituality, have all come through the discipline of these rituals.'

I also did another main thing one is supposed to do at Benares—I bathed in the Ganges to wash my 'sins' away. Of course a little sprinkling with Ganges water is purifying; but immersion, some feel, is even more beneficial. My courage failed me at the crowded ghats, however. Too much rubbish along the shore for one thing; and for another I felt ashamed of the awful pallidness of my skin in contrast to the lovely natural suntans of everyone else. So Raoji and I hired a boat and went out to the middle where I swam for a few minutes. The water was clean and not too cold. It was only as I was leaving India weeks later that I found out this gesture had missed producing any merit. Since, as one would do when he is swimming in deep water, I had kept my head up, I had missed the point of the whole act. You have to submerge yourself completely in the Ganges if a Ganges immersion is to count!

The cremation activities of Benares interested me enormously. Walking through the lanes near the river, you may be brought to attention by loud calling behind you and the bouncy tune of a three-piece band. Then stand aside, for it is a funeral procession. The body goes past on a bamboo stretcher covered with a clean white cloth. At the front of one procession I saw, ahead of the band, a man with a bagful of small coins, which he was tossing to the people in the roadways. This is supposed to be an indication of the wealth of the departed and an act of charity.

The whole burning procedure was far less repellent than I had imagined. It appealed to me as possessing a civilized dignity, a sense of aseptic good taste, proportionate to the stark fact of death. But I think you have to be a realist to feel this. For there is no pretty scenery at Manikarnika Ghat, no recorded light classical music oozing from shrubbery to distract you, not a single reassuring motto carved on statuary. *This is a thing.* What made it a person has vanished. This thing is unfit for human society and is growing more unfit every minute. Get rid of it in the most efficient way possible.

About seven maunds—around five hundred pounds—of wood are used in the average cremation. This costs about ten to fifteen rupees, depending on the kind. Bel and mango are preferred. With such a good quantity of fuel a large and hot fire can be made. Wood is placed above as well as below the body; thus the onlooker cannot see anything horrible, and besides the corpse becomes blackened and undistinguishable from the burning brands in a short time. Two hours are required to consume most of the body. The abdominal section takes the longest, two additional hours being needed to burn that. Especially large pieces of fuel are placed beneath this section originally, which continue to burn longer than the rest.

I did not see much of priestly participation or even much of mourning families. Just twice, though, I witnessed paroxysms of grief which surpassed anything ever seen at an American funeral. Both were on the part of women, who tore at their clothes, threw themselves on the ground, and screamed terribly, so that they had to be forcibly restrained. Perhaps such manifestations are partly custom; but they also may be more healing in the long run than Anglo-Saxon restraint.

For him who dies in Benares, it is his last birth. This is the tradition. Some say it is one's sure faith that the Lord will indeed deliver him if he dies in Benares that causes God's grace thus to work. Some explain it in this way, that you are not drawn to residence in Benares if you have not pretty well completed your spiritual struggle anyway. Conversely, it is said that if your karma has not as yet been pretty well worked through, you will not succeed in dying in Benares, however hard you try. Examples are given of persons waiting in Benares for years, only to step outside the city briefly on some trifling errand, to promptly expire.

So strong is their faith that they are nearing nirvana that many of the old people living in Benares look forward to death quite happily. The Ramakrishna Order maintains an ashrama in the city for elderly monks. I remember how one, Swami Divyananda, used to say to me in the merriest way: 'I have had one heart attack. In a few weeks the hot weather will come on and the temperature will rise to 122, 123, 124. I will probably have another heart attack and die.' In the most casual, good-humoured way he told me this.

Sri Ramakrishna, it will be remembered, confirmed this belief about Benares through his own mystic vision. Standing in a boat outside Manikarnika Ghat he saw a tall, white person with tawny matted hair—Shiva—walking with solemn steps to each pyre, raising tenderly each soul, and whispering into his ear the mantra of the supreme Brahman; while on the other side of the pyre he saw the universal Mother sitting, untying all remaining knots of samskara, or karmic debt, opening with her own hands the door to liberation.

When they heard the content of this vision the local pundits said respectfully to Sri Ramakrishna: 'It is written in the scriptures in general terms that any soul dying here is granted liberation. But it has never been stated exactly in what manner this was done. Your vision has supplied the modus operandi. Your experience has confirmed, has gone beyond, and has supplemented the scriptures.'

Anyone fond of Swami Vivekananda wants to see the Advaita Ashrama at Mayavati. Especially anyone from the West, since one of Swamiji's ideas in starting this Himalayan retreat was to provide a residence in a temperate climate for Europeans and Americans whom, in his words, he did not want to kill 'by forcing on them the Indian mode of living and the fiery plains'. It was to be a centre of work and meditation, he said, 'where my Indian and Western disciples can live together, and them I shall train as workers, the former to go out as preachers of Vedanta to the West, and the latter will devote their lives to the good of India'.

In the some sixty years since its founding, the first of Swamiji's objectives for Mayavati has been fulfilled. Many of the present leaders of Western Vedanta societies are Mayavati alumni. But the dream that American and European Vedantists should live and work in India has as yet materialized but in slight degree. It is not known, of course, just what Swamiji had in mind or when he expected this development to work out. The lack of those material fundamentals the Westerner has known since his birth and his consequent susceptibility to physical breakdown—even in a place like Mayavati where some concessions to Western ways are a part of the tradition—make math life for him in India a hard undertaking. And what can the Westerner do in India to help Indians anyway, beyond demonstrating a few technical skills— which is probably done better by the foreign aid programme of the US government or the agents of Western charitable foundations? I was to discuss this topic later with Gurudas Maharaj—Swami Atulananda— one of the few examples to date of a Western devotee spending long years in India with genuine success.

Also, perhaps the Western mind is too set on distraction for easy adjustment to India. Certainly it can be questioned whether this mind is up to the asceticism of Mayavati. The place is so remote, so devoid of any atmosphere of man and maya, as to be genuinely frightening. Even the Indian Swami who was to become its sixth president felt this way about the Advaita Ashrama at first. Writes Swami Pavitrananda in the January, 1950, *Prabuddha Bharata*: '. . . I found the silence of the place quite oppressive. . . . I confess I was seized with some unknown fear. . . . the next day's experience also was no better. In the morning, after breakfast, as I sat in a relaxing mood on the bench in the veranda out- side, I felt as though I was a prisoner in that place and as I looked at the surrounding hills, I felt as if they were prison walls. . . . But as days passed by and I began to enter into the spirit of the place I liked it more and more, and no monotony seized me.'

Is there a hint in this highland country of what jnana is like? May there be found in this awesome sensation of divestiture a suggestion of how it feels to follow the yoga of knowledge? A shocking mode for the average aspirant, indeed—the paths of love or work or meditation being far less demanding. Yet this is what Swamiji intended for Mayavati. There would be no dualism practised there, no worship of aspects or incarnations. The Advaita Ashrama in the Himalayan impersonality of its setting should forever keep fresh the Himalayan formula of non-dualism: All this is not; God is.

It takes three days to get to Mayavati from Benares, and two days again to, as they call it, 'come down'. You take the train north from Benares to Lucknow, then change to a narrow-gauge railway, which carries you west and north again to a town called Pilibhit. Here Mongolian types begin to appear. One can tell from the gypsy style of dress on the women, the more frequent use of wool, the Chinese cast to the face, that one is approaching Nepal and Tibet. From Pilibhit a very small train saunters up the last few miles of the plains which tilt north to the foothills of the

Himalayas. The end of the line is Tanakpur, and here one waits overnight for the 'up' bus which leaves at dawn. A drab town, practically
closed down in the summer, because of heat and malaria. One sees
many wandering sadhus at Tanakpur on their way into the mountains.
On the opposite bank of the stream which skirts the town is Nepal.
Crossing the river are lines of little Nepalese men—identical in dust-
coloured pyjama suits and peaked caps like so many brownies—carrying
on their backs into poor India from poorer Nepal, goods which they
hope to sell.

I have written in previous chapters of bus trips. Now ahead of me was
one more, also formidable, from Tanakpur to Lohaghat, sixty miles
away and six thousand feet up, where one gets out for Mayavati. (In
Swamiji's time one walked to Mayavati, or went by horseback or palanquin.) For safety's sake all vehicles navigate the mountain roads in
convoys. They go together also because there is in this hundred miles or
so of mountain trail hardly any place wide enough to allow passing, so
that it is necessary for all the up traffic to get through in the morning,
in order to allow the down traffic to use the road in the afternoon. The
convoy plan is necessary no doubt, but in practice it requires all travellers,
with the exception of those in the leading vehicle, to breathe dust the
entire ascent.

A wild ride, with thousand-foot drops a few inches from the front
wheels. But lovely scenery all the way. Views of deep valleys, of ice-
water rivers, of blood-red rhododendrons contrasting with the fresh
green of young grain plants in the terraced fields. The houses are of stone
with slate roofs and decorations of carved wood, looking surprisingly
Swiss.

Lohaghat at 2.00 in the afternoon. Rama Chaitanya and Brahmachari
Madhav are waiting for me, with a pony to carry my luggage the three
and a half miles up to the math. I think the boys are happy, after the
cold and lonesome winter, to have a visitor from the outside world.
There will be others as the summer comes on, but I am the first this
spring.

The boys have brought a thermos bottle of hot coffee. We sit down in
a stony upland pasture bright with Alpine wildflowers and enjoy a cup
of it. Hills above and below. The bell at the pony's neck jangles merrily
as he munches grass. It is like a scene in *Heidi*.

'But the snow-capped Himalayas?' I question. 'Where are they?'

'Out there to the north,' Madhav points. 'Maybe fifty miles to the
north. Any cloudiness in between obscures them. Sometimes they don't
appear for weeks at a time, but I hope you will be lucky.'

'Oh yes,' I answer, 'I must see the snow range. To miss that after
coming this far would be an awful blow.'

First the coffee, then the British look of the old tea-plantation buildings when we reach the Advaita Ashrama, make me feel at home. Comfortable late Victorian, it all is, like Captain Sevier and Mother Sevier must have been—the English disciples of Swamiji who founded Mayavati. How good it feels to walk and sit upon wood floors after months of nothing but cement and stone! I am given as quarters the famous old publication office of *Prabuddha Bharata* where such eminent former editors as Swamis Yatiswarananda, Ashokananda, and Pavitrananda in years gone by worked and lived. In the room beneath, the first hand-set editions of Swamiji's works and life were printed on a press lugged all the way up here from the world below.

There are six people in residence—three swamis, the two brahmacharis, and the doctor in charge of the small mountain hospital run by the math. There are, besides, a number of servants to help with the housework and care for the kitchen gardens maintained on the terraced slopes. The Tibetan-looking scullery boy, Jaydev, a born scamp, greets me every time he sees me with a grand bow and an amused English 'Good morning'.

I take several walks in the hills with *Prabuddha Bharata*'s then current editor, Narayan Maharaj, Swami Vandanananda. I know that he is an almost certain candidate for an assignment to America. (He eventually becomes assistant in Hollywood.) We talk very often about work in the West. He speaks of the frequently encountered idea that a major requisite for a swami in America and Europe is unusually good speaking ability. 'But we don't feel that way at all,' I remark. 'The United States is full of entertaining speakers—whom probably no foreigner could hope to excel anyway. The only thing that will make an impression in America, we all feel, is the example of a genuine holy life.'

Then one day it happens. Without prelude, noiselessly, the curtain parts, and there it is, the awesome tableau of white silent peaks stretching from extreme left across the horizon to extreme right. More than 25,000 feet high, some of them. All day the vision remains, as of some reclining, slowly breathing God. Sunkissed but cold, inviting yet alarming, the most advaitic sight it is given an earthling to see. And the next morning, gone.

In a comparable location, two hundred miles to the west of Tanakpur and a hundred miles north of Delhi, are Hardwar and Rishikesh. Both are important in the religious life of the Hindu because of their situation at the Ganges gateway to the Himalayas.

At Hardwar the river comes out on to the plains from between two facing hills. It is the objective of the pilgrim to bathe here. A legend tells of a battle between the demons and gods of old for possession of the nectar of immortality. In the contest some of that precious food fell to earth, into the Ganges, it is said, at a spot now in the centre of Hardwar, called the Brahma Kund. Here the river forms a narrow channel, passing the ghats in a cold, clear rush. But, undaunted by its icy temperature, the pilgrim bathes at Brahma Kund all the year. There is a feel of Benares about the place, especially at the vesper hour when the arati bells are ringing in the temples. And one of the pleasant features is the custom in the evening of sending off down the river leaf boats with flower offerings and lighted candles as cargo, as an earnest of one's prayers.

The Brahma Kund is the focal point of that periodic religious festival called the Kumbha Mela—'mêlée' would seem to be the more correct term, I often quipped—attended by several million pilgrims here every twelve years. At the Ramakrishna math near Hardwar during the 1950 Kumbha Mela a thousand guests were housed on the ashrama premises, with eight thousand medical cases being attended to by the math hospital staff.

Rishikesh, sixteen miles upstream, has been since ancient times sought out by renunciates wishing to live in a lonely, sylvan place conducive to the full-time pursuit of God-knowledge. Here in the old days the imperious monk, possessing nothing, depending on God for alms, was monarch. M., the compiler of Sri Ramakrishna's Gospel, maintained a cottage in the woods across the river which can be seen to this day. And there is an old custom which requires men of the Ramakrishna Order, where possible, to spend a while at Rishikesh in concentrated spiritual struggle between the time of taking brahmacharya and application for sannyas, a few huts being maintained by the Order for their use. And remember the aspirant mentioned in the Gospel who became a holy man through the single spiritual discipline of chanting all day, 'How beautiful! How beautiful!', standing wonder-struck in admiration of the Lord's goodness in creating a place like Rishikesh.

Now the sadhu has it easier. Simple facilities for his living are provided by endowment trusts supported by leading citizens from all over India—a kind of Community Chest setup for the sponsorship of spirituality! Field kitchens furnish free meals, and a large camp of simple shelters allows non-cost housing. (For those whose path is absolute possessionlessness, complete nakedness is permitted here.)

And lately Rishikesh has caught on with the general public also. Many ashramas catering to householders have been built on the Ganges edge in the manner of holiday resorts. It is now possible to combine a week-end of relaxed outdoor living with the acquisition of holy vibrations.

One of these ashramas, as a result of widespread advertising in India and abroad, is world-famous. I wanted to see it and its founder, who is depicted in the scores of publications his organization has sponsored— all well illustrated with photos of himself—as a great yogi, even the living incarnation of Shiva. 'He who desires prosperity should worship the Knower of the Self,' says one booklet, a travel guide describing the attractions of the headquarters. 'Nowadays it is a common sight at the Abode of Bliss to witness mass as well as individual worship [of its leader.

He] who stoutly refused to accept such worship three years ago, had to yield to the devotees' almighty will. . . . Through such egoless personality flows divine grace in abundance.' In another place one reads: 'You can have darshan at 9.00 a.m. in the office where he attends to his correspondence work till 11.00 a.m. Tell him frankly all you desire in a few words as he has to attend to a lot of work in the ashram.'

I timed my call so as to reach the Abode of Bliss at the darshan hour, my visit happening to coincide with the arrival of the Ambassador of Thailand, his wife, and a party of friends. We were led into the presence of, as they called him, Gurudev, a big man, reclining in a deck chair, naked from the waist up, entertaining, loaded with personality, and dynamic in spite of a certain fleshiness. The room was crowded, all eyes upon the leader, while a small army of his sannyasin disciples ran about snapping photos, bringing in books for him to autograph, herding people forward and back. Gurudev addressed a few words to each caller, then rose to sing some rather revival-type songs in English, accompanied by little dance steps. At one point some youngsters came in and demonstrated yoga exercises.

Gurudev explained his objective—the making of life pleasant and religion easy. (On the occasion of a visit to the Abode of Bliss by another member of an American Vedanta Society, who was not even a monastic probationer at the time, Gurudev offered immediate sannyas!) 'Through the practice of yoga postures and breathing exercises,' one of his books says, 'you attain longevity, good health, smoothness of skin, and everlasting beauty and youth.'

The Ambassador and his wife prostrated at full length and implored Gurudev's blessings, which he gave in a very frank and hearty way. Movie cameras ground to record the moment. I tiptoed out, remembering once more that in religion as in everything else the old slogan is right: You can have anything you want in this world and usually get exactly what you are willing to pay for.

Going back to Hardwar, at a corner where a small road started up into the hills, I saw a sign that made my pulse quicken: 'To Kedarnath.' Kedarnath, one of the great holy places of India, 12,000 feet up in the Himalayas. Now only March, a pilgrim could never make his way along the 128 miles of trail, the snowy route being passable only from May to September. But I had seen Kedarnath in a movie in Calcutta, a story about a band of pilgrims and their experiences in struggling up to Kedarnath—an account which, though fictional, had been filmed on the actual sites. There was the young girl, making the journey for fun and excitement. Her old chaperone, to fulfil a life's ambition. The fake sadhu, the rascal of the tale. The young man in search of some meaning to his life. Then the thrilling picture of the destination, the old Shiva temple with the great snowy peaks behind it. And finally a long scene taken inside the temple itself where the pilgrims walked around and around the deity—a jut of rock in the centre of the floor—singing a triumphant hymn to express their joy in having reached their heart's goal.

I remembered, too, another story about Kedarnath, of how a certain swami had gone there late in the season, only to find the temple closed and the place cold and deserted. Yet, hating to leave without gaining the darshan of the temple, he waited, wondering what to do. Then a stranger approached him and said, 'Why not wait overnight? You can visit the temple in the morning. We can have a game of dice to pass the time away.' They played all night. When daylight came the stranger told the swami he might now enter the temple and went away. And lo, birds were singing, the snow had gone, mountain flowers were opening, and it was spring. Then the swami perceived that the night he had gamed had been all winter and that his opponent and protector could have been none other than the great Lord Shiva.

In Hollywood, Ida Ansell—Ujjvala—was my special friend. I had first been drawn to this lame old lady because she had known Swami Vivekananda in San Francisco in 1900. Then we came to work together in the Vedanta Society office, so that we became close acquaintances. Every few weeks, I noticed, Ujjvala wrote to India; and as frequently, composed in a small, neat hand, the replies came back. It was Swami Atulananda—Gurudas Maharaj—to whom she wrote and who responded so faithfully. This correspondence had been going on for a long time, so that when Ujjvala died in 1955 the letters from Gurudas Maharaj—tied up and labelled by years—made up a considerable part of the small legacy she left.

Ujjvala used to talk about Gurudas. His childhood name was Cornelius Heyblom. Born in 1870 in Holland, he had come to the United States as an immigrant at twenty-one. In 1898 he had met Swami Abhedananda in the eastern United States, from whom he took brahmacharya in 1899. He met Swami Vivekananda in 1900. Later he had lived in San Francisco, where Ujjvala had known him. Then he had gone to stay in India; and Ujjvala had travelled too to that land of her dreams—through Gurudas's letters.

I was anxious to meet Gurudas Maharaj because of his friendship with Ujjvala, and most especially because he is an example of a Western aspirant successfully transplanted to monastic life in India. There were the Seviers, Sister Nivedita, Sister Christine, Tantine, Frank Alexander, and perhaps one or two more, who had lived and worked in India, but none of them had spent the major portion of his life there, or had gone on to become, as Gurudas had, an ordained swami of the Order.

Not only a swami, but a big swami. Gurudas is recognized as one of the Order's present-day great. Swamis and brahmacharis from all over

India try to make it a point to journey to Hardwar in order to meet him. He is considered a man of spiritual attainment. See photo 5b.

The most striking thing about Gurudas Maharaj, when I bowed before him in his comfortable room at the Hardwar math, was the sight of his blue eyes. Blue eyes were a rarity I had not seen for many months; and blue eyes above gerrua—that is a singularity one must go a long way before expecting to find again! He was little and seemed frail, but one felt he was very wise and possessed of that steadiness of mind—call it holy indifference—that one is told is a mark of the genuine sadhu.

Gurudas's frankness I found delicious. We talked man to man about the fascinating problem of making the grand shift from one world to another so utterly different. I found myself confessing to him my numerous faux pas and the anxious times I had had in trying to adjust myself to India. He smiled at it all—kindly, though unconcerned. It was familiar to him, but he was, one could feel, quite above all that now.

He told me his story. He had first gone to India as a brahmachari in, I think, 1906. He had plunged into the life and had tried to become a complete Indian, to the extent of carrying a handkerchief with him to meals so that the others would not see the tears pouring from his eyes as he ate chillies along with them. He had had a back injury earlier, and this, plus his efforts to Indianize himself, resulted in a breakdown after five years. Back to the United States he went to recover. But the call of the East, as he amusedly referred to it, attracted him again, so that he returned for another five-year trial. Again the same difficulties, so back to America once more. In 1922 he attempted it for the third time, and on this occasion he was able to make the shift permanent. He received his sannyas the next year.

I asked Gurudas Maharaj to tell me frankly what he felt now about how his life had gone. He said it had turned out very happily. But he advised any Westerner considering moving to India to work and live, not to deceive himself that he could become the complete Indian. He must have more comforts, a better balanced diet, completer accommodations of every sort, than the average Indian—as Gurudas himself had arranged to have from his third trip on. And to do that—since these are things the Order cannot afford to furnish—means that any Western devotee who might wish to work and live in the Order in India must come backed by some regular and permanent income, although this need not be large. Then, Gurudas said, he thought the transfer might work.

One got the impression Gurudas was enjoying life hugely. 'Even if I had had any regrets about never seeing the West again,' he confided, 'I could have none now at eighty-three. It is nice to be old in India. In the good old USA you're not wanted when you're old. But here elderly people are respected. Look at the way they love and spoil me.' He twinkled: 'In India old age is really an advantage.'

Gurudas wanted me to take something back from him to Ujjvala. We thought about it and decided a new cane would be a nice present. So I cycled down to a store beside the Brahma Kund and bought her a good handmade stick. I took it back to Ujjvala; and Gurudas's Hardwar cane was a part of her from then on till the day she died. Even then we did not separate her from it, so that she and that memento of the land she knew but never got to see were cremated together.

When God descends as man, we call it the advent of a divine incarnation. He assumes an individual name and dresses himself up in a particular form. Each disguise he takes is not only unique and eternal but is, as it were, deliberately designed to appeal most fully to the highest aspirations of the struggling people of the age in which he comes.

Of all the masquerades the Lord has used when putting in his appearance at this harlequinade we call the world, the one he wore as Govinda must be considered, many contend, his masterwork. We have in the adolescent Krishna a beautiful lad combining the sweetness of a young virgin with the virile promise of a teen-age boy. He is a youth every other boy must claim as his best friend and yearn to be with constantly, arm in arm. He is a boy no girl can resist as intimate playmate, confidential comrade. He is a boy all men and women must long to have as their own, to dote on, to spoil, to adore as darling son. Govinda is cocky, flirtatious, a tease—yet a fountain of love when he wants to be. A flute-playing cowherd boy, dressed in a short gown, a blue peacock feather riding jauntily in his long hair.

Govinda has danced across the imaginations of Hindus since before anyone can remember. The scene of his gambols was Brindaban: Brindaban, a city of twenty thousand inhabitants a short distance from Agra and Delhi in northwest India, rather hot, rather dry, full of temples —a city like any other, the Jamuna river flowing past, high at flood stage, low in the dry season.

The traditional site of Krishna's birth at nearby Mathura was well known. But the locale of his divine play with Radha and his cowherd companions had long ago been lost. Then Sri Chaitanya four hundred years ago, his longing heart like a Geiger counter, searched through the area and discovered it again. Vibrations from Govinda's ancient visitation remained still in the soil, which Chaitanya's adoring sensitivity was able to discover. He identified the place of every scene that legend claimed had occurred there. Thus Brindaban came to life again.

When Sri Ramakrishna journeyed on from Benares to Brindaban in 1868 he confirmed Sri Chaitanya's findings. This is his account, in his own words: 'No sooner did I see the Kaliyadaman Ghat than a divine emotion surged up within me. I was completely overwhelmed. Hriday used to bathe me there as if I were a small child. In the dusk I would walk on the bank of the Jamuna when the cattle returned along the sandy banks from their pastures. At the very sight of those cows the thought of Krishna would flash in my mind. I would run along like a madman, crying: "O where, is Krishna? Where is my Krishna?" On my way to the sacred pools of Shyamakunda and Radhakunda, when I saw the meadows, the trees, the shrubs, the birds, and the deer, I was overcome with ecstasy. My clothes became wet with tears. I said, "O Krishna! Everything here is as it was in the olden days. You alone are absent".'

The city of sticks and stones may be like any other. But not the real Brindaban. For Brindaban, it seems, is not a place, and Govinda is not a boy. They both stand for ever so much more.

If one would know this larger meaning, he may read Girish Ghosh's *Vilwamangal*. This play, like the *Canterbury Tales*, is a story about a group of assorted characters on a religious pilgrimage. There is the bewildered rich young man, Vilwamangal, disappointed in love, searching for someone truly and forever his own. We meet too Chintamani, Vilwamangal's erstwhile mistress, crying now—after having traded in its counterfeit so long—for real love. There is a jewel-thief seeking, according to his own lights, excitement, beauty, satisfaction. There is a childless couple wanting comfort for their old age. All have been told they may find something in Brindaban, to which they journey, hungering, hoping.

They reach Brindaban, and they do find their heart's desire. To each Govinda appears, perfect, divinely desirable, to each as he would have his love be. To Vilwamangal the Lord is noble attachment; to Chintamani, real, pure love; to the beggar, security; to the virtuous couple, a comforter. Even the Mother of the universe, who appears in the play as a madwoman—symbol of that maya which obscures man's goal yet leads him to it—bows down before the miracle of Brindaban and its young king.

Then the characters turn to the audience and sing:

> With sight by love made bold, see now the eternal play
> In blessed Brindaban, the shrine within the heart.
> There look, and there alone, if thou dost yearn for peace:
> There peace and freedom find, where is the source of all.
> Since Heaven's richest treasure within thyself lies hid,
> Why wilt thou trifle longer; why, restless, wander more?

The reward from a trip to Brindaban, Girish Ghosh tells us, is the sight of Brindaban. The gain from the vision of Krishna is—the vision of Krishna. Thus with any spiritual pilgrimage, and most particularly with that larger pilgrimage which should take us to God. To make what is 'out there' come 'in here'. Or, more properly—since what is 'out there' is said by those who know to be 'in here' all the time—to see the glorious destination within—by his grace—soon.

CHAPTER IX

BENGAL BETHLEHEM

IN his valuable biography of Sri Ramakrishna, Swami Saradananda says that all the divine incarnations except Rama and Buddha were born in poverty and hardship. He mentions, as having come from poor families, Jesus, Shankara, Sri Chaitanya, Krishna, and Mohammed. And he says he believes this is as it should be.

'If we think deeply,' Saradananda explains, 'we find that there is a subtle connection between that condition of poverty and the future life of the incarnations. For, unless they had from their early years known and sympathized with the lot of the poor, the oppressed, and the miserable, how could they have, in later years, wiped the tears of those people and brought them solace?

'That, however, is not the only thing the incarnations were out to to accomplish. . . . They came to earth mainly to stop the decline of religion. To fulfil that object they had to acquire an intimate knowledge of the principles underlying the past religions and, by a study of the causes of their decline, to bring out new and perfected forms of those religions suited to particular times and places. It is in the huts of the lowly and not in the palaces of the rich that that intimate knowledge can be gained; for it is the poor man, deprived of the enjoyments of worldly pleasures, who clings to God and his dispensations as his main support. Although, therefore, religion declines everywhere, a little flash of the old teaching still brightens the poor man's hut. That is perhaps the reason why these great souls, the world teachers, are attracted to the huts of the poor at the time of their birth.'

Now I was to journey into that rural part of Bengal, some seventy-five miles northwest of Calcutta, to the hamlet of Kamarpukur where Sri Ramakrishna had been born. I was to see for myself those scenes of hardship and poverty such as Swami Saradananda speaks of. Holy Mother's birthplace at Jayrambati, two or three miles from Kamarpukur, I was also to visit.

And finally, on this same trip away from Belur Math, I was to be the guest, at the nearby small city of Bishnupur, of the family of my teacher, Swami Prabhavananda, and to view scenes of his boyhood days.

Bishnupur is the place where one gets off the train when one travels to Ramakrishna's birthplace by rail from Calcutta. The railroad had not yet been put through even to Bishnupur during the Master's life; one of the interesting stories of those days is about Holy Mother and how, when at eighteen she went to join her husband in Calcutta, she walked through fields and forests all the way, the journey consuming the better part of a week. It is difficult for an American to imagine any inhabited place not situated on a through road; and yet such was the case with Kamarpukur and Jayrambati even until recently. These hamlets were isolated in the middle of farmland, with nothing but footpaths along the edges of fields to connect them with the outside world. Even after the railroad had been extended into this part of Bengal the line did not go anywhere near Kamarpukur or Jayrambati. Bishnupur, the nearest rail junction, is some twenty miles distant. After a rest and an early start, one made the journey to these interior villages by bullock cart or man-carried palanquin, neither of which could average more than two or three miles per hour. Sometimes the trip required two days.

On my journey to Ramakrishna's village I was transported from Bishnupur in a jeep provided by friendly officials of the district government. This was the only kind of motorized conveyance capable of negotiating the dirt trail with its frequent mudholes at that time. I understand that now, however, good roads are being pushed through to Kamarpukur and Jayrambati to accommodate the quickly increasing number of pilgrims wishing to gain the blessing of attendance at the birth shrines of the Master and of Holy Mother.

Kamarpukur and Jayrambati would be typical of the really small, remote villages of India, said to number about half a million. Such hamlets have a population of from one hundred to five hundred people. Bishnupur, on the other hand, would be considered a fair-sized market town. Its population is approximately 26,000. The business district encircles a large pond, somewhat as towns in the American midwest centre round a green square on which sits the county courthouse. Several hundred years ago Bishnupur was the capital of a dynasty of provincial kings. Whatever palaces they built seem to have vanished, but some dozen or more temples constructed during their reigns still remain. Set here and there in grassy or wooded places around the town, these shrines are in various states of preservation, but all abandoned. It gives the visitor a peculiar sensation to wander in and out of these old sanctuaries, trying to picture the way things must have been in the 1500s and 1600s, before the British came, before famines swept the land, when this was a centre of booming prosperity and culture. I found that the deities had been removed from the temples and had been placed

all together in the storeroom of one temple—carved stone gods, goddesses, devas, and devis, all lying side-by-side on the floor behind iron
bars, cobwebby and dirtied. As I gazed in at them I thought, 'If I could
only bring you home to Hollywood we would love you again and give
you a place of honour. We would set you up and many would come to
see you.' But it would be unfair to the devotion which installed them to
kidnap the deities, I suppose. Better to let them await their end near
where their original worshippers placed them.

Swami Prabhavananda has three brothers—one older and two
younger than himself. He has two sisters. These, with all the children
and in-laws, add up to a large family. I was to meet many of these
'relatives' of mine. The elder brother, Sri Amulya, was a West Bengal
state assemblyman and lived a good deal of the time in Calcutta. Sri
Gokul, junior to Swami, was the principal of the Bishnupur High School.
And Sri Aurabindo, the youngest, is a lawyer in a village fifty miles
from Bishnupur named Khatra. It was Sri Gokul who met the train
and took me to the place where I was to stay, an ashrama on the out-
skirts of Bishnupur.

I had experienced examples of Indian hospitality before, but nothing
compared to what I was to be accorded now. I was to be given a demonstration of that ancient provision of Hindu dharma that a guest is to be
treated as God. In addition, this was a 'bhakta family' such as Swami
Saradananda speaks of, 'clinging to God and his dispensations'. The
members were devoted to Ramakrishna, Holy Mother, and Ramakrishna's disciples. Some in the older generation had seen the Master; and
since in later years the Holy Mother customarily got off the train in
Bishnupur on the way from Calcutta to her village, many of those alive
during her time had seen her. The family members had mostly taken
their initiations from swamis of the Ramakrishna Order. On top of all
this, they were eager to do honour to the sadhu brother in America by
showing special cordiality to his child who was coming to see them. I
was thus to experience the code of behaviour of the householder functioning according to the classic rules.

I was taken to stay in a small ashrama. It was not as yet affiliated with
the Ramakrishna Mission; newer religious installations must demonstrate stability and self-support before their responsibility can be taken
on by an already overstrained Order. This was instead an independent
centre run and frequented by local citizens, where Ramakrishna's pre-
cepts were taught and practised. There was a staff of one independent
swami, assisted by a servant or two.

Let me describe the ashrama. It is made up of a line of three rooms
opening on to a veranda, facing a walled courtyard. The rooms are more
or less individual Indian huts side by side, with thick earthen walls and
peaked thatched roofs. Inside, the rooms are shadowy, the furnishings
sparse. The walls of the courtyard are of adobe too. The court is bright

and full of life like the busy patio of a Spanish hacienda. Here clothes are washed and hung out to dry, water is heated over an open fire made of coconut hulls, meals prepared. A family of pigeons—referred to in Bengal as birds of happiness because they are thought to frequent only places where there is love and harmony—chatter softly all day in their boxes under the eaves.

At the bottom of the yard is a gate which leads to a big lake. The water stretches out, calm and bright. All through the day there is along its shores an air of drowsy peace. In the morning I could watch as a dozen or two children, together with a few mothers with babies in their arms, lined up, each holding some small container, to get his ration of lique-fied powdered milk distributed through courtesy of the ashrama.

Beside the lake, beneath an old twisted tree, sits a neighbourhood shrine. After washing themselves, people come here to bow and perhaps leave an offering. At evening arati is held. When the twilight has so far advanced that, glancing at your arm, you can no longer quite distinguish the hairs one from another—that in India indicates the time when night and day meet and the proper moment for the commencement of vespers. At that hour bells are sounded and lights waved in the wayside sanctuary.

The accommodation given me at the ashrama proved to be the one sleeping room in the place, very private and comfortable. It included the unusual luxury of an attached washroom, which contained a portable commode, a pitcher and washbasin, and a cemented place with a drain-hole where one could stand and take a shower by pouring water over himself. This concession to Western style (for, as I have said before, bathrooms in India are usually a fair walk's distance from the living quarters) had been built two or three years before when Swami Prabhav-ananda had made a trip to India and had occupied the same room. The sadhu in charge of the Bishnupur ashrama was named Swami Shivat-mananda. He was a man with a gentle, loving nature. I learned later that the reason this swami was staying in the second of the three chambers—the crowded storeroom—was that he had moved out completely so that his room could be given to me.

The third of the rooms making up the ashrama was given over to the shrine. There was no electricity at the ashrama and the nights when I was in Bishnupur were very dark. One or two compressed-air-gasoline lanterns such as campers use in the United States, served to light the place. In the evening we would sit in the small worship hall for our meditation while the lights hissed and made violent shadows and great moths flopped about. Many village elders would come for the arati. Then, swinging a hurricane lamp to light his way, a servant would arrive from Sri Gokul's house downtown, bringing my supper in a tiffin carrier. Later all of us would sit on the veranda in the dark, talking a little, making efforts to bridge the Bengali-English chasm. There was an intense feeling of friendliness, even if the conversation consisted substantially of smiles and gestures.

As I have indicated, each meal was sent to me from Sri Gokul's house at least a mile distant from the Bishnupur ashrama. The women of the family would not have heard of anyone else's cooking for the American visitor. On one occasion I had noon dinner at the family homestead in Bishnupur. Going first to the family shrineroom to bow to the deities, I then was shown the bedroom which my guru had occupied as a boy. The older male members of the family and I ate together, sitting in a line on the floor of the porch, with the women of the family serving us, and the children watching. This visit to the house of Sri Amulya and Sri Gokul gave the female folk a chance to look at me and made it possible for me to see them. Sri Aurabindo's family sent food to the ashrama where I stayed at Khatra (his daughter actually baked a genuine American nut cake), and once I had a meal at Aurabindo's house. Both at Bishnupur and at Khatra the family members went to such a trouble to serve me foods they thought I would like that I felt embarrassed. For example, Sri Gokul made a journey of seventy miles round trip to Midnapore by train to get a few Western provisions for my stay.

The serving of food to guests and to that most important guest of all—the Lord, in all ritualistic worship—is a major concern in India, and its practice was well illustrated on my stay in the Bengal provinces. Hence, it seems appropriate in this chapter to make some further mention of Indian food. I do not pretend to understand this complex subject thoroughly, nor will I discuss it in detail; my purpose rather is to convey general impressions.

It would be hard to find any two major human interests more totally dissimilar than Western and Indian feeding and eating practices. In the first place, in Europe or America there would be a mixing of the sexes. 'Balancing the table' would be a first consideration in any well planned meal, with men and women paired off in such a way as to add as much piquancy to the situation as possible. In India men eat together, with the women serving them in the attitude of mother-provider. If strangers are present, young women will not appear at all, although a rustling at the entrance leading to the inner part of the house might indicate their presence, excitedly watching from behind the door. Nor will a woman eat a meal until after she has fed her husband, no matter how late he may be in getting home. In the West, the meal is as sociable as possible, often greatly stretched out, and may be the prelude to further social contact. Dining in India seems to be devoted mostly to the simple taking of food. There is little conversation (I think talking is considered distracting) and the event ends with the dessert, people taking their leave or lying down for a nap directly afterwards. Nobody, of course,

M

entertains in restaurants or cabarets in India. In fact, that most important feature of Western maya—going to the stylish restaurant where opportunities are available to enjoy many taste and sight experiences— is almost completely absent there.

Settings and utensils could not be more disparate. A dinner party in America or Europe would be an elaborate presentation with polished furniture, snowy napkins, flowers, glistening silverware, many changes of dishes. On the other hand, it is possible that the food itself might receive relatively little personal attention from the hostess, being mostly prepared elsewhere by strangers—canned or frozen or bought already cooked. In India simplicity of arrangement is the plan, whereas the foods are complicated and require hours of cooking time and are almost all done at home. Your seat might be a small rug or wooden slab on the floor, and the dishes consist of a banana leaf or brass plate, a brass bowl, and a bell metal tumbler. You would eat with your fingers and go outdoors to wash your hands and mouth at a spigot afterwards. Conversation would be anything but animated. But you could be sure that an enormous amount of attention and long hours over a brazier or open fire had gone into the preparation of the food to make it good, and further to guarantee what the Indian considers most important of all—an absence in it of unwanted 'vibrations' of the unclean or the irreligious.

The structures of the two meals are different. It can be said approximately that the typical Western—or at least American—meal is composed of five parts. One-fifth is served first—an appetizer such as soup, fruit cocktail, or salad. Then follow three-fifths: meat, potato, vegetable. Finally comes the last fifth, the dessert. Along the side, toward the beginning, there may be breads and relishes. Toward the end there will be a beverage such as coffee. In the food naturalness of taste and appearance, and a separation of the components, would be striven for. That is, most foods would look and taste—ready to be eaten—much as they do in their natural state: a trout would look like a trout, a tomato like a tomato, a pear like a pear. Things best cold would be served cold, and those meant to be hot would be served hot.

The Indian meal is somewhat the opposite. Almost everything is placed before the diner at the same time; many foods are mixtures, with those that are not mixtures being blended together before being brought to the mouth, and nothing is especially hot or especially cold. Nor will many elements of the meal look raw or natural; indeed, the approximation to nature so striven for in sophisticated Western cooking would, I think, dismay the Indian—as though the cook had not gone to sufficient pains to improve on nature through the application of art. I remember having heard an Indian remark, while consuming a Western meal: 'Phew, these carrots look, smell, and taste like carrots.'

I shall describe the composition of an elaborate non-vegetarian meal in Bengal. It is the actual menu served me at the home of an Indian I had previously known in Hollywood, Amal Dey. The rationale, it is said, is that one is to progress from bitter through pungent to sweet. Directly before me is a brass plate about two feet in diameter. On it is a small mound of neem leaves—bitter greens looking and tasting something like cool cooked spinach. On the plate are also a large mound of rice, several airy fried pastries something like cream puff shells, called puries; a whole fish with head and roe included, fried; some fried cauliflower; and some potato and eggplant curry. Arranged in a circle around the plate from left to right (more or less in the sequence in which the dishes are to be approached) are small brass bowls containing the following: some sourish vegetable in a curry sauce, maybe turnips; curried shrimps; a curry made of fried chana (solidified cottage cheese) mixed with potatoes; a piece of fish in a curry sauce; curried mutton; a bowl of yogurt to be eaten toward the end of the meal, considered a digestive; and a dessert called payas. Payas is a sweet, runny rice pudding, sometimes garnished with nuts or pieces of fruit. At the Dey's there was also chutney to mix with the rice and curries; and to eat after the payas there were squares of sandesh: dry, crumbly candy made from cheese and brown sugar. Sandesh is normally cream-coloured, but if one wants to be a bit more festive, he may buy it in cakes dyed in bright greens, reds, and blues.

Of course one doesn't eat like this in the monasteries of the Ramakrishna Order. Rice, vegetable curries, dal, and chapatties would make up the main diet. Yogurt, too, is popular, often eaten blended with the rice. And fruit—papaya is a favourite kind—would constitute a dessert. Of course rice is the basic staple. To me, rice is rice; but not to the Indian. Its proper preparation is very important to him. Rice must be cooked sufficiently so that no graininess remains in the kernel, yet must not be mushy. In properly cooked rice each kernel will be separate, yet moist. Indians are expert in the numerous grades and varieties of rice. Many can identify by taste the locality in which any given example was grown.

Breakfast at a math might consist of tea mixed with milk, puffed rice, and fruit. In the south good strong coffee made by adding hot milk to what they call decoction (concentrated coffee syrup) would replace tea, and there might be idali. This is a thick, moist pancake made of cracked rice or wheat, eaten with a tartar sauce composed of fried lentils, coconut, yogurt, and ground chillies.

For supper, likely there would probably be dal and chapatties, with a bowl of milk. Dal is a gravy made of lentils and spices. It can be very good and is said to be high in protein. Indeed, if one has nothing else, rice and dal—sometimes served mixed in a dish called kichuri—will support life well, somewhat in the manner of the European's bread and cheese. The chapatti is the Indian counterpart of bread. In size and shape the chapatti resembles the tortilla of Mexico, but tastes different. Torn into pieces and dipped in the dal, or rolled into a scoop to lift the dal, chapatties are hearty and filling. The milk, with which one may finish supper, will probably be boiled, boiling being the Indian's approximation to pasteurization. Milk is expensive and is considered a luxury. It is served to old and sick swamis and to Western guests, usually warm and heavily laced with sugar.

It is considered proper for any devotee 'going to see the Lord'—that is, visiting a monastery with its shrine—to bring a food offering. Like as not, this will be some Indian sweetmeats, which are a cross between dessert and candy. I have already spoken of sandesh. Another is the rasagollah, which I shall mention farther on. A third is the jellabi.

The jellabi is the Indian sweet I liked best from the very start. I was gratified to learn that Sri Ramakrishna fancied jellabies, too; when you read in the Gospel of his having some sweets in his room, or of his giving a sweet to someone he wanted to show affection for, it is quite possible that it is the jellabi that is meant. This is a pastry the colour and shape of a large pretzel. But here the similarity ends. The jellabi is tender, juicy, and very sweet. The making of jellabies takes skill. If the fat in which they are fried is not the correct temperature they will grow tough, while if they are not dipped in the sugar syrup for the correct number of seconds, or if the syrup is too thick or too thin, the result may be soggy. For the reader who may want to try making jellabies I am including a recipe. This formula has been tested by me—and is guaranteed to produce an uproar in the kitchen and engender an appreciation for Indian culinary skill.

With two cups of flour mix a sufficient quantity of water to make a batter the consistency of thick cream. Let the batter stand in a warm place for twenty-four hours to ferment.

When ready, have a pan of deep boiling butter or other fat ready (not oleo). Fill a small funnel (with the finger over the outlet) with the batter, or one of those kitchen 'eye-droppers' may be used. Let the batter run into the fat in a continuous figure-eight. Allow it to set, then turn. When quite crisp and of golden colour, remove from the fat and drain.

One should have ready the syrup in which the jellabies are to be soaked. This is made as follows. Place together in a saucepan four cups of sugar, four cups of water, a few sprigs of saffron, and the inner seeds of six cardamoms. The mixture should be boiled until it is heavy; keep it warm.

The jellabies should now be dipped in the syrup, turned, and drained. They may be kept in the syrup long enough for the syrup to penetrate the pipes of the jellabies, but not long enough to destroy their crispness.

Jellabies are highly perishable. Fresh, they are delicious. By the next day they will have become rubbery. But this is assuming there will be some left till the next day, which is certainly unlikely!

Indians are convinced that their diet is not suited to Westerners. Before going to India I was told by the head Swami of an American centre that I should take all my meals when in his country in Western-style hotels or hire an English-trained cook to prepare my food individually. And the concern felt toward keeping me successfully nourished at every math I visited was touching. I believe the good monks were relieved to get me on to the next stop on my itinerary with my health still intact.

In some places my hosts, with their keen wish to serve their guest adequately, would try to give me something they thought I was used to at home. But Indians' ideas of Western cooking are naturally not very authentic. In one centre there was a brahmachari who had an interest in European food and proposed to make me some French toast. Of course I was delighted. But when the dish came I found the egg batter in which the bread had been fried had had mixed in it chopped onions and ginger. On another occasion this good young man proposed substituting an omelette for the safe and sane boiled eggs I often took at breakfast. This proved to be filled with chillies.

More usually the Indian's efforts are based on the idea that in America all food is separated and totally unseasoned. This would result in my being given quantities of plain boiled vegetables. Here they would be on my plate: a mound of turnips, some carrots, a few potatoes. Having been boiled for a long time, they had had all the good cooked out of them, and they were now cold. I would sprinkle on some salt and sadly chew them down. When I said I preferred their own diet, I meant it; they did it better than their approximation to mine. But my hosts thought I was being polite or noble. And I am sure that the note I was given by the head of one centre to carry on to the head of the next place I was to stay in—always written in an Indian language I couldn't read—probably said: 'Although the Yankee will tell you he wants to eat as we do, he is just being tactful. Don't take him seriously. What he really likes is plain boiled vegetables.'

At the same time that I stated I would rather have straight Indian food at maths, I also explained that I would simply take myself out to get a Western dinner at an hotel if and when the needs of my system should demand it. I did eat out once in a while without encountering serious opposition from my Indian brothers. But dining out would not be a pleasure to them. I tried on several occasions to entertain Indian friends by taking them with me. Once or twice my invitations were accepted. But always these dinners were failures. The men felt out of place and I know the dining-room stewards and waiters—Indians also, of course, —experienced an uneasiness. My guests didn't know how to use silverware, the food was unimpressive and the menu confusing, and I believe they were nervous about the emanations arising from the kitchen. The appropriate way to entertain monastic friends in India is to give a sum of money which can be used to buy provisions for a feast held right at the math.

There are indeed some adjustments to be made by any visitor to India trying to live on the local diet. But I believe strongly that if you don't try to participate with others at meals—especially if you are a member of the Order—you will lose out on a great many useful experiences. You will fail to learn something about a totally different table etiquette and cuisine thought to be attractive by millions of people, and will shut yourself off from valuable contacts only possible when eating with others.

They do their own diet best; it belongs to the country, and eating it helps you belong to the country; and on its own terms it is good. A basic idea we hold concerning Indian dishes, that they are all terribly highly seasoned, I did not find to be the case, or not more so than, say, Mexican cooking. Many preparations I learned to eat with genuine enjoyment and would choose them again any day if in some international food mart I were offered a selection of all the good things to eat of the whole world.

If I were to criticize Indian food I would do so on two counts: that it is often—to Western eyes—unattractive; and that while it fills it somehow fails to sufficiently nourish.

Dining in a squatting position from a leaf laden with damp and often yellowish mixtures, and sucking the food from the fingers, is just not our idea of delightful dining. It has an impromptu quality that is reminiscent of grabbing something from the icebox and eating it hanging over the kitchen sink. We are taught from birth to sit up straight at the table and to keep our hands tidy. The setting, in fact, may be more important than the food itself. The Indian will tell you he doesn't feel satisfied unless he eats in his own way: it is clean, unfussy, and direct.

As for the nourishing effect of the food, my experience was that far more bulk is required, with Indian than with Western preparations, to supply a comparable amount of food value. I never could learn to load up my stomach, and consequently felt unsatisfied and very soon hungry again after eating. Probably this effect would hold anywhere where vegetables and grains were to take the place of meat. It may be especially true in a country where there has been for so many centuries such an intense drain on the soil. I noticed a change in my system. As the weeks passed I lost weight and felt more and more dragged out. My eyesight grew blurry. Perhaps the climate had something to do with this. In any case, I began to be able for the first time to sympathize with the Indian's easy-going attitude toward life.

Although, as I say, I felt this physical ennui, on the other hand, I experienced, and was appreciative of, a noticeable lessening in the pressures of lust. Would this be the natural concomitant of any general condition of reduced physical vitality? Or the mainly vegetarian diet? I think not. Undernourished and sickly people nevertheless have large families. Sparrows are vegetarians but are extremely lustful, whereas the lion, although a meat-eater, manifests sensuality but infrequently. Rather I should say that the effect I speak of was the result of the relatively small 'amount of maya' in India, together with the influence of holy association. There is, as I have said, an almost total absence in India of the subtle sexual lures so common—and so unrecognized for what they are and what they can do to one—in the USA (To the usual Western mind India can easily appear sterile, uninteresting, and drab for this reason; and this is mainly why I believe the country will not develop into a popular world tourist destination.) This feeling of dharma in the nation, together with the religious atmosphere of the monasteries I lived in, produced in me a sattwic effect.

Hence, from the evidence of my own interior experience I am convinced that there is something to the Indian theory of being particular about the vibrations one imbibes through food—which ultimately is through association.

Many sweet memories of food experiences come back to me.

I recall the happy occasion when there was a feast at the big orphanage and boys' home operated by the Order at Rahara across the Ganges north of Dakshineswar. A celebration is held there every year, to which all the Ramakrishna sadhus in the Calcutta region are invited. Dozens of us, dressed in our freshest dhotis and chadars, piled into buses and jeeps to go from Belur Math, and others came from the many other centres in the area, perhaps two hundred altogether. The boys of the home were all set to put on a drama following the after-dinner rest period. An outdoor stage had been prepared, with scenery painted on paper in bright water colours. But a sudden splash of rain came up to melt the sets and ruin all hope of their being a performance. However, the meal was a huge success—lines and lines of us sitting on the floor in a big upstairs classroom, while the boys passed back and forth, bringing round the many dishes, including treats the sadhus rarely got. The staff of the orphanage, some of them perhaps 'old boys' of the institution who as grownups had stayed on and taken to the monastic life, moved about, addressing everyone in a familiar Bengali phrase meaning: 'Eat unashamedly'. Hands held over the plate in a gesture of refusal signified: 'No more; that is, unless you talk me into more'. Bending determinedly over the plate with arms outstretched: 'I really mean it when I say no more'.

For dessert there were rasagollahs, literally thousands of them, served fresh and oozing out of great crocks. These are spherical 'donuts' about the size of a plum, made of cheese and soaked in heavy rose-flavoured syrup. The eating of these developed into a contest, to see who could consume the most. There were merry shouts as various contestants dropped out and a few champions stayed in the race until one triumphed. I regret that I cannot remember the quantity of rasa-gollahs eaten by the winner, but it was a large number. As the banquet drew to a close there was a kind of community song service. Someone would call out in Sanskrit the first lines of a stanza from one of the scriptures; then the concluding lines would be answered by all the men in a ringing chorus. A new line and a shouted reply. Finally, it being 1.00 or 2.00 p.m., everyone retired to the dormitories for a nap, before returning in the downpour to his post.

Another memory: the chapatti production line at Belur Math. I can see the kitchen still, part of it a dim, open-air shed, with concrete floor and tin roof. It is practically devoid of counters, cupboards, refrigera-tors, labour-saving accessories. Canned or frozen provisions are un-known. Many of the supplies are bargained for and bought fresh every day and carried from the markets along the Grand Trunk Road. Bulkier supplies are transported by river boat, unloaded at the Belur ghat. The cooks and their helpers rush about busily, as in kitchens all over the world. In another section the big brass cooking pots are scrubbed with sand and sluiced with water, which runs away to the outdoors in a small cement canal.

The gong sounds to inform us that the Lord has been served. Then the prasad is brought back through the tunnel leading from the shrine, to be mixed with the rest of the food. The brahmacharis who are to take meals to those senior swamis and sick members who will not be coming to the dining hall are filling trays.

I know that we shall soon be eating, for the chapatti production line is going full tilt. Chapatties are made by kneading whole-wheat flour with water and a little butter. At a table a couple of cooks are rapidly and expertly rolling out small balls of the dough into perfectly circular discs about six inches in diameter. These are passed to the men who do the cooking. The red heat reflected on their faces, these men stand over the clay firepots, baking one chapatti after another. The disc warms, squirms a bit, then swells up like a balloon. The cook flips it over. It swells again and is done. The cook removes it, bangs it down to make it flatten out, and passes it on to the final man on the line. With the bottom of a pan dipped in melted butter he anoints the chapatties one after another; piles of them grow tall before him.

I can see yet the two lines of diners facing each other as we eat in the long, narrow Belur Math dining hall. I shall never forget Vikash Maharaj, the head of the kitchen, and his kindness in going to the bother, with all the other people he had to look after, of trying to give me a few extra things he thought would appeal, principally the best rice (the variety which had been offered to the Lord) and plenty of sweets.

I recall Govinda Maharaj, the dining room steward. A young swami with a benevolent nature, he ran up and down, up and down, that line three times a day, dhoti rolled up to the knees for unencumbered movement, seeing that everyone was served, placing favourite foods on individuals' plates, encouraging everyone to eat. He always seemed to be smiling. His joy was in other people's happiness. His presence made the dining room pleasant.

I met and admired another cook swami, the head of the kitchen at Kankhal, Swami Sushantananda. He had varicose veins and probably shouldn't have been in such an active job, yet daily he energetically presided over the big kitchen which served many monastics, guests, and hospital inmates, personally seeing to it that everyone was as well and agreeably fed as possible.

As I watched these men I thought that maybe Brother Lawrence might have been something like them.

At the end of the meal in India it is customary to take a few spices to clean the mouth and freshen the breath, or to chew betel. Sri Ramakrishna used both. I can still see the brahmachari at Belur Math standing on a raised place outside the dining room door holding his wooden boxes of spices. We go first to the taps to rinse our hands and mouth, then pass him. He drops on to the outstretched palm a few flavoursome seeds. Betel, or pan, I had just once. That was at the Advaita Ashrama, the publishing office in Calcutta. It being suggested that the American should try betel, after dinner someone was sent out to buy enough pans for each of us to have one. A pan is a betel leaf garnished with lime and a few nuts and spices. It comes folded into a small packet, secured with cloves. A pan makes a fairly big wad in the mouth as you first start to chew. As you continue, it turns the lips and saliva red, and with habitual use stains the teeth black. Betel is supposed to aid digestion and at the same time to give the user a pleasant lift. I regret to report that I got no effect at all and not even much taste. I was just as glad when I could conveniently remove the leafy mouthful and throw it away.

Food is, as I have indicated, a subject of enormous importance in India. And it has far more layers of complexity than ever I was able to observe. Yet despite my being—from an orthodox standpoint—a person of nonexistent, or certainly dubious, caste, I was never aware of being discriminated against in the matter of food. Nobody, so far as I am aware, ever hesitated to eat with me or to let me eat with him. The Ramakrishna Order and its friends are liberal and progressive.

The only sanctions I encountered are ones concerning the feeding of the Lord. I will explain. In many places where I went, the sight of a Yankee, a sahib, who was also a Vedanta brahmachari, was a surprising curiosity. In their ingenuous way, people would gather to stare and to ask direct, personal questions. Did the American actually love the gods and goddesses of the Hindus? Had he truly come all this distance and spent all that money for the purpose of revering them in India? Were other Westerners practising renunciation in the midst of the West's fascinating materialism? Were the Ramakrishna centres in America successful? And did we perform the puja of Sri Guru Maharaj?

The subject had come around to food. 'Do you do the worship of Ramakrishna?' implied a further question: 'Do you offer food to the Lord in the West?' When I said: 'Yes. Why not?' the wonderment would grow and would elicit the final and most interesting question of all: 'And what is the Lord offered in Hollywood?'

How you answer depends on where you are. In Madras among old-line brahmins, one might sidestep giving any reply, because what they really wanted to know was: 'Do you practise and cause the Lord to practise vegetarianism?' When asked the question in Bengal, I could answer: 'We try to give Sri Ramakrishna the things he liked as a Bengali, including fish.'

The ultimate query, too shocking even to utter, was of course: 'Surely you haven't Westernized the Lord so much that you give him beef?'

No, we haven't and we don't, because we know better. And yet I believe that if, in ignorance but with devotion, someone were to offer Guru Maharaj beef, he would not turn away. He said when he came as Krishna: 'Whatever worship you choose to give me, if you worship sincerely, I will accept it.' Buddha accepted and ate the blacksmith's offering of pork that he knew was to kill him, because he was too compassionate to offend the profferer by saying nay. But it is better not to be ignorant; it is better to give the Lord what he prefers.

We know that God as God needs nothing at all, and that there is no favour anybody can do for him. But as an incarnation he assumes a human side. That he does for our sake, because in doing so he allows himself 'characteristics' which we can see, can emulate, can love, can cater for. He lets us feel he needs things, for *our* delight.

We begin to understand why this subject of food is so important to the Hindu. The psychology of it is wonderful. Giving someone a good meal is a tangible act you can perform for that person's pleasure. The Lord invites us to feed him, because to do so makes us forget ourselves and think of him. His assumption of eating 'prejudices' makes the process slightly more difficult and so reinforces the impression. It is human nature to adore somebody you are able to do something for, especially if you have to fuss a little. Feeding a human guest is almost the same to the Indian as feeding God, because the old ethic requires him to treat the guest as God, and this produces a like effect. Worship becomes hospitality; and civility is transformed into a sacrament.

I am going to cook for the Lord (or for his proxy, my guest). So I shall bathe and put on fresh clothes. I am going to entertain the king. Hence I shall find ingredients which are agreeable and will cook them nicely.

My beloved is coming. Therefore my house must be aired and swept. My mind I will keep clean too. The theory is that thoughts are material; they have a subtle chemical content which can get into other matter. I am putting good vibrations into the meal, just as I am getting a good effect in my mind as I prepare it. I present it to the Lord (or my guest) with my love behind it. It is the utmost I can do. He accepts it and in doing so makes love stir in me.

What has happened? I have spent my time thinking high thoughts and improving myself. And God has accepted my offering, perhaps not for his own sake so much as for mine. The guest who eats, or my family, or I, will absorb the essence of these thoughts and be helped. (This is completely irrespective of whether God's acceptance and consequent 'prasading' of the food does anything to it.)

This is how to make a routine and sometimes dreary labour more pleasant. This is the way to take the drudgery out of housework and convert it into spiritual practice. This is why food and its preparation is so important in India and why people are particular about who feeds the Lord, as well as the source of what they themselves consume.

One day Sri Gokul drafted me into giving a talk to the student body of the Bishnupur High School. The Bankura Sub-Regional Officer sent his jeep to transport me from the ashrama, and also presided. At the school there was the usual garlanding, followed by the presentation of a neatly written scroll bearing the following message of welcome:

Dear Brother:
Words only fail to express our sincere admiration for your wonderful devotion to Vedanta religion professed by your Master and for your pious and noble endeavour in taking the trouble of visiting this land of your dreams, the sacred birthplace of your revered Guru, thousands of miles away from America.

We are really proud to feel that your Swami was once a pupil of this Institution where the seed of his future greatness was first implanted. We take the liberty of offering you our heartfelt welcome, on the occasion of your kind visit to that holy alma mater.

Your splendid example of renunciation and vast erudition fills us with inspiration and it will, forever, be preserved in our memory.

With best love and good wishes,
Yours fraternally,
The Staff and Students
of Bishnupur High School

I felt quite uneasy. Me—an example of renunciation! Of course it was the white cloth of the brahmachari I was wearing that they were showing respect for. Or rather, not me at all, but the fact that I was a tangible extension of one of the town's most valued native sons. I gave my usual talk about the work of Vedanta in the West, Gokul translating my words into Bengali paragraph by paragraph. Visions of my teacher as a youngster ran through my mind as I looked out into the crowded auditorium. I could see him as a boy, very much like one of those before me, the same 112 pounds he is today, wiry, energetic, human-hearted. Before I had been born he had sat in that very hall to study. The fact of his being an alumnus made the room, the entire high school, precious to these people. Why, this whole town is bhakta, I decided, 'clinging to God and his dispensations'.

Upon sitting down, I found a quickly scribbled note at my place, which brought me back to the present:

Sir:
We, the students of this school, venture to approach you with the humble prayer that you would be pleased to grant us two days' holiday in honour of your visit to our school, once the alma mater of your revered Guru.

Looking at Gokul and realizing that my informing him of the message might put him on the spot, I slipped the letter into my pocket and said nothing. But since then I have had misgivings. Perhaps we should have declared the holiday, at that.

On another day in Bishnupur Aurabindo came over from Khatra, and he, Gokul, and I went to the birthplace of my guru. Its location is at Surmanagar, two or three miles outside the city limits of Bishnupur. We proceeded by bicycle rickshaws till we came to the place where the road left off, or rather became a wagon trail, between fields. We walked from there. Surmanagar is a tiny hamlet of a dozen huts at the edge of a small lake. There was one two-storied brick house, in ruins, which had been the home of Swami's mother's people. It was here—the custom in India being for a wife to go to her parent's place at the time of her confinement—that on December 26, 1893, the birth took place.

At the time when I was there the brothers were already making plans to give over the property to the public as a community centre. This has now been done. The old house is gone, and on the grounds it occupied there is a medical dispensary, a small prayer hall, a library, and a dedication stone marking the place of birth—all in honour of the Bishnupur boy whom God made a sannyasin and a preceptor of many.

At Khatra, Aurabindo's town, I was also housed in an ashrama. This was a new building consisting of a meeting room with a wide veranda, and a shrine. The swami in charge was named Kashishwarananda. He resided in a small cabin at the back of the property. Special preparations had, as at Bishnupur, been made for my comfort. The rear half of the main room of the ashrama had been curtained off to make a bedroom, leaving the front half as a living-dining area. And a completely new bathroom had been constructed just outside the building, having a roof of tin, burlap walls, and a cement floor not yet quite dry by the time of my arrival.

Because the presence of an American was a real novelty in Khatra, even more people came to call than had come at Bishnupur. I was busy receiving delegations all day and all evening. Government officials and other leading citizens of the town came in to talk about America and the amazing fact of Americans' interest in the religion of Vedanta. There were many other callers who didn't talk at all but sat at a distance, regarding me silently. One day Aurabindo and I walked around town to see the sights and were accompanied by a retinue I believe of fully two dozen. When I went into a jewellery shop and bought a few 'primitive' handmade pieces of the district—rather than the fashionable stuff imported from Calcutta—amazement over the doings of this curious stranger was profound. (This was due partly to the fact that the kind of ornaments I had chosen to take home to American ladies were—unknown to me—of the type customarily worn only by the poorest servant women of the area.)

On this walk, by the way, I got a good look at the evidences of 'dharma worship' done by some of the people of that part of Bengal. Under an old tree or in the corner where a wall turned one would come upon huge piles of clay horses and elephants. Some would be beautifully made, reminiscent of those valuable Ming figures of China. Most were small, crude clay representations such as a child would model. People must have deposited them there year after year, I suppose with a prayer for some boon. It is said that they were never moved, and none was ever taken away (although the big ones would be sensationally desirable as decorative pieces if shipped to the USA). No one seemed able to offer an explanation of the origin and purpose of the practice except to say that there was in it some throwback to the worship of dharma (righteousness) dating back to Buddhist times.

On Friday night, February 6th, I was to give my talk at Khatra at an outdoor mass meeting. Blankets had been spread on the ground to make a comfortable place for the people to sit, with lanterns strung up to give light. But just an hour before lecture time a wild thunder and lightning storm came up. Everything had to be dismantled quickly. Aurabindo was upset over the disappointment he said everyone would feel. Finally he decided to crowd the men on to the veranda of the ashrama; and converting my living quarters back into a meeting hall again, to squeeze the women and children in there. This was done. Three or four hundred very wet folks came, and the Indian genius for getting a multitude into a very small space was again demonstrated. Aurabindo estimated that a thousand (one-fifth of the entire population of the town) would have attended if it had not been for the storm. We had a good time, with Aurabindo giving the translation. I was presented with an asana and two scrolls, one of which read as follows:

Dear Brother:

We, the children of this Ashrama, want to welcome you. That you have come, we are glad. Of course, we do not know how to receive you, how to honour you, yet we are not hesitant as we know quite well you love us and have taken us as your own. So, in return, take our love and regard.

We are really proud to see you here. We are young learners with only prattlings and without knowledge. Let your curiosity to know things inspire us. Let your ideals too awaken us. May God brighten your path and bless you.

We remain, Dear Brother,
Yours affectionately,
The Children of Sri Ramakrishna Ashrama

You are blessed, I had been told early in my stay in India, if you can manage to visit the site of a great soul's birth, the place of his enlightenment, the place where he gave out his message, and the location of his death. A spiritual power is thought to remain in such favoured precincts which can be beneficial to anyone visiting them in an attitude of love and longing.

I had thus far been fortunate in my travels. I had stood on that hill at Mathura where Krishna is believed to have been born, and had stopped a few days in Brindaban where as a lovable youngster he had by his wonderful play evidenced God's doctrine of bhakti. At Puri I had actually entered the great temple of Jagannath where Sri Chaitanya was wont to stand enraptured hour by hour, in demonstration of his preaching of the efficacy of prema, of consuming love for God; and I had gazed from the Puri beach into the waves of the Bay of Bengal beneath which he is said to have given up his body. Buddha I had made obeisance to at Gaya under the descendant of the original Bodhi Tree, and I had visited the site of his first sermon at Sarnath near Benares.

As for Sri Ramakrishna, I had been to the Cossipore Garden House near Calcutta and had meditated in the very room where he had breathed his last. I had made several visits to the Dakshineswar Temple where he communed with God and had given out his message, had on one occasion even so much as touched with my forehead the couch on which he had sat when uttering his gospel. And now, at last I was to go to the place where Ramakrishna was born, twenty miles from Bishnupur.

It is the second Sunday of February, the same month and within a few days of the very date of the Master's birthday. It is mid-morning, sunny and quiet. Swami's brothers and I are chugging ahead toward Jayrambati and Kamarpukur, in the government jeep. We move slowly, bouncing over the dirt roads. Now and then the road disappears for a distance beneath a bog or mudhole. To pass these places, at a sharp angle we take to the edge of the bordering field. We traverse a tiny town or two, shadowy under heavy dark green trees, where are a few mud houses with steep thatched roofs, and several shops. Dogs lie in the yards stretched out fast asleep. Here and there one can glimpse a wayside shrine, nearly grown over with vines. Most of our way is past fields of young rice plants. Small fields, one after another, in which the rice is sprouting yellow-green, stretch away flat and vast like a calm yellow-green ocean. Palms rise regally in black silhouette against the extravagantly blue sky.

At Holy Mother's town of Jayrambati there is a large temple built over the spot of her birth. At a pump out in front people wash their hands and feet before going in to bow before Mother's picture. (There is a white marble statue of her there now.) In a room behind the shrine many relics of Mother's life are kept. See photo 6b.

Nearby is the home where Holy Mother spent her girlhood days. It was to this house that Swami Prabhavananda and a companion came when they were teen-agers, to take a curious look at the wife of the already celebrated Sri Ramakrishna. As Swami relates it, Mother seemed to know in advance they were coming and had lunch ready by the time they got there. She bid them sit right down to eat, serving the boys affectionately. Swami was a bit shy of this important lady at first, but soon he was bewitched by her naturalness into concluding that she was like his own mother. The two youngsters ate heartily. Respect reasserted itself enough to prompt them to offer, after the meal, to help tidy up. 'What would you do if you were in your own home?' Sri Sarada Devi asked. So they just got up and departed, leaving the Mother of the Universe to wash up after them.

There is another house in Jayrambati, which Swami Saradananda built for Holy Mother to live in in her later years. It is a quite ordinary earthen house having a dirt porch. Perhaps the reader will recall the photo of Mother which shows her sitting on that porch, her bare feet on the ground. At this place I collected a bottle full of earth from the spot where Holy Mother's feet had rested.

It is amazing how the Bible comes to life for you in India. Those remote scenes from the New Testament which were only much too highly coloured illustrations in the Sunday school lesson sheets are to be seen in Jayrambati and Kamarpukur today in full reality. India, like Judea at the time of Jesus, has an agricultural economy. One's daily existence there, as in Christ's land, is spent near the soil, continually at the mercy of nature: of the seasons and the weather. You share your lot with all living beings. Like your animals, you live close to the food supply. Like theirs, your housing may be scanty; and your dress at times may not be so very much better than that which providence has given them.

There is a slow and steady rhythm to the life of the Indian village. Nothing changes, you feel, or ever has changed or ever will. Women walk to the well, straight and tall, with pots for water balanced on their heads. The town pump or reservoir is the meeting place for people and their flocks. In the river, in the shade of bending trees, women wash clothes and take their baths. Little children run about, with their stomachs sticking straight out in front of them, possibly wearing nothing more than a piece of jewellery at the ankle or wrist, or a nose ring. You hear a creaking sound, and a team of oxen drawing a crude cart pulls slowly by, stirring up a cloud of dust from the powdery road. Paddy is piled in barnyards, ready to be threshed; later the straw will be used as fodder or roofing material. There are storage bins, perhaps fifteen feet tall, made by winding a strong rope made of straw round and round until it forms a conical container, capable of keeping rice grains in good condition for up to twenty years.

You see the bare or sandled feet known from Bible pictures; the staff for aid in walking on rough paths and for guiding animals; and the home-spun mantle variously adjusted to keep off the sun or the rain, or to protect a man against the cold.

We drive the three miles from Jayrambati to Kamarpukur and stop in front of the homestead of Ramakrishna's family, the Chatterjees. The house looks exactly like it does in the pictures one has seen of it—a three-roomed adobe dwelling with pointed roofs of thatch. Across the street is the Shiva temple where Ramakrishna's mother, Chandradevi, experienced the vision which was also an annunciation. See photo 7b.

It takes but a moment to walk around the town. Towards the market place we come upon the nat mandir, open at the sides and roofed with corrugated tin, which was the schoolhouse in which Gadadhar studied. A little farther on is the place of Dhani's house, where there is now a shrine, with a painting of that good midwife nursing the holy child.

Back the other way is a piece of vacant land, recently acquired by the Ramakrishna Mission, where once stood the home of Srinivas. This old man was the first to recognize the youngster for what he was, and to place a garland around his neck and offer him sweetmeats—jellabies, I am certain—in worship:

And it was revealed unto him . . . that he should not see death, before he had seen the . . . Christ.

Then took he him up in his arms, and blessed God, and said,

Lord, now lettest thou thy servant depart in peace, according to thy word:

For mine eyes have seen thy salvation.

Continuing on past Ramakrishna's house, one comes to the old cremation ground, still in use, with the big banyan tree at the far end. And beyond this is the mango grove of Manik Raja, where Gadadhar and his young friends used to go to rehearse their plays.

To stand before the very spot of the Master's birth is, of course, my ultimate purpose. Passing through a gate and under a mango tree planted by Ramakrishna himself when he was a young man, I enter the Chatterjees' back yard. It doesn't seem possible that I am actually here! Straight before me across the compound is the back of the Laha house, quite an impressive mansion in its day, I can see, but now in ruins. To my right, a few feet behind the Master's home, had been the old shed of sticks and straw where the birth took place. It had been preserved for years, but it finally mouldered away; in its place has been built a small stone temple, its altar right over the point of Ramakrishna's advent. Nearby is another shrine housing the Chatterjees' family deity, Rama, represented by the salagram stone which Khudiram found in a field a few months before his son's birth, and installed in their home. See picture 7a.

Everything is in good repair, presided over by the Ramakrishna Mission, which has a staff of monks living on the premises. New tanks have been built, with pumps for irrigation. Model kitchen gardens are maintained. A guesthouse has been opened across the street. And down the road past the cremation ground and the mango orchard on the way to Jayrambati, a thirty-acre agricultural demonstration station has been started.

But how small and close together everything is! All the scenes of the incarnation's early days could be placed within the space of one or two city blocks. For years you read and hear about the doings of world figures such as Sri Ramakrishna and Holy Mother and their families and associates, so that you grow to feel that the physical environment in which they lived—like their doings—must be of heroic dimensions. But this is not the case. Ramakrishna's is an ordinary house like thousands of others; and the lying-in room was nothing but a shed such as would be found at the rear of any rural homestead. These great souls seem deliberately to have chosen the most ordinary scenery available against which to enact their fabulous lilas.

We are back to what Swami Saradananda said. Incarnations often select parents of simple goodness, and an environment of poverty, for their purposes.

It is that quiet and very dark hour a few minutes before sunrise. The Chatterjees' back yard is dewy; possibly a slight breeze brings fresh smells from the grass and trees. The tank across the way lies still. The date is Wednesday, February 17, 1836. Chandradevi has been feeling that the time of delivery is near. Dhani has been staying with her since the evening before. Now labour pains come on. Dhani helps Chandra to

N

go the few steps across the yard to the old shed, and assists her to lie down, probably on some straw such as Mary rested on in the stable behind that crowded inn of Bethlehem. A piece of farm equipment for hulling rice stands at one side; and across the room there is a crude fireplace of the kind often found in summer kitchens. I feel that a few cattle may have been standing nearby, munching hay, and pigeons beginning to rouse themselves in their boxes under the eaves. Very soon Chandra gives birth to a boy. While Dhani is busy with the mother, the baby slides into the fireplace, where he lies all covered with ashes. For a second Dhani cannot find the newborn child; she is terrified. Then she spies him, looking like an infant Shiva, clothed in the garb of renunciation, staring up without a murmur. Dhani picks up the boy and washes him, marvelling at his size and handsomeness. Word is sent to the women of the Laha house. They streak across the yard to see how Chandradevi is and to take a look at the new arrival. And at this auspicious moment when night yields to day, conch shells are sounded to announce to the whole village that a new being has joined the human race.

The February sun rises on a lovely day. Cows low and the pigeons commence their homely chatter. What does the conch say, and the voices of the birds and beasts, and the excited talk of Khudiram, Chandra, and their friends? 'Unto us a child is born; unto us a son is given. And his name shall be called Wonderful, Councellor, The mighty God, The everlasting Father, The prince of Peace.'

Leave it to the rich believers of later years to place a temple over the shrine and then erect a cathedral above the temple. Permit them to pave the Chatterjee lawn with marble and encase their mud hut and the Shiva sanctuary in weatherproof steel and glass. Let them frost everything with jewels. As for us of this day, we are happy to look at the evidences of poverty and hardship which Saradananda described. The grandeur of the incarnation is not in anything we or individuals in the future can do for him. It is in his own possession of a double personality —or rather in the fact of his having, along with his divine aspect, a human side. He is one of us; the lowliest of us. The divine we go toward; but we must start with the human.

Tears fall. I am here. I can see this with my own eyes. I am blessed forever. I feel a wish to intone a carol to the newborn saviour. It must needs be of my own idiom, my own tradition; that is all I know. From out of my young days in some literature class the words of the seventeenth-century Richard Crashaw return:

> Poore world (said I) what wilt thou doe
> To entertaine this starrie stranger?
> Is this the best thou canst bestow
> A cold and not too cleanly manger?
> Contend, ye powers of heav'n and earth,
> To fit a bed for this huge birth.

Welcome, all wonders in one sight!
   Eternitie shut in a span,
Summer in winter, day in night,
   Heaven in Earth, and God in man:
Great little one! whose all-embracing birth
Lifts earth to heav'n, stoops heav'n to earth.

CHAPTER X

'MAY HE ILLUMINE US'

I HAD now been to many Ramakrishna maths and had met scores of swamis and brahmacharis. I had made the acquaintance of juniors who were struggling to get established in a life of religion. I had touched the feet and talked with seniors of the Order, men of high levels of spiritual attainment. As a pilgrim I had gained the darshan of many of India's sacred spots and temples. I had walked in the footsteps—had stood on the stages where their lilas had occurred—of many saints. I had felt an acquaintance growing in me toward Sri Ramakrishna and Holy Mother and Ramakrishna's disciples. Dakshineswar I dared believe had turned me into a bhakta, a serious spiritual seeker; and the power felt at Jagannath had convinced me as no scriptural authority, no philosophical proof, no example even of holy life could have done, that the word 'God' represents something real, actual, knowable.

Gradually the answers were coming to the wonderings that had motivated my journey of research: Is Ramakrishna Vedanta a great new force capable of revitalizing Hinduism and freshening and broadening the other religions of the world? Is the Order a good instrument for carrying Ramakrishna's revelation forward? Do I want to throw in my lot with this unmaterial and, to me, foreign movement forever?

A significant part of the answer to all these wonderings was still to be supplied by the events of what might be called the Ramakrishna movement's annual holy week, which comes each spring and includes Shiva Ratri, the anniversary of Ramakrishna's birthday, and the annual brahmacharya and sannyas initiations of the Order. I experienced this holy week from the best vantage point, Belur Math.

When I returned from South India I found every building at headquarters bulging with sadhus who had arrived for the big events. The second floor of the old guesthouse, which I had occupied alone in November, was now filled to overflowing. Swami Vishuddhananda, the Vice President, had returned and was occupying the inner room—

Tantine's old bedroom which contained the big bed in which Swami Vivekananda had slept at Ridgley Manor, brought by Tantine to Belur Math. On the veranda that made up the balance of the quarters a dozen or fifteen men were now encamped, their bedding rolls and small bundles of possessions occupying narrow spaces side by side on the concrete floor.

Shiva Ratri means 'Shiva's night'—a yearly event devoted to the veneration of that aspect of God which emphasizes austerity and impersonality. The night is celebrated with four worships three hours apart, commencing at sundown and coming one after another until dawn. Those who celebrate Shiva Ratri properly not only stay up all night and attend the four worships, but begin a complete fast the day before, eating and drinking nothing until the final watch is over. The idea is that at least once a year in this way one may declare that one is verily other than the body and show one's independence of its demands for sustenance and rest.

In the centre of the auditorium of the main temple at Belur Math a roped-off section had been prepared, containing the implements for the worships, and a big basin into which, as events progressed, the worshippers were to make their oblations of water and vilwa leaves, which is all in the way of offering that the indulgent Shiva requires.

As the first watch ended, a clamour of shouting, clapping, and drum beating surprised me from the direction of the door, and in marched a costumed company moving to calls of 'Byom, byom; Hara, Hara'. Around the worship centre they paraded, many of the seated sadhus getting up and joining in. At the head of the group danced a very realistic Shiva, or Lord Hara, with trident—a swami from the Ubdodhan Office—followed by two or three brahmacharis outfitted to represent Shiva's 'demons' or attendants.

Thus with joy and realism was recalled Shiva's aspect as Nataraja, the divine dancer in whose ecstatic movements the whole world has its being, and from the sound of whose booming drum creation evolves.

Another aspect—of Shiva as the austere renunciate seated alone in meditation in the wilderness—was also commemorated that night. In the yard outside the dining hall a fire of big stumps had been built. To this place everyone adjourned between worships, as to a dhuni fire, that special fire of the monk, which symbolizes his unhoused mode of life and the incineration of any worldly objective. Here the same representative of Shiva in his role of ideal ascetic held court.

Back and forth throughout the night, which stretched on and on, moonless and black, sleep pulling at one, thirst and hunger making the stomach pinch and the head pound. Then at last, 7.00 a.m. and a big feast in the dining hall. Outside the fire was still burning but looked, in the strong rays of the morning sun, queer and unreal, as remote and unlikely as the events of Shiva's night, just passed.

Sri Ramakrishna's birthday is celebrated throughout the Order on two days. The first is that of the actual birth anniversary and may, of course, fall on any day of the week. This time is reserved for devotees, who come for special worships and other programmes and usually remain for a full meal of prasad. And on this day the monastic initiations occur. The second is the public anniversary and is always set to fall on the following Sunday: for Ramakrishna is a national hero in India, and all maths of the Order there must hold on his anniversary a giant open house and rally to which the general public is welcomed.

The public celebration fell on February 22 the year I was in India. I became aware that something special in the way of numbers was expected as, days in advance, teams of workers began preparations: added fencing for control of the coming crowds; temporary bamboo, palm thatch, and canvas shelters; enlarged washing and toilet facilities; a new ghat into the Ganges. The kitchen was extended, and a fresh bank of mud firepots built. Five new earthenware bins nearly the size of cisterns were constructed, into which food, as it was cooked in big brass vessels, was deposited for storage. The courtyard was roofed over to make a covered dining area. Some thirty extra brahmin cooks were hired, plus a platoon of kitchen servants.

The day commenced—as days generally do in India—at 4.30 a.m. Conch shells sounded. Then music began—full and very loud through a public-address system—which, except when interrupted by speeches, was to continue all day. At sun-up the gerrua flag bearing the seal of the Ramakrishna Order was raised above the main temple. The special buses which were to depart from Howrah Station every minute on the minute all day long began letting out their loads at the gate. People, more people than I had ever seen before at one time, began to arrive.

The half-mile long drive leading from the Grand Trunk Road to Belur Math had been turned into a market place. Here, and in the math precincts as well, merchants had been allotted free space in which to set up shops. Someone told me 500 businesses operated that day, and maybe counting the mobile food and betel hawkers, there were; my count showed about 150 actual emporiums. On sale were: images and pictures of deities; dishes and crockery; eyeglasses; furniture and toys; sweets, fruits, cool drinks, tobacco, and betel chews; kitchen utensils; notions; jewellery; ice cream—'Shanti' or 'Peacefulness' brand; and sugar cane and sugar cane juice (heavy presses had been moved in to make the latter). There were several places where a person could get weighed and a number of stands where publications representing many viewpoints were available. See photo 6a.

Everything was handled efficiently. Direction was in the hands of

150 swamis, assisted by 1,000 volunteer workers, mostly students from Ramakrishna schools. Three hundred policemen from the Howrah constabulary patrolled the grounds. The following were provided: first-aid, with a small tent hospital; pure drinking water at five booths; a lost-and-found service for restoring misplaced children. There was a free 'restaurant tent' for sadhus, with all provisions and services provided free by householder devotees who thus annually played host to their monastic friends. What fun the devotees had in stuffing the brahmacharis and swamis with all the rich foods that are popular in India but which monks rarely get because of their high cost! A dozen sweepers, contributed by the local municipality, worked constantly to keep things tidy. Two shoe-check rooms did a rushing business. Coast guard rescue teams to care for too-venturesome Ganges bath-takers operated from boats opposite the ghats. And a legally constituted magistrate's court carried on right there on the Belur Math grounds, administering immediate justice to anyone caught stealing, picking pockets, or committing any other offence.

During the day several orchestras played from different places throughout the grounds, and at one point three kirtan parties were going on simultaneously. At 2.00 p.m. a party of men, singing and dancing, arrived from Calcutta whence they had come on foot, bearing on high the whole way a picture of Ramakrishna festooned with flowers. Before the day was over the crowd totalled 400,000.

On the private puja day several days earlier ten thousand people had been given complete sit-down meals of potato curry and kichuri. On this public day twenty-five thousand were given their prasad in earthenware cups, which they ate standing or moving about.

One of the main things the visitors wanted, of course, was to have the darshan of Sri Ramakrishna. This was arranged for by placing a number of relics, such as clothes he had worn, in glass cases and displaying them outdoors on the lawn. Past these relics people filed reverently all day. Also, everyone wanted to bow before the statue of the Master in the big temple, and this was made feasible through use of a valve system. Outside the front steps people lined up, then were allowed in small groups (and through the use of barricades) first to climb the steps, then to move into the auditorium, then to approach the shrine, then to bow before the shrine, and finally to depart immediately through a side door, other similarly regulated groups following. The shouts of joy as the visitors entered the temple reminded me of similar outbursts at Jagannath. The great day ended at 7.00 in the evening with a fine display of fireworks.

As the tent city had sprung up mysteriously the night before, as magically that evening did it disappear. The whole area was a shambles the next dawn, camp fires yet smouldering, foundations for the stands still in place, a great deal of litter lying about. It looked like a gypsy camp after the gypsies have moved on, or perhaps like a bivouac ground just abandoned by an army in the field. But lorries and sweepers arrived early, and putting things to rights again was soon accomplished.

It was a big, relaxed fair, an Indian counterpart of the Kentucky Derby, New Year's Eve in Times Square, or the annual Rose Bowl parade and football game—a demonstration of what we are told by and about Indians, that religion is meant to be enjoyed.

The Ramakrishna order, as we know, was started by the Master himself when toward the end of his life in 1886 he distributed gerrua cloths to his boys and sent them out to perform that symbolic first act of the new renunciate, begging food from house to house. The next year the formal establishment took place when the brothers met at the Baranagore monastery, and under the guidance of Swami Vivekananda, performed the ceremony of sannyas, taking the vows of lifelong celibacy and poverty and assuming swami names.

But the antecedents of the Order go back much farther, to the ninth century, and I found it interesting to trace down from those times as much as I could of the organization's family tree. The beginning was with Sri Shankara, that amazing philosopher-saint who lived, it is believed, in the early 800s. Although his life is clouded in legend, it is generally agreed that Shankara was born in south India, that he gained his illumination while in his teens, that he became a monk and made successful preaching tours to all parts of India, that he wrote some two dozen books, and that he died in the Himalayas at the age of thirty-two. His greatest accomplishment was the purification and revitalization of Hinduism through the formulation of advaita Vedanta.

Shankara came at a time when Buddhism, then more than a thousand years old, was fast decaying, and the balance of India's religion had become a matter of ritualistic observances tightly controlled by a hereditary brahmin priesthood. Shankara's mission was considerably advanced through his establishment of a band of ascetics, this being the first time that monasticism had ever been organized in Hinduism. In doing this Shankara was not only trying to obtain for Hinduism the disciplinary advantages of the Buddhist church, but was attempting as well to aid those who wanted to devote their lives to seeking God exclusively. There had always been wandering monks in India. Now the ascetic could live in one place without needing to spend so much of his time in the mere search for physical sustenance.

Shankara selected four places in India where he established monastic centres, in the north, east, west, and south. He organized ten orders of monks, each with a different name, two or three to operate out of each headquarters. The headquarters of interest to us is that of the south, Shringeri, a few miles from Mysore.

When Sri Ramakrishna took his sannyas vows he received them from a monk named Tota Puri. Tota Puri arrived at Dakshineswar toward the end of 1864. Thought to have been born in the Punjab, he was in any case known to have been the head of a big monastery in that province. He was a person of tremendous self-discipline, an advaita Vedantist, and a realized soul. One begins one's religious course formally, it is held in Vedanta, with that ceremony in which the aspirant receives from a teacher a mantra appropriate to the spiritual path he intends to follow. This is known as initiation. He who initiates one into religion is the 'diksha' guru. Somewhat comparable ceremonies are held to induct one into monastic life. A monk thus receives three initiations: dikhsa, brahmacharya, and sannyas. He may take all three from the same guru or each from a different guru. Tota Puri, who initiated Sri Ramakrishna into the path of sannyas, was a monk of the Puri order of Shankara.

As in all monastic organizations, upon acceptance members of the Ramakrishna Order are given new, religious names. The system of naming works like this: Suppose one's childhood name is, for example, Gopal Ghosh. He enters the Order as a probationer. He is then known as Brahmachari Gopal, or Gopal Maharaj (anyone taking to a religious life becomes a king—of himself and of maya!). After a novitiate of at least five years, Gopal takes his formal brahmacharya initiation. He is now given a new religious name—say Bhakti—along with a second name shared by all initiated brahmacharis—Chaitanya. This has nothing to do with the sixteenth-century Bengali saint of that name, but is simply a Sanskrit word meaning 'one who realizes God as consciousness'. The man is then known properly as Brahmachari Bhakti Chaitanya, remaining, however, to his intimates Gopal Maharaj. (With Western brahmacharis a different plan is sometimes followed. To help a man break his identification with old associations he may be given an Indian first name soon after he comes to the Order, which becomes his Maharaj name; or after he is initiated into brahmacharya the first word of his Chaitanya name may be adopted as his familiar and Maharaj name.) After a minimum of four to five years more, if he is considered fit, Gopal may take sannyas. Then he is given a name ending in 'ananda' or 'bliss'—let us say Kripananda. He is now known as Swami Kripananda, although his intimates will still call him Gopal Maharaj.

Naturally I was curious about the mother house of the Puri order. But when I inquired about it I was told that no relations were maintained with this centre, and indeed it was doubtful whether many of the Ramakrishna monks had ever visited there. Here again was a good example of the 'unorganizedness' of Hinduism. From Sir Charles Eliot's monumental *Hinduism and Buddhism*, however, I was able to find out something about the Shringeri math. Eliot says that it is one of the most important religious institutions in India. The abbot in power at the time when Eliot was writing, about a generation ago, was said to be thirty-third in succession from Shankara. The math has a good-sized financial endowment instituted by local kings. The abbot is treated with great respect.

It would be very good to go to Shringeri one day and see it all!

A few days before the big public celebration at Belur Math, in a pre-dawn ceremony the annual brahmacharya and sannyas initiations had taken place. There have been also in the past dozen years, several brahmacharya investitures in the West. The rites are limited to the candidates and to ordained monks, who do not reveal much about what occurs. But since there is a deep interest in these ceremonies on the part of devotees and probationers, with very little published information available about them, it seems useful to explain what they consist of. While the exact words of the rites must remain restricted, I have been permitted to compose for publication the summaries appearing below.

For brahmacharya initiations in India this is the routine. The candidates come from various parts of the country several days before the appointed time. Each man meets with the President, or Vice President, who counsels him as to the meaning of the step he is about to take. In the West the initiations have been small and until 1959 limited to the disciples of one guru who has himself conducted the initiations in the presence of at least two additional swamis serving as co-sponsors. Each candidate provides himself with a new white dhoti and has his head shaved cleanly except for a tuft left at the crown, which is retained until sannyas.

With what attitudes do candidates approach the ceremony of brahmacharya? No novitiate can come other than confidently, with faith in the power of the rites and the guru who administers them truly to grant him a new birth in spirit. Yet at the same time one may experience considerable awe or trepidation. It is natural to feel nervous when entering formally upon a stage of life whose demands cannot be known fully in advance. The contrast between his own known shortcomings and his sincere resolve to fulfil excellently the obligations he is about to assume cannot help but give a man anxious concern. In a word, you are eager but scared! In addition, to me the unfamiliar experience of being obliged to have my head shaved for the ceremony constituted a hazard, as did the prospect of having to take a new and foreign name. But in whatever condition the candidate takes his brahmacharya vows, if he remains a steady aspirant he is certain to develop in actuality those qualities which he may have taken on only potentially. The meanings of the affirmations he makes he gains the power to realize.

The candidates sit before a sacramental fire. The guru and other seniors take their place behind. First comes a prologue in which is declared the purpose of the ceremony and the step the initiate is about to take: 'The purpose of my life is to cultivate dispassion, to attain union with God, and to be immersed in the bliss of divine love. To attain these objectives I will do my utmost to live according to the ideals of brahma-charya.'

These ideals are then enumerated, and constitute the vows proper:
To meditate every day with regularity.
To pray for devotion to God and feel the purity of one's true nature.
To do work as service to God.
To be calm, sweet-tempered, enthusiastic, and fair in one's dealings.
To be moderate, constructive-minded, and self-effacing.

To ever remember that the consuming passion of the brahmachari's life must be to find God, who is dearer than any enjoyment, any personal relationship, any worldly responsibility.

To be practical in a practical world: 'When I have known the Truth that these vows lead to—but only then—I will try to help others reach that Truth.'

Finally comes the actual vow of brahmacharya, of continence in word, thought, and deed, the practice of which is a necessary instru-mentality for realization of the other ideals.

In the West a short final sentence has been added, said first by the administering guru and repeated by the candidate. With its enunciation formal entrance into the Order is effected: 'Om; I take refuge in the holy Order of Sri Ramakrishna, as the Lord helps me.'

Last of all, all present repeat the ancient prayer addressed to that Presence in the fire which, even as it consolidates one's good intentions, equally consumes one's ignorance: 'I, who am an embodied being, endowed with intellect, life-breath, and their functions, now offer up all my actions and their fruits to the fire of Brahman. No matter what I may have done, said, or thought, in waking, in dreaming, or in dreamless sleep, with my mind, my tongue, my hands, and my other members: may all this be an offering to Brahman. We offer ourselves and all we have at the feet of Sri Ramakrishna.'

In India the head of the Order now gives sacred threads to those who do not have them, for everyone becomes a brahmin on becoming a brahmachari if he is not a brahmin already, the new cloth, and the new name ending in Chaitanya. In the West the thread-giving is omitted, but one is told his new name by the guru just at the close of the ceremony.

For sannyas the routine is more complex. There is the same shaving as for brahmacharya. On the day of the initiation a complete fast is observed. Clothes of gerrua are obtained. In addition, the candidate must perform the obsequies of his father and mother and indeed of himself. As a monk, he henceforth can have no family duties such as participating in memorial services for parents. Nor will he have any offspring to perform the last rites for him when he dies; so he completes the funeral services for those of his elders who are already dead and for himself once and for all before becoming a sannyasin. Also these funeral rituals symbolize his death to the world. Performed a few hours before the sannyas investiture, the rites make the candidate a veritable 'ghost' until he gains his new birth upon becoming a swami.

To me this was very interesting. A swami not only cuts himself off from the line of his heritage religiously, but throughout India does so legally also; for according to law an ordained monk is considered as not related any more to his former family members. He may be the only son and his father may die leaving millions, but he cannot now inherit a cent; equally, his family, whatever may betide them, can have no further claim upon him.

At the appointed hour before the fire the vows are spoken. (Sannyasins are initiated ahead of brahmacharis.) It is a long ritual, consisting of many prayers and affirmations. Its purpose is utter renunciation for the sake of God. Some of the mantras are given in English in Chapter XV of Book II of Swami Saradananda's *Sri Ramakrishna the Great Master*. It is a ritual, essentially, of disavowing forever matter's false illusions, and espousing Spirit as the one true ingredient of man and nature. For example, here is a typical affirmation:

> Om. Oblations to the supreme Self.
> May my skin, flesh, blood, bones, fat, marrow,
>   and nerves be purified.
> Free from ignorance, the root of all evil,
>   may I realize myself as the Light
>   of pure Consciousness,
>   the self-luminous Brahman.

Thus the body, mind, and senses are purified, one's ego is surrendered, one's mind relieved of all impressions of past deeds, thoughts, and limiting memories, by the enunciation again and again of: 'I am the Atman, the non-dual Brahman, pure and free.'

Now the candidate proceeds to the sannyas guru, prostrating himself before him. The guru cuts the tuft of hair. This, along with his sacred thread, the man consigns to the flames, signifying his severance from caste, sex, and society. The guru then hands the candidate the ochre cloth. He gives him his name and teaches him the secret mantras known only to monks, by which any sannyasin of any order can identify any other as ordained and genuine. The man dresses himself in the clothes of renunciation. Last of all he burns in the fire, with all that is holy as his witness, his desire for enjoyment of life here and hereafter—all cravings for wealth, for progeny, and for name and fame. (These are vows of poverty and chastity nonpareil. Obedience is taken for granted, for no initiate would feel he can be anything but dutiful to the source and channel of his blessing.) The man utters the sacred promises attesting that no living being need ever in future have anything to fear from him, avowing all creatures to be extensions of himself. Thus the cere-

mony, which really turns a mortal into a God, ends. Through utter
renunciation of humanness one has gained divinity.

Then the new swamis prove that what they have just enunciated—
that the life is more than the food, and the body than the raiment—is
true. Two by two they perform that symbolic act of total abandonment
to divine providence, begging food from door to door. For three days
they go out into the neighbourhoods around Belur Math, those who do
not speak Bengali paired with those who do, obtaining their entire fare
by mendicancy. They bring back whatever they collect for their own use
and for sharing with the other members of the brotherhood, who subject
them, of course, to much friendly teasing about the feebleness of their
talents as providers! And during this time each new swami greets all
seniors, telling them his new name and having the joy of hearing himself
addressed by it.

The gerrua flag raised above the main temple at Belur Math on the day
of the public birthday had borne the seal of the Ramakrishna Math and
Mission. I had noticed this emblem carved into the lin-
tels of doorways at some of the other maths. It appears
too as the colophon on the Order's publications. I made
an effort to find out what the emblem means.

The seal shows a choppy lake with a pink lotus in the
water, lighted by a rising sun and encircled by a snake.
On the waves rides a white swan. Below is a band of
Sanskrit lettering.

At first the symbol struck me as somewhat bizarre. But if one makes an
effort to understand it, it grows meaningful and attractive. Designed by
Swami Vivekananda, it is a powerful ideogram showing his design for the
harmonious balance and development of the religious aspirant. In another
place he established as the objective for the Ramakrishna monk that he
should work for his own liberation and for the good of the world. In the
Math seal he carries the idea farther. The tenets of work and worship
are incorporated into the seal and more besides. Swamiji said in his great
lecture on 'The Ideal of a Universal Religion': 'Would to God that all
men were so constituted that in their minds all these elements of philosophy, mysticism, emotion, and work were equally present in full!
That is my ideal, my ideal of a perfect man'. He designed the emblem
to illustrate this objective and show the way to it. The rough water
stands for karma yoga, for spiritual progress through unselfish work;
the lotus for bhakti yoga, for development through love of God; and
the rising sun for jnana yoga, for the practice of discrimination and
knowledge. All are held together by raja yoga, concentration and meditation, which arouse the 'serpent' of spirituality. The swan in the centre
symbolizes the Supreme Soul. Supported by all these modes must
emerge Swamiji's ideal man, serene, blissful, perfected, alight in the

beauty of his own Self. The motto states Swamiji's ultimate aim for his children, to which all work, all worship, all vows and efforts and struggles should lead: 'May He Illumine Us'.

One of the most popular books during the latter 1950s was *The Nun's Story* by Kathryn Hulme. This is a beautifully written and most moving tale in which Sister Luke, a Belgian nun, after seventeen years of dedicated service in a Catholic nursing order, eventually feels she must leave her convent, and does so. The failure that sends her away is her inability to develop to the required extent the virtue of total obedience. The book is not condemnatory in spirit, but its theme is that the severe external disciplines which Christian monasticism imposes with the object of eliminating natural weaknesses succeeded too often in crushing natural humanity, generosity of heart, and spontaneity instead. Sister Luke could never overcome the idea that this result was at odds with God's purpose for her.

The way of life followed in Sister Luke's order was based on the Rule of St. Benedict. This code, which largely set the pattern for Western monasticism for fifteen hundred years, contains seventy-three chapters of minute rules. Other manuals developed since Benedict's time are as detailed, or more so. In such codes every phase of a monastic's deportment is prescribed—how to walk, how to hold a book, how to tabulate and publicly confess one's infractions of the rule, observing a proper balance between a dangerous reticence and an equally perilous self-condemnation. Penalties, including personal indignities and even corporal punishments, are prescribed for failure to obey. 'Ours is a life against nature,' Sister Luke is told again and again. 'The nun dies a little every day. Singularity in virtue, even in the adoration of God—as is excessive humility—is a sin of pride. Your one purpose here is to reduce yourself to a Living Rule.'

Whether appealing to the touch of masochism in human nature, or to one's sense of the dramatic, I don't know; but such ideals of asceticism do attract. To practise them should, I think, also give one a tangible sense of accomplishment. The monastic may know exactly where he stands in relation to his obligations, and if he obeys the rule precisely he may presume himself to be successful in his religious life. To manage matters through codes should have advantages for the directors of the religious, too. Superiors can govern according to the book.

But a thoughtful person finds something very disturbing in such practices. To read such codes or stories about how they are practised makes you feel sorry. Is one who is trying to renounce all for God an incorrigible who must be broken? Is a cloister a disciplinary barracks? Most important, do these methods produce saints? One recalls the pitiless logic of Mira Bai, the sixteenth-century saint of Rajputana:

> If by renouncing women one could attain God,
>   What about eunuchs?
> If eating roots and fruits could make Him ours,
>   What about monkeys?
> And could baths in sacred rivers wash one clean,
>   Then what about fish?

No, says Mira Bai, that's not the way at all:

> No, seek for devotion.
> Without that intense love, God,
> Who is the embodiment of love,
> Cannot be found.

Then how should monasticism be ordered? If not according to rules, what is the way? Some established policies are necessary, no doubt, but the real spirit of monasticism, the Ramakrishna Order teaches, cannot be achieved through codes. It is an intangible something yearned for, struggled after, and if one is fortunate—caught.

Swami Brahmananda always urged that the progress of the individual is more important than the expansion of the organization. And Swami Vivekananda declared many times that freedom is the first requisite of growth. Swami Shuddhananda, the fifth President of the Order, told the following story at a conference of senior monks at Belur Math in 1935: 'After Swamiji's return from the West, a brahmachari requested him for some well-defined rules. At Swamiji's instance all assembled ... when Swamiji said: "Our objective is to transcend all rules, for we are sannyasins and free. Still there is need of eliminating bad rules with the help of good ones, and then to reject the latter also. This is the goal of rules. Rules by themselves are of no avail unless we ourselves are good. Rules invite an attempt at breaking them. Monks should never take a wrong step. The purpose of establishing an organization and framing rules is to enable newcomers to imbibe through them the ideal, which is: For one's own salvation and for the good of all." '

The rules that Swamiji established, when he did do so, were however not rules in Benedict's sense, but instead broad and general objectives for individual spiritual growth and for the future direction of the Order. A summary of them may be found on pages 135-139 of the *History of the Ramakrishna Math and Mission*. In 1935 and in 1937 a few additional tenets were adopted, but again these were more for the ordering of the business procedures of centres than for the detailed direction of behaviour. Certain specific individual regulations, however, were included in the 1935 legislation, and these we shall examine.

Concerning entry into the Order, the rules simply state that a candidate should be healthy and adaptable, may not be over thirty (in India —thirty-six in the West), must have been known at the centre where he expects to make his postulancy for at least a year, and should be a sincere aspirant after spirituality, having 'due regard' for the ideals of Sri Ramakrishna and Swami Vivekananda.

I noticed this difference between Vedanta probationers in India and the West, that the former would average as a rule possibly up to ten years younger than the latter. Men in India tend to go more or less directly into the Order from high school or college, often having been closely associated with a math during their student days as pupils in one of the Order's educational institutions.

Of the two dozen monastics at the Vedanta Society of Southern California in the autumn of 1959, one-third entered at an early age (seventeen to twenty-five), whereas two-thirds joined when around thirty or somewhat older. This later entrance age is not so very desirable (for too much contact with the world fills the head with appetites and memories hard to efface later), but is inevitable at the present time because of Vedanta's newness in Europe and America. Vedanta there is not widely known or available. A person is unlikely to have heard of it as a child or to be aware of its existence at the end of his school career, so that most who come to Vedanta do so only after having made an examination—which takes time—of other religious possibilities first.

In India parents frequently are devotees. And while it must surely be as hard for a father or mother in India to give up a son as for those anywhere else, the acquaintance of parents with the Order would appear to make the lots of both parents and children easier. Of the two dozen monastics at the Vedanta Society of Southern California in the autumn of 1959, only a fourth had parents knowing anything of Vedanta at the time of their postulancy. Indeed, the parents of at least half were originally hostile to this unknown foreign influence.

Other tenets of the 1935 regulations are that monastics must meditate every day, must be circumspect in their relations with women, should not go out without informing the math head of their intention, and may be expelled if they flout fundamental monastic principles. That is about all.

But the most essential qualification of a monastic aspirant, as the Ramakrishna Order sees it, cannot be codified nor its development legislated. That is possession by him of devotion, or at least the potentiality of devotion, to God. It is as impossible to identify the promise of this inner quality in a postulant as it is to define it. It is impossible to force its appearance later in the monastic career. Yet without it excellence in other characteristics is held to count for little.

This matter of devotion—of somehow striking a gusher of divine love in one's heart—is central to Ramakrishna monasticism. The highest ideal of human existence is held out—realization of God in this life; others have realized him; I too can and must: 'May He Illumine Us'. To realize him I must somehow develop this love for him, this devotion.

It is hastened by initiation, by affection for and service to one's teacher, by unselfish work, by meditation: 'Think, meditate, and love will grow'. No set of rules can produce devotion. Outward penances may not speed it at all.

> If the Lord is worshipped, what is the need of austerities?
> If the Lord is not worshipped, what good can they do?
> If God is within and without, what use have penances?
> And if he is not, what good can they do?
>
> Hence, O aspirant, give up.
> My child, there is no need for austerity at all.

Instead—

> Approach the Source of Love.
> Win love, win strong devotion,
> And with devotion as a sword,
> Cut apart your bonds of wordliness.

As I understand it the Ramakrishna plan is simply this, to hold high the ideal of realization and trust God that the necessary devotion may come. One successful guru explained the Vedanta training technique in this brief formula: 'We insist upon regular daily meditation; and we let go but keep watch'. It is as simple as that! The Christian plan seems to be to legislate the outside in the expectation that the inside will change. The Vedantic idea is to let a person largely have his head until he arrives at his own comeuppance and consequent insight, which will begin to make a man of God out of him and result in the outside's taking care of itself.

The steady meditation—the first ingredient of the recipe—is counted upon to refashion every tissue, nerve, and capillary in the aspirant. The movement of grace and the ability to co-operate with that grace may be expected to occur if one is persistent in meditation. The hands-off part of the formula, which allows a man to run his own course—checked only if he gets dangerously far out of line—permits self-understanding to come and self-discipline to take over. A progressively purified mind— a mind filled with devotion—is the only effectual rulebook there can ever be.

Where the emphasis is on inner rather than outer discipline, trainees will not always appear to be perfect saints. To those who come with Catholic ideas of deportment, processes in the Ramakrishna monastery may now and again seem helter-skelter and the residents discomposed. New observers may be puzzled by what they see; and monastic aspirants at first are likely to find the unsubstantialness of the training programme and the liberality allowed them to seek and follow almost any path they find congenial, quite unnerving.

o

But watch closely. I do not believe you will find literal-mindedness, martyrishness, or spiritual self-satisfaction in the Ramakrishna monk. Wait a bit, and you will see that this Hindu method—intangible as it seems—actually works. Anyone who has been around a Vedanta centre very long has beheld examples of revolution in personality that are amazing. Sometimes they come gradually. Sometimes an individual who has been wayward, intractable, apparently incapable of improvement, will become suddenly transformed.

And this intensive remaking of personality, is after all, what monasticism is for. Not merely the remaking of personality, but the creation of saints. The man who has seen God is earth's most valuable being. Living in peace with himself, he brings peace to others. As a present and visible testimony that joy in life can be had, he guarantees that every man's instinct toward happiness is not ill-founded. Attainment of God-knowledge is the real, the only objective of the religious life. That it can produce this result is proved by the presence of perfected persons among us.

Most people can still remember the excitement which surrounded the entrance a few years ago of Hollywood actress June Haver into a convent, and the even greater attention focused on her when she departed therefrom eight months later. If a prominent figure renounces, or if a known or even unknown person decides to give up monastic life, the occurrences produce intense speculation. One must conclude that the man in the street is more idealistic than is generally supposed. Any act of eschewing wordliness (although he would not choose to do it himself) attracts his admiration; if it is not carried through he is genuinely disappointed. But if an individual progresses satisfactorily in a religious vocation, as most do, there is nothing in this of a sensational nature, even though quite newsworthy changes for the better in him are probably taking place. Well, so it is, and so it should be.

What are the facts about growth and stability in monasticism? I have always wanted to know, and everyone else I have ever talked to about this is also vitally interested in the topic.

I had hoped to gather sufficient data to present the full facts concerning membership, expansion, and turnover in Catholic and Episcopalian monasticism, and to compare these with the data I have been given on the same factors in the Ramakrishna Order. But considerable library research, as well as numerous personal and written inquiries of Roman and Anglican sources, failed to produce very satisfactory figures.

The only figures that are fairly complete are those on numbers. As far as membership goes, monasticism in the Roman Catholic Church is expanding. The *National Catholic Almanac* of 1956 published data showing a more than 14 per cent world-wide rise in men's orders from 1948 to 1954. Statistics reported in the British journal, *The Life of the*

Spirit, in its July, 1954, number, gave the figure of 19 per cent as the membership increment for men's orders over the period from 1940 to 1954. The only growth estimate I have for Catholic women's orders is that the number in them in the United States has tripled since 1900. with the contemplative orders growing faster than the active. Total membership in the numerous Catholic orders and congregations throughout the world is at least 270,000 men and 575,000 women at the present time. I have no figures on numbers in Episcopalian communities.

Second, as in any other specialized field nowadays, in Christian monasticism really first-class individuals are hard to attract. There are no figures to be had on the shortage of gifted trainees in the religious vocation, but candid Roman and Anglo-Catholic authorities will admit that it is a fact that such a dearth prevails.

Third, there is a good deal of coming and going in Western monasticism (as there is, for example, in the institution of marriage and in place of residence. Restlessness and impermanence are prominent features of the Western temper at present.) What the dropout rate is I have not been able to determine. A mother superior of a contemplative order told one of the members of the Hollywood society that the turnover in active orders of women is 'large' but in contemplative orders is 'small'. One Catholic monk who visited the monastery at Trabuco some time back made this statement: 'If everyone who had come to our place had stayed we'd have 5,000 by now'. His abbey was organized in 1900 and presently has a membership of 240.

The figures on Hindu monasticism are even scantier than those for Christian monasticism. Since Indian monasticism is not organized in the Western sense, no statistics for it have ever been compiled or probably could be. But if the total in Indian orders were known, and to them were added the figures on wandering sadhus, the number would certainly be a staggering one; the estimate usually given is eight million.

Satisfactory figures for the Ramakrishna Order—which is one small and new organization within Vedantic monasticism—are however available. They were supplied by the General Secretary, Swami Madhavananda, partly in the long interview I had with him in India, and partly by letter since.

Total number of sannyasins on March 1, 1956, was just under 500. There were approximately 110 ordained brahmacharis. The number of probationers, who are not registered on the Orders' official roll, was estimated to be something over 100. The average number of initiations for the prior six years was 20 into brahmacharya and 15.5 into sannyas yearly.

Is the Ramakrishna Order growing? Yes, its growth rate would compare favourably with that of Christian orders, producing a net increment of perhaps 25 men per year, or something over a 20 per cent rise in the previous five-year period. If one were to figure the rise in Hollywood where there was one monastic in 1940 and more than two dozen in 1959 the expansion factor would be in the nature of 2,500 per cent!

The Ramakrishna Order also finds it hard to attract sufficient material of high quality. What the reason is for this no one in the Order seems to know. But a real manpower shortage exists, so that no new projects requiring added personnel may be started anywhere in the Order without permission from Headquarters; and it is only with difficulty that men can be spared to be sent to the West as assistants in established centres, let alone to father new societies.

The turnover rate in the Ramakrishna Order is very low. The total over-all shrinkage figure has been estimated to be less than 20 per cent. That is, of all men entering, four-fifths remain for the rest of their lives. As would be expected, most of those who depart leave during the probationary period. It is rare that an initiated brahmachari leaves, less than an average of two doing so yearly, while the percentage of sannyasins resigning from the Order is even lower—not more than three or four annually. In other words, of the total 600 in the Order, fewer than half a dozen leave per year, making the annual dropout rate less than 1 per cent. When one considers that the average labour turnover in business in the United States runs around 4 per cent per year, one sees that the stability factor in the Ramakrishna Order is indeed considerable.

Ramakrishna Vedanta, as it becomes a world movement, must face many hard decisions. It must preserve its Hindu character and the purity of Ramakrishna's revelation, yet be flexible enough to adapt itself to many different cultures. How can it do so and yet avoid being modified too much or diluted past recognition? A look at the struggles of Buddhism and Christianity in China may suggest some answers.

In the year A.D. 62 Ming-Ti, emperor of China, had a dream in which he beheld in the West a marvellous golden man. To discover who or what he might be Ming-Ti sent emissaries to India, who brought back the glad tidings of Buddhism. This story may be only legend, but it is known that about this time Buddhist missionaries did arrive in China and were welcomed at court. This great religion, which grew out of Hinduism and which eventually the Indian people were to disregard, had by then been in existence some five centuries.

What Gotama preached, as did every other avatar, was the perennial philosophy—pure Vedanta. By the time Buddhism reached China, however, it had been subjected to various interpretations, and several schools of thought had grown up; but its great monastic system enabled Buddhism to retain a considerable identity through the years. Wherever it came the people saw it before their eyes not as a theology, but as above all a religion of monks, of holy men, dedicated to their faith. As elsewhere, so in China, the first missionaries were monastics from India, and it was primarily through the settling down of such men to lifelong service in China that this foreign faith was able eventually to take root there and become part of the indigenous culture of the Chinese people.

One would have thought China an extremely unpromising field for Buddhist expansion. The Chinese were practical and outward-looking, whereas Buddhism is world-denying. And a fundamental conviction of the Chinese is reverence for the family and for the duty of begetting sons, while Buddhism praises celibacy. Their monastic status could not be given up by the Buddhist missionaries, but they learned how to make themselves useful to the Chinese family. They adopted into their teaching the ideal of filial piety. They established masses for the dead, enlisting much sentiment in their favour. Buddhism appealed also to the natural human hope for life beyond the grave.

While the upper classes remained Confucianist in outlook and tended to hold somewhat aloof from the new religion, on the other hand the Taoist system, also prevalent in China at the time, contained much that was compatible with Buddhism; and after some three generations there began to be a real exchange of ideas between the foreigners and the Taoist mystics. Taoism had already prepared the soil with its own ideal of inwardness and passivity in the doctrine of the Tao, as presented by Lao-tzu in the Tao-te Ching. Instead of attacking Taoism, Buddhism almost adopted it. It took over some Taoist deities into the Buddhist cycle as attendants of the Buddha; some of them it even made into Bodhisattvas. It became common to say that Lao-tzu—when he disappeared as legend claimed he had in the sixth century B.C. into the Gobi desert—was on his way to India to become reincarnate as Buddha. With Taoism thus blended into Buddhism it became possible to claim that Buddhism was not a foreign sect but a universal religion, and Buddha a world saviour.

In the second century A.D. several outstanding figures were teaching Buddhism in China. The main emphasis at first was on the translation of Indian scriptures into Chinese. By the end of the fourth century there began the practice of Chinese believers making pilgrimages to the holy places of Buddhism in India. Returning, they brought more scriptures, stories of the dramatic life of Buddha, legends of the Jatakas, some knowledge of Indian culture—and enthusiasm. By A.D. 363 Buddhist missionaries were given permission to receive native Chinese into the order as monks. Hitherto Chinese converts had been laymen only. With this important happening the church became national, independent, and self-guided. Chinese Buddhism became, as it was from then on to be, a local religion, its adherents loyal to their own country and emperor.

By the fifth and sixth centuries many people of quality became interested, and numerous Buddhist monasteries and convents were established, to which Chinese flocked. By 900 the influence of Buddhism in China was very strong. By this time it had developed into many sects.

Chinese Buddhism had its own orthodoxies, neo-orthodoxies, reform movements, quietisms, fundamentalisms, and modernisms. But it had incorporated itself into Chinese life so thoroughly that today one finds many Chinese words to be Sanskrit in origin, Chinese deities who have been evolved from Indian originals, and much in Chinese mythology, literature, and art traceable back to the homeland of Gotama. Sir Charles Eliot in his *Hinduism and Buddhism* says that Buddhism was perhaps as great a power in China as was ever Christianity in Europe.

Consider, in contrast, the fate in China of the religion of Jesus. There is evidence that Christianity reached the Far East some six or seven hundred years after the death of its founder. However, this religion made little headway there until re-introduced in the sixteenth century by Jesuit fathers. Francis Xavier tried to reach China but died just outside her shores. He was followed by Matthew Ricci, who was a very able man and whose way of spreading Christianity permitted him a considerable success.

The story of Matthew Ricci is a fascinating one. It has recently been set forth in an engaging book called *The Wise Man from the West*, by Vincent Cronin. Ricci was an upper-class Italian who joined the Jesuits as a young man, in 1571, and reached China some ten years later. The China of that day was still the unknown and impenetrable Cathay—extremely distrustful of outside interference—and Ricci had to spend many years of struggle in achieving any attention for himself and the faith he represented. Actually then it was Ricci's great gifts in secular fields, as a linguist, astronomer, and pioneer geographer, which finally commended him to the influential people of the country and permitted a grudging sufferance of this theology. Dressing first as a Buddhist monk, in an attempt to make it clear that he was a man of religion, Ricci soon learned that this identification did not recommend him to people of the higher classes. So he adopted the dress and manners of the Confucianist graduate, or mandarin, a mode which his learning and austerity of life allowed him to carry off successfully.

Eventually Father Ricci reached Peking where he became known to the court and the Emperor. He lived quietly, carried on a social intercourse with the aristocratic men of the capital, made a few converts, and gave his main attention to translating Christian doctrines into Chinese. These books came to be accepted as excellent Confucian-type moral treatises, some eventually to find their way into the roster of recognized Chinese classics.

Ricci died in 1610. Other Jesuits followed and, working in Ricci's way, caused Christianity in China to continue to be taken seriously. An edict of toleration of Christianity was given by the Crown in 1692.

Ricci had perceived that Christianity could never succeed in China as an exotic import. It must adapt itself to Chinese ways of thought, graft itself to all that was good in an established and fastidious culture.

Ricci respected Chinese susceptibilities, believing that to do otherwise was bad manners and worse religion. He had used tact and gentleness, understanding how anyone must feel when confronted with a brand-new creed. He had contended that the mysteries of his faith must be unfolded gradually. Most particularly, after an intense study of the Chinese mind, Ricci had decided that converts must be permitted to fulfil their two traditional duties, the veneration of Confucius and of the dead members of their families.

But now things began to change. Franciscans and Dominicans entered China. Their method of evangelizing was direct, uncompromising. They walked through the streets holding up crucifixes and proclaiming all unchristian dead to be lost, with the living headed for the same fate. They disregarded a culture older than their own, which contained much of wisdom and beauty, and made no attempt to adapt themselves to the country. When these men discovered Ricci's toleration of Confucius and ancestor worship they protested to Rome that a tainted form of Christianity had been introduced into China.

A hundred-year dispute followed—one of the most serious and far-reaching controversies ever to face the Catholic Church. Finally the decision was rendered. The Church chose to be rigorously inflexible. 'Integrity', it phrased its final word on the subject, 'must precede charity.' The veneration of Confucius and dead ancestors was declared superstitious and Christians were forbidden such ceremonies. Ricci's policy of tolerance and adaptation was revoked.

Thus the imperial power in China was confronted with the pontifical will, and to the enraged government of China Christianity appeared no longer a faith of reasonable men, but a swashbuckling and fanatical cult. The emperor responded with a declaration of *his* own, a rule that all missionaries, if they wished to remain in China, must obtain an imperial permit, which would be issued only to those who agreed to abide by the practices of Matthew Ricci.

So as the years passed Christianity declined in China. Through the eighteenth and well into the nineteenth centuries what Christianity remained there had to be practised almost in secret. As the military and commercial invaders of the Western nations made themselves felt after 1850, China was again opened up to 'Christian influence'. Even so, by the twentieth century China counted only 2,500 native clergy and three million Catholics, the second figure representing considerably less than 1 per cent of the population. Mass was still said in Latin. Under the protection of Western guns Protestants sent in representatives who did good work in founding schools and hospitals. But at every turn the ideals of Christianity were refuted by Western treatment of China.

Eventually China did open her heart and mind to the outside world. Going beyond her instructors, she reached out for the one idealogy which it seemed people were enthusiastic about and willing to sacrifice for—

the most extreme form of Western materialism there is, namely communism. China learned the lessons the Christian nations taught better than they meant her to. She accepted Ricci's mechanical advances; his faith she dashed to the ground. And the result today is that China has become again as of old the difficult and inaccessible Cathay.

Most curious of all, the saving hope clung to by those who fear recent developments in China is that her present detour from virtue (as they see it) cannot be lengthy or serious because of the fundamentally Buddhist adherence of her vast masses!

I take this look backwards in the hope that things past may reveal things to come. The future of the Ramakrishna movement is a subject very interesting to conjecture about. In many particulars the Ramakrishna Order, as its monks move out as teachers on every continent, must meet the same challenges as did Buddhism and Christianity when they went to China. Will Vedanta follow the way of 'integrity' or of adaptation?

Ramakrishna died in 1886. Within ten years his apostle had introduced his message to the world. When you recall that it took centuries for Buddhism, and equally centuries for Christianity, to reach China, what a commentary this gives on the speed-up of communications in our time.

If one thinks in terms of numbers of churches or of membership, it cannot be denied that Vedanta is, however, after two generations, still an alien growth' outside India. With its probably not more than two thousand members in the United States and Europe, it is not possible to claim that Vedanta is at present, except in its homeland, at all a popular movement.

Yet again, something has happened, and it is good. Consider the remarkable broadening out that has occurred in Christian nations in the past few years. Suddenly it is no longer a dangerous heterodoxy to hold that the spirit of the one God may be manifest in faiths besides Christianity. College comparative religions courses, in which all viewpoints are treated with respect, are numerous. Anthologies of spiritual literature published today regularly include passages from the Bhagavad-Gita or the Upanishads. Members of Christian church groups are often to be found attending Vedanta temples as visitors. In 1956 a book recommending the mysticism of Ramakrishna—Colin Wilson's *The Outsider* —became a runaway bestseller in England and the United States; and Arnold Toynbee's *A Historian's Approach to Religion*, which predicted the emergence of a broad new Oriental-type faith, was nearly as popular. The Bhagavad-Gita in a news-stand edition has sold in the hundreds of thousands in America and England. *Time* and *Life* have run sympathetic stories about phases of what we would call the perennial philosophy. And the 'illiterate' priest of Dakshineswar has even been quoted in *The Reader's Digest*. A new world of reconciliation seems to be dawning.

The Vedanta movement says that the spirit of God who appeared on earth as Ramakrishna is the cause of this.

In so saying, is Vedanta then following the way of 'integrity'? Is taking satisfaction in this new saviour the admission that Vedanta is just another proselytizing religion, using sweet words of universality as a more than usually clever missionary come-on? A case could be made for this position. In one place in his rule Swami Vivekananda declared that India must conquer the world with her spirituality. The Order has not been adverse to publicity of a refined sort, and throughout India and the rest of the world its men have been as busy translating the life and words of Ramakrishna into local languages as were all the missionaries of the past in disseminating knowledge of their founders. The Ramakrishna sadhu has shown himself willing to be taken seriously by the leaders of thought of our time, just as were the early Buddhists and Ricci when they were trying to get footholds in China.

But a little deeper enquiry will show that it will be next to impossible for Vedanta ever to be an evangelizing movement. Two fundamental tenets of Vedanta must, it would seem, keep this from happening: the doctrine of the avatar; and the evolution-involution view of history. The syncretist outlook of the Indian which permitted the Buddhist to live with Taoism and Confucianism and to add something to them as well as to gain something from them, is as strongly at work today as in the past.

Will adaptation, then, be Vedanta's mode of working? So it seems. Vedanta will spread, not by saying it is right and all others are wrong, not by remaining firm and making all others conform, but by accepting people as they are, telling them that what they are doing is fine, showing them that they can do better.

On the shrine of the typical Ramakrishna centre you will see Jesus and Buddha side by side with Sri Ramakrishna. Vedanta gurus in initiation give the mantra of Christ to those who are drawn to him as Chosen Ideal, as well as the mantra of Ramakrishna and other incarnations. Also those who do not believe in avatars have a place in Vedanta. Vedanta's principal is that any aspect, if it is helpful, if it is purifying, is therein divine. No church council will declare it superstitious or anathema.

Such an absence of contentiousness is, of course, maddening to the religious segregationist, who complains that Vedanta would caddishly swallow up Christ as early Buddhism incorporated Lao-tzu. But what is wrong in this? Is he who is the World Soul to be kept secure in some sect's small iron safe of exclusiveness? Which was better for the sincere Chinese—Catholic 'integrity' or the Buddhist way of reconciliation? Each time the Lord comes he says, "Think not that I am come to destroy the law, or the prophets; I come not to destroy, but to fulfil.'

There is a chance that his pronouncement will be, this time, heard everywhere and actually understood. This is what Swamiji visualized in his directive, that Vedanta's message of harmony should be broadcast throughout this one world.

But adaptation is a two-way movement. If Vedanta would adapt truth and truth-seekers to itself, Vedanta must expect to find itself adapted. This is exactly what is happening. Practices have always differed in the Ramakrishna installations of north and south India. They will differ most markedly in the West. In time an occidental Vedanta will emerge, as did a Chinese Buddhism. This is in accordance with the principle of religious freedom, and will be necessary if Vedanta is to grow.

The changes which have appeared between the practices in America and those of the Mission in India are not tremendous, but they *are* changes: Substitution of rose leaves in the daily worship for the leaves of the prescribed vilwa, which does not grow in the West; replacement of venerable Sanskrit by upstart English in rituals; officiation on the part of swamis at funeral services for devotees who have died; and dozens more of a like nature.

Swamiji said that any religion, to take root, requires a philosophy, a mythology, and a ritualism. Vedanta philosophy is not being adapted in the West. There is no need for it to be; its principles overleap racial differences and continental boundaries. The variegated Hindu mythology, however, is being modified a little by the omission of parts too strange, too excessively exotic, and the addition of stories of the feats of Western heroes and heroines, some of which even in these few years have been adjusted in the telling, so that cool fact has softened into warm fable; while ritual, like the Sabbath being made for man and not the other way round, is being changed quite considerably in America and Europe, to attune it to the convenience and mode of those who would practise it. And all this is as it should be.

Some would say that a religion of renunciation like Vedanta can never be adapted to the occidental mind; to make Vedanta available in the West is not to adapt it but to degrade it. But fear of Western inability to live up to Vedanta is not the attitude of the Ramakrishna Order. In the interview I had in India with Swami Madhavananda, I asked him about this problem, and the answers he gave to me, an American, were reassuring. In the first place, it is certainly true that not everyone in India is spiritual; there, as everywhere else, materialists are to be found. And in the second place, Vedanta may very well become conscientiously followed in the West for the very reasons some might say it won't. Having had so much luxury and enjoyed so much self-expression, and seeing they don't answer the soul's need, Western people may now have had their surfeit of these things and thus may be quite ready for renunciation.

Time will tell. But the intentions of the Westerner who comes to Vedanta must not be underrated. To come to Vedanta in the West is still a considerable step, at odds with the trend of the times and a man's apparent best interests. Serious sacrifices may be called for. To become a member of a Vedanta centre may result in some social ostracism. To join the Order may subject one to a lower standard of living than he has been used to. Both devotees and monastics must fight hard against the beguilements of the maya still ample in this time and place. For example, so thoroughly are many forms of communication seasoned with sensual appeal that Harvard sociologist Pitirim A. Sorokin calculated not long ago that in the United States everyone encounters some kind of sexual lure every nine minutes of the waking day. The Western Vedantist must not be sold short. If he takes to Vedanta he does so with the zeal of the rationally convinced. Adapt Vedanta he must, but ruin it he will not.

Thus there are Western devotees; and Western outlanders are being ordained with full privileges in Shankara's aristocratic order of Puri. At present 10 per cent of the total members of the Order are occidentals. Since 1947 brahmacharya has been given in the West. On his world tour in 1956 Swami Madhavananda ruled that qualified brahmacharies from the West will be in the normal way eligible for sannyas, which happened in 1958 when a brahmachari from Hollywood received his initiation as swami, and in 1959 when five brahmacharinis from the same centre became sannyasinis. While at least the male candidates must go to Belur Math for their investiture, they may thereafter live and work in their homeland. To preserve a needed coalescence throughout the Order a swami from India should probably head every centre as spiritual director. But there is no reason why Western sannyasins should not in time become preachers and operating managers of Vedanta societies anywhere in the world. These occidental swamis will adjust things according to local needs, and the adaptation of Vedanta will go on.

Does this mean that there will be no institutionalism in Ramakrishna Vedanta of the sort which permitted a Rome to dictate details of Christian practices in a far-off China? Does it suggest that the Ramakrishna movement will split up into pockets as isolated from the source as Buddhism became in the Far East?

Yes and no. Rigid institutionalism is as un-Vedantic as denominationalism. Where the avatar theory and the idea of historic cycles are held you will not find anybody preaching that his institution has all truth for all time. The Order supports a viewpoint which, as antagonistic to strong organizationalism, must eventually undermine the organization itself. Instead of preaching its own unassailability it regards itself as a necessary evil and speaks freely of its own equally inevitable eventual decline.

Yet again, Swamiji instructed his followers that total Hindu 'unorganizedness' is not right either. A valuable revelation requires a body of trained workers to hold it purely and hand it on.

The opinion of the seniors of the Order is that a blend of Western institutionalism and Indian laissez-faire will emerge. What will probably result is a loose federation where freedom and self-determination exist side by side with the easy working relations likely in brothers who have received their ordination from the same line of sannyas gurus.

The answer is clear. There is 'something to' Ramakrishna Vedanta. A great revelation is at hand. And the instrument, the Order, established to hold and expend it, is good. We are alive now. All things are favourable. This is a most auspicious moment to 'awake, arise, and stop not', as the Upanishads direct, 'till the goal is reached'.

I am still at Belur Math. It is the day after the public ceremony. Things have quieted down. The 400,000 of yesterday seem a fancy of the mind. Many of the new swamis and brahmacharis have left, on the pilgrimages to the holy spots of Hinduism customary after these initiations. Tantine's guesthouse is comparatively deserted. I too am leaving, by train tonight for the north, where from New Delhi I shall depart from India by air. This is farewell to Headquarters.

In the morning I make a last trip to Dakshineswar. In the afternoon I begin taking leave of the many swamis, brahmacharis, and servants who have been so good to me. It requires some time. I see I have started on these rounds too late. I shall never get through. I remember one swami advising me to devote a whole day to it, starting first thing after breakfast. Now I see what he meant. Everyone wants a final chat along with the good-bye. The swamis I take leave of by taking the dust of their feet. When I rise some embrace me. The brahmacharis I know best embrace me too.

At teatime there is a going-away party for me in the guesthouse. Those men who have been my closest acquaintants attend: Mahavir Maharaj, Manik Maharaj, Raoji, Vishnu Maharaj, the new Swami Kritananda of Mauritius, and a dozen more. I happen to have a jar of instant coffee sent as a Christmas present from home. Milk is procured and heated. Indian sweets appear. We have American coffee, Indian style, and the sweets. We sit around on the floor in a circle, feet bare, dhotis nicely smoothed across our knees, the strangest stag party I have ever been to. In turn each man gives his testimonial, some who are not adept in English anyway bravely doing the best they can. The burden of these remarks is that when they heard that this formidable Yankee was coming they didn't know what to expect. But, having known him, they find the foreigner to be just like one of them. The Western brother is a brother indeed. In my reply I say that I had had fears on my side too, but now also feel the same way about them. Is not the scene an illustration of what we preach—undoubted diversity, yes; but unity in diversity?

Now it is dark; time to leave for Howrah Station. The industrial school jeep is waiting. In the main temple arati is going on. Through the doorway I can see the bright nave and at the far end the marble

statue of Sri Ramakrishna lighted by candles. The monks and devotees
are singing the old, sweet vesper songs.

My last act is to say good-bye to President Swami Sankarananda.
Months have gone by since that first meeting when at his invitation I
sat down in a chair in his presence. The memory of the sweetness of his
gesture in asking me to do this, and my impropriety in accepting, is still
strong. At least I have learned not to do that again. I enter the old headquarters building where so much of the history of the Order has been
enacted. Leaving my shoes at the bottom of the stairs, for the last time
I go up to the second floor. Before me runs the River, lighted by a
passing boat. On this balcony Maharaj used to sit, and here my guru
first met his guru and in that exchange was sealed the fate of many. To
the right is Swamiji's room. As usual when passing the door I wonder if
it may not feel something like this to be in the vicinity of a working
uranium pile.

I tap at the portière-closed doorway of Swami Sankarananda's room.
A soft 'Enter' from within. Here is President Maharaj sitting in his
armchair, patriarchal, with indrawn eyes. I bow before him, feeling sad.
He smiles and gives me several messages to take to swamis in America.
Then he speaks tenderly his good-bye: 'Always remember that you have
a home everywhere'. A final pranam. I leave.

On the surface President Maharaj's words mean that a member of the
Order is welcome in any of the Order's places on four continents. It is
nice to know this and gives you a feeling of being a forerunner of the
new world citizen. But I believe the spiritual father of the Order means
something additional—that if we find the Self we enter the sanctuary.
That tearing sense of isolation which plagues us from our babyhood
we may lose when we rest in the Source. The pain we feel from being
separate, desiring, ego-bound 'Yankees' will cease when we take our
place in the unlimited realm of the spirit, when we achieve Swami
Vivekananda's objective: 'May He Illumine Us'. The refuge sought
through a thousand weary incarnations each man carries within. 'Always
remember that you have a home everywhere.' And remembering,
enter in.

NOTES ON ILLUSTRATIONS

I have gathered together some pictures illustrative of Sri Ramakrishna's life and of his monastic order. I wish there had been space for many times this number, for the people and the places of India are very photogenic. Instead, full captions have been supplied so as to aid the illustrations in supplementing the text and to make it possible for each illustration to do the work of several.

1. Frontispiece: map of Dakshineswar. Here are shown the principal spots associated with Ramakrishna's adult life as temple priest at Dakshineswar. See Chapter II. Several terms used in the map are not mentioned in the text of this book but are nevertheless used frequently in the Master's Gospel. 'Chandni', for example, refers to the resthouse at the head of the landing ghat. 'Natmandir' is an Indian term for the meeting hall or audience chamber often found facing shrines. The term 'Radhakanta' refers, of course, to the shrine of Radha and Krishna. The Bakultala Ghat is the one used for her daily bath by the Holy Mother. The Pine Grove is where Ramakrishna went to answer calls of nature.

2a. Belur Math on the Ganges. The headquarters of the Ramakrishna Order occupies a park-like grounds fronting the river a few miles north of Calcutta. Temples dedicated to Swami Vivekananda (left), Sri Sarada Devi, the Holy Mother (centre), and Swami Brahmananda (right), rise above the ghats; and farther back stands the big main temple of Sri Ramakrishna.

2b. Dakshineswar: see Chapter II. The picture was taken from the south end of the great central courtyard. Behind the photographer, not shown, is the Ganges landing ghat and the twelve identical Shiva temples which line the river. The nine-spired main temple in the centre houses the Kali image; entrance to her shrine is through the central archway facing the reader. At the right is the meeting hall. Its balancing structure toward the left contains the shrines of Radha-Govinda and of the broken Krishna image repaired by Sri Ramakrishna. At the very left is the building which, as it stretches farther to the left and toward the river, contains Ramakrishna's room. Holy Mother's nahabat and the Panchavati are behind.

3a. Tantine in her later years. The bonnet of black lace had been made many years before by a London society milliner; it was the only hat she ever wore; she was believed by some to possess at least six of the same model. The pendant, which Tantine referred to as her jewel, was made for her by her friend, the famous French jeweller and glass maker, René Lalique.

3b. Swami Sankarananda, President of the Ramakrishna Math and Mission, known as President Maharaj. I have written of him in Chapter I and again at the very end of the book in Chapter X. This picture was taken by an American monastic of the Vedanta Society of Southern California, George

NOTES ON ILLUSTRATIONS

I have gathered together some pictures illustrative of Sri Ramakrishna's life and of his monastic order. I wish there had been space for many times this number, for the people and the places of India are very photogenic. Instead, full captions have been supplied so as to aid the illustrations in supplementing the text and to make it possible for each illustration to do the work of several.

1. Frontispiece: map of Dakshineswar. Here are shown the principal spots associated with Ramakrishna's adult life as temple priest at Dakshineswar. See Chapter II. Several terms used in the map are not mentioned in the text of this book but are nevertheless used frequently in the Master's Gospel. 'Chandni', for example, refers to the resthouse at the head of the landing ghat. 'Natmandir' is an Indian term for the meeting hall or audience chamber often found facing shrines. The term 'Radhakanta' refers, of course, to the shrine of Radha and Krishna. The Bakultala Ghat is the one used for her daily bath by the Holy Mother. The Pine Grove is where Ramakrishna went to answer calls of nature.

2a. Belur Math on the Ganges. The headquarters of the Ramakrishna Order occupies a park-like grounds fronting the river a few miles north of Calcutta. Temples dedicated to Swami Vivekananda (left), Sri Sarada Devi, the Holy Mother (centre), and Swami Brahmananda (right), rise above the ghats; and farther back stands the big main temple of Sri Ramakrishna.

2b. Dakshineswar: see Chapter II. The picture was taken from the south end of the great central courtyard. Behind the photographer, not shown, is the Ganges landing ghat and the twelve identical Shiva temples which line the river. The nine-spired main temple in the centre houses the Kali image; entrance to her shrine is through the central archway facing the reader. At the right is the meeting hall. Its balancing structure toward the left contains the shrines of Radha-Govinda and of the broken Krishna image repaired by Sri Ramakrishna. At the very left is the building which, as it stretches farther to the left and toward the river, contains Ramakrishna's room. Holy Mother's nahabat and the Panchavati are behind.

3a. Tantine in her later years. The bonnet of black lace had been made many years before by a London society milliner; it was the only hat she ever wore; she was believed by some to possess at least six of the same model. The pendant, which Tantine referred to as her jewel, was made for her by her friend, the famous French jeweller and glass maker, René Lalique.

3b. Swami Sankarananda, President of the Ramakrishna Math and Mission, known as President Maharaj. I have written of him in Chapter I and again at the very end of the book in Chapter X. This picture was taken by an American monastic of the Vedanta Society of Southern California, George statue of Sri Ramakrishna lighted by candles. The monks and devotees are singing the old, sweet vesper songs.

My last act is to say good-bye to President Swami Sankarananda. Months have gone by since that first meeting when at his invitation I sat down in a chair in his presence. The memory of the sweetness of his gesture in asking me to do this, and my impropriety in accepting, is still strong. At least I have learned not to do that again. I enter the old headquarters building where so much of the history of the Order has been enacted. Leaving my shoes at the bottom of the stairs, for the last time I go up to the second floor. Before me runs the River, lighted by a passing boat. On this balcony Maharaj used to sit, and here my guru first met his guru and in that exchange was sealed the fate of many. To the right is Swamiji's room. As usual when passing the door I wonder if it may not feel something like this to be in the vicinity of a working uranium pile.

I tap at the portière-closed doorway of Swami Sankarananda's room. A soft 'Enter' from within. Here is President Maharaj sitting in his armchair, patriarchal, with indrawn eyes. I bow before him, feeling sad. He smiles and gives me several messages to take to swamis in America. Then he speaks tenderly his good-bye: 'Always remember that you have a home everywhere'. A final pranam. I leave.

On the surface President Maharaj's words mean that a member of the Order is welcome in any of the Order's places on four continents. It is nice to know this and gives you a feeling of being a forerunner of the new world citizen. But I believe the spiritual father of the Order means something additional—that if we find the Self we enter the sanctuary. That tearing sense of isolation which plagues us from our babyhood we may lose when we rest in the Source. The pain we feel from being separate, desiring, ego-bound 'Yankees' will cease when we take our place in the unlimited realm of the spirit, when we achieve Swami Vivekananda's objective: 'May He Illumine Us'. The refuge sought through a thousand weary incarnations each man carries within. 'Always remember that you have a home everywhere.' And remembering, enter in.

Fitts, when he went to India in 1958 to take his vows of sannyas, becoming Swami Krishnananda.

3c. Relying on conceptions of artists, devotees in the past could never be quite certain as to the appearance of incarnations. But in the case of Sri Ramakrishna, who lived after photography had been invented, it is possible to know exactly what he looked like. Three photographs were made during Ramakrishna's lifetime. The one shown here was taken at a kirtan at Keshab Sen's house in Calcutta. He is in samadhi, supported by Hriday, a relative. This picture was made from an old print acquired by Swami Prabhavananda when in India in 1959.

3d. This is a picture of Sri Sarada Devi, the Holy Mother, with the English disciple of Swami Vivekananda, Margaret Noble, known as Sister Nivedita. The original of this photo, whose existence had been previously unsuspected, was discovered in the home of the Earl of Sandwich, who was related by marriage to Tantine. I carried it to India with me and gave it to the seniors of the Order, who were astonished and delighted that it should have come to light. A picture taken of Holy Mother on what must have been the same occasion was well known; but that she and this large, energetic Western woman had also posed together was an interesting surprise.

4a. Swami Vivekananda. The original of this photograph was given to me in Hollywood by Ida Ansell, known as Ujjvala. (See Chapter VIII.) The picture was taken in San Francisco in 1900, I believe Ujjvala said on a Sunday afternoon. Swamiji had been lounging on the lawn talking to several Vedanta students. Someone asked, 'Please, let us take your picture'. He immediately sprang up and smiled, and this wonderful likeness was caught, against a background of plum blossoms.

4b. Swamiji at Greenacre, Maine, in the summer of 1894. In Chapter IV I have tried to appreciate Swami Vivekananda's qualities as an awesomely austere sadhu and powerful spiritual force. But it is gratifying too, that, like other saints one reads about, Swamiji had a charming lightness and humour in his make-up, which I feel are attractively caught in this photo.

4c. Swami Brahmananda, or Maharaj, in the old headquarters building at Belur Math. See Chapter IV. The steps behind him lead to a balcony where he used to sit watching the Ganges flow past, surrounded by the young monks whom he was preparing to become, in many cases, the present seniors and spiritual leaders of the Ramakrishna Order. At the top of this staircase also are Swamiji's room and the quarters of the President of the Order.

4d. Sri Ramakrishna's great-grandnephew, Kanai Ghoshal. Part of his time is spent at Dakshineswar, and part at Kamarpukur, where he carries on priestly duties. When I was introduced to him he appeared to be still in his teens. Because of his youth I made no particular obeisance to him, but later realized I had been wrong in not doing so. Despite his youth, he is highly revered, in accordance with the Indian concept that members of any family into which an incarnation chooses to be born must be possessed of extraordinary spiritual endowments.

5a. This is the group photo taken at Madras to which I refer in Chapter I. The seniors are on the front row, with the brahmacharis in back. Several individuals mentioned in the text are in this group. President Maharaj is in the centre. Priti Chaitanya (Chapter VI) is behind him, to his left. Ramamurty (Chapter VI) is in the back row, the third from the reader's right, next to Sunil, with whom I went to Jagannath (Chapter VII). I am shown (with unshaved head) behind President Sankarananda, to his right.

5b. This is Swami Atulananda—Gurudas Maharaj—who is described in Chapter VIII. Born Cornelius Heyblom in 1870 in Holland, he lived for a time in the United States. Then he moved to India where he took the vows of sannyas in 1923, to become the fourth and until recently the only living Western swami of the Ramakrishna Order.

6a. Belur Math on Ramakrishna's birthday (see Chapter X). To the left is the main temple, described by Christopher Isherwood as follows: 'Although I had seen pictures of it, I had always had dark forebodings that a building which attempted to be, as this does, a combination of Gothic, Oriental, and Mohammedan architecture, couldn't possibly be anything but a rather absurd hybrid. But, after close inspection, I think it really is a very beautiful building of noble proportions, especially inside.' A few booths can be seen in the right foreground. The structure in the centre with the festoons is the viewing place where relics of Ramakrishna's life are on display. The tent at the left is a shoe-check room or first-aid station.

6b. Holy Mother's native village of Jayrambati, typical of many rural hamlets throughout Bengal. In the foreground is a tank where people bathe, wash their clothes, and obtain water for irrigation. Banana trees and coconut palms overhang the water's edge, and small homes hug the shore. The domed building is a temple built to honour Holy Mother, over the place of her birth.

7a. Ramakrishna's native homestead at Kamarpukur as it is today. The thatched building is the original Chatterjee house. The pointed structure in the centre is a stone chapel built over the place of Ramakrishna's birth, and has a 'music hall' facing it where meetings can be held or people can sit for meditation. The small shrine at the left houses Raghuvir, the family deity. See Chapter IX for details.

7b. Sri Ramakrishna's birthplace at Kamarpukur, as described in Chapter IX. The homestead is of earthen construction, with thatched roof. In the yard behind the house originally stood an old shed of sticks and straw, where the birth took place. On the right is the neighbourhood shrine before which Ramakrishna's mother had a vision that she should bear a divine child. The big tree at the left is a mango, planted by Ramakrishna as a young man. This photo was taken in 1949 before the new constructions were carried out which are shown in picture 7a, and conveys the atmosphere of this Bengal village as it must have been during Sri Ramakrishna's time.

THE END

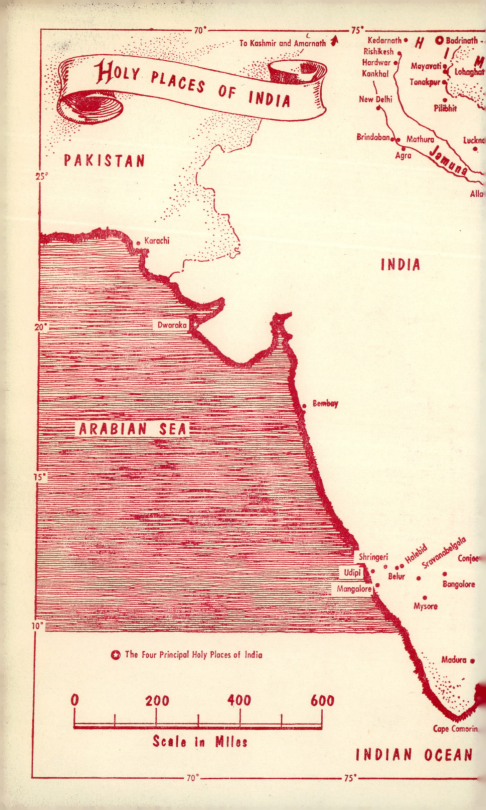

HOLY PLACES OF INDIA

To Kashmir and Amarnath

PAKISTAN

Karachi

Dwaraka

ARABIAN SEA

Bombay

INDIA

Kedarnath
Rishikesh
Hardwar
Kankhal
New Delhi
Brindaban
Agra

H
Badrinath
Mayavati
Tonakpur
Pilibhit
Mathura

I
Lohaghat
Lucknow
Jamuna
Alla

M

Shringeri
Udipi
Mangalore

Halebid
Belur
Sravanabelgola
Bangalore
Mysore

Conjee

The Four Principal Holy Places of India

Madura

0   200   400   600

Scale in Miles

Cape Comorin

INDIAN OCEAN

25°
20°
15°
10°

70°   75°